T0299964

Migration,
Prostitution,
and
Human
Trafficking

Migration, Prostitution, and Human Trafficking

The Voice of Chinese Women

Min Liu

Routledge
Taylor & Francis Group

LONDON AND NEW YORK

First published 2011 by Transaction Publishers

Published 2017 by Routledge
2 Park Square, Milton Park, Abingdon, Oxon OX14 4RN
711 Third Avenue, New York, NY 10017, USA

First issued in paperback 2018

Routledge is an imprint of the Taylor & Francis Group, an informa business

Copyright © 2011 by Taylor & Francis.

Library of Congress Catalog Number: 2011003367

Library of Congress Cataloging-in-Publication Data

Liu, Min, 1969-
    Migration, prostitution, and human trafficking : the voice of Chinese women / Min Liu.
        p. cm.
    Includes bibliographical references.
    ISBN 978-1-4128-1505-5
    1. China—Economic conditions—2000   2. Migration, Internal—China.   3. Women migrant labor—China.   4. Prostitution—China.
5. Humantrafficking—China.   I. Title.
    HC427.95.L584   2011
    363.4′40951—dc22
                                                                    2011003367

ISBN 13: 978-1-4128-6531-9 (pbk)
ISBN 13: 978-1-4128-1505-5 (hbk)

Contents

List of Tables and Figures

Preface

China has gone through a wide-ranging transformation in the last three decades since the Chinese government initiated economic reform and an open-door policy. A series of reform strategies, while producing an economic miracle in China, has, however, resulted in myriad social problems. The resurgence and prevalence of prostitution is one of these. Rarely have there been any attempts to explore prostitution in relation to human trafficking. This study tries to explore questions such as whether Chinese women in the sex sector are victims of trafficking, what are the factors causing Chinese women to get involved in prostitution or become victims of trafficking, how authorities respond to these issues in terms of laws and policies, and so on.

This study was conducted in Shenzhen—China's best-known boomtown since the 1980s, where many sex establishments involving internal migrants have been set up. Guided by qualitative methodological approach, a total of sixty-four interviews were conducted: forty with women working in sex venues, nine with sex-ring operators, and fifteen with law enforcement officers. Eight field observations were also completed. Participants included women practicing prostitution in four types of sex venues: nightclubs and karaoke lounges; massage parlors; hair salons; and the street.

A variety of factors relating to women's involvement in prostitution were discovered. Different paths to prostitution were identified and described. Six out of forty women were identified as trafficking victims. The organization and operation of sex venues and the life of women on the "job" were examined. In addition, China's responses to the expanding sex industry were analyzed in terms of law and administrative regulations, as well as policies. The ineffectiveness of campaign-style policy and reasons for its failure to contain prostitution were also explored.

While this study helps improve our knowledge and understanding of prostitution and sex trafficking in contemporary China and provides information for the Chinese authorities on the nature, magnitude, and gravity of these problems, some issues emanating from this study remain unanswered, such as the definition of terms such as exploitation, coercion, or forced work, which are key elements in defining human trafficking.

Acknowledgments

This book is the result of two years of research and investigation, including two months of fieldwork at the research site. As with any qualitative study, it has gone through many phases: research design, IRB bureaucratic obstacles, data collection and analysis, and finalizing of the writing. Accomplishing this task would have been impossible without encouragement, support, assistance, and inspiration from many people.

First and foremost, I would like to express gratitude to Drs. James O. Finckenauer, Ko-lin Chin, and Ronald V. Clarke. Their contribution to my academic and scholarly achievement is invaluable, and is not merely limited to this study. The idea for this study was crystallized while I was a research assistant for Drs. James O. Finckenauer and Ko-lin Chin. Their guidance and advice on this research was forthcoming even before the actual commencement of the study. Similar gratitude is due to Dr. Ronald V. Clarke who was the chair of my Core Exam. His advice and guidance during the preparation of the Core Exam was immeasurable. It helped me to understand the Rational Choice Perspective, which later provided the theoretical framework of my study. Special thanks to Dr. Chin for his inspiring fieldwork, and his generosity in reaching out to me during my own.

Thanks are also owed to my friends in China who introduced me to their friends or acquaintances, some of whom became intermediaries or subjects in this study. Special thanks to those women who trusted me and shared their life stories with me. Their consent to participate in this research constitutes the most significant contribution to this study—it would be an unaccomplished mission without them.

I also would like to express my gratitude to Rutgers University School of Criminal Justice and Graduate School for their financial aid towards my fieldwork and during the writing of this book.

Last, but not least, I would like to express gratitude to my family for their ongoing support, and my daughter, Jamie, who is always a source of joy.

1
Economic Reform, Migration, and Prostitution

Prostitution, one of the oldest professions in the world, has existed in China for over 2,000 years (Ren, 1993; Gil and Anderson, 1998; Zhou, 2006), despite economic development, cultural traditions, changes in social systems, and authoritative suppression. Historically, prostitution has been a topic of research in differing disciplines, such as law, psychiatry, penology, sociology, history, geography, and social work (Davis, 1993). To date, however, few studies have examined the relationship between the increase in prostitution and the development of a society, that is to say, the extent to which economic development, industrialization, and urbanization affect the development of prostitution. In the United States, it has been observed that prostitution evolved into a highly visible business along with the economic development, industrialization and urbanization of the mid-nineteenth century (Barry, 1995). In China, although prostitution prospered under several dynastic reigns, it did not reach its peak until the country opened its door to the outside world during the second half of the nineteenth century (Zhou, 2006). Coincidently, from 1978 onward, as the Chinese government began implementing economic reform, and adopting an open door policy, and as China began experiencing rapid economic development, moving towards industrialization and urbanization, prostitution has seen a revival. It is increasing rapidly after approximately 30 years of purported abolition.

After examining changes in prostitution in Shanghai from 1849 to 1949, Henriot (1996) concluded that prostitution could only prosper in a context where the population is growing rapidly and is diversifying; where foreign trade has opened, and people from all walks of life relocate with the hope of making a better living and attaining prosperity. Even if it is accepted that the advancement of a society, especially in the form of economic development, is inevitably accompanied by thriving prostitution, the question still remains: Why has prostitution in contemporary China been developing so rapidly in the presence of Western culture and a growing economy? Does the current climate of economic reform inevitably engender prostitution? What social changes have occurred in China since 1978, and how do these changes give rise to prostitution? The present study attempts to examine prostitution in China within the context of a society in transition—an isolated, agricultural and underdeveloped country transforming into an open, industrialized, and urbanized one.

Economic Reform and Floating Populations

When China ended its isolation from the outside world in 1978, the government initiated a policy of economic reform and opening to the outside that has profoundly changed people's lives. One of the most prominent results of these new policies, in other words, China's economic boom, has been double-digit economic growth rates, lifting millions of people out of poverty and bringing the poverty rate down from 53 percent in 1981 to only 8 percent in 2001(Ravallion and Chen, 2004). In 2001, there were 400 million fewer people living in extreme poverty than 20 years previously (World Bank, 2005).

The economic reform and open door policy, however, has also restructured the lives of Chinese people in a negative way. Not all the reform strategies have achieved their intended results, nor are all beneficial to people from all walks of life. These less desirable changes, especially noticeable in urban areas, include the abolition of government subsidies for education and the loss of free housing and medical services provided by work units. The loss of these benefits, along with a high unemployment rate, has affected the welfare of the Chinese people very significantly.

Significant Economic Reform Policies

Chinese economic reform has gone through a number of phases, affecting people's lives in different ways. With the initiation and enforcement of a range of reform strategies, many people have become unemployed and have consequently sought jobs in areas offering more opportunities, while others were encouraged to migrate in search of alternate sources of income.

Changes in economic strategies resulted in a large number of unemployed and underemployed people in urban areas, and surplus labor in rural areas. Generally speaking, three significant nationwide reform measures gave rise to this high unemployment rate and the huge floating population. The first is the rural economic reform policy. The initial reforms in the late 1970s and early 1980s targeted the agricultural sector, which is the most important economic sector of China, through the institution of the Family Production Responsibility System (the FPRS) in agriculture. The FPRS contracts farmland to individual households to be cultivated for whatever purposes they see fit as long as they meet the crop quotas for their collective unit. Those who meet the quotas keep the surplus harvests and net profits. Later, in 1993, the government abolished the 40-year-old grain rationing system, leading to more than 90 percent of all annual agricultural produce being sold at market-determined prices (Findlay and Chen, 2001). This reform gave more power to each family to meet its individual needs, and as a result, the farmers have become more energetic and productive. They have been able to retain a surplus from their individual plots of land.

However, although China's agricultural output is the largest in the world, only about 15 percent of its total land area can be cultivated (*The World Factbook: China*, 2008). As China's industrialization continues, vast amounts of agricultural land are being converted into industrial land, aggravating the historical problem of limited space for farming. Farmers displaced by such urban expansion often become migrant labor for factories. They are encouraged to leave their rural homes to seek jobs outside of the depressed agricultural sector and to find multiple income opportunities in urban areas.

The abolition of the rationing system (whereby only urban residents could have rations of food, clothing, etc.), the loosening of recruitment policies governing urban enterprises, and the demand for labor by newly established private and joint-investment companies have motivated farmers to move to urban areas, especially those along the southeastern coast, for economic reasons. With differences between urban and rural life becoming increasingly more prominent, more and more rural farmers are enticed by the diversity and high quality of city life. Incomes from jobs in the cities are much higher than those from farming, especially in areas where the land was not arable to begin with, providing another incentive that motivates farmers, especially young people, to join the increasing "floating population." With China's urbanization accelerating over the last decades, more than 200 million people have left the land. Currently, over 120 million rural workers are "on the move," making their way into towns (China Labor Bulletin, 2007a).

Unlike rural residents who are emancipated from the land, the floating populations from urban areas are people who are unemployed or underemployed as a result of a series of reform measures carried out in state-owned enterprises. During the Maoist period, the majority of urban residents in China were attached to a work unit, an enterprise or institution which provided comprehensive social security for its employees in the form of housing, children's education, pension, and health services. Most urban residents spent their entire lives in the same work unit upon entering the labor market. This was referred to as the "Iron Rice Bowl." One of the hallmarks of China's socialism, the Iron Rice Bowl gave urban residents the promise of employment, and virtually lifelong tenure, by recruiting local urban residents, particularly family members of its current employees. This is one of the reasons why rural residents did not have any chance to work in state-owned enterprises (SOEs) during the pre-reform era. Urban residents were allocated by the local government to a work unit which provided them with a comprehensive benefits package. This employment policy was once touted as one of the advantages of socialism over capitalism. However, the inherent problem with the Iron Rice Bowl raised its head soon after its implementation. The unintended consequences included overstaffed industries, and a reduction of workers' incentive due to job security. As a result, reformers regarded the labor market as unproductive, and a number of strategies were introduced to address this issue. One of these strategies was the termination of the Iron Rice Bowl, which meant that a lot of urban residents lost their jobs, and many young people were no longer guaranteed a job as they entered the labor market. As the economic reforms progressed, government-controlled job allocation declined sharply from 76 percent to 52 percent of the total job market between 1980 and 1992 (China Labor Bulletin, 2007b). The Iron Rice Bowl was shattered, and guaranteed lifetime jobs were replaced by performance-based labor contracts. Those worst affected by these changes were poorly educated, unskilled workers. As a result, unemployment has become one of the Chinese central government's most pressing problems.

Another policy contributing to the high unemployment rate in urban China was the reform of state-owned enterprises (SOEs) in the late 1990s and early 2000s. Economic reform entered a new era with the dismantling of inefficient and unproductive state-owned and state-managed industries and enterprises, and the development of social security systems (Ren, 1999). The most affected areas were provinces with a high concentration of state-owned enterprises established by the Communist Government, especially those in northern China. In some severely affected areas, SOEs started to lay off employees, or were shut down due to economic reasons. Families with several members working in the same industry or work unit were the most adversely affected. Unfortunately, such situations, in which several family members worked in the same unit, were very common because of the Iron Rice Bowl employment policy. Thus, unemployment began to increase significantly at the end of 1990s, as the government's big push to reform SOEs got underway. About 20 million SOE employees became unemployed as enterprises restructured, merged, or declared bankruptcy (China Labor Bulletin, 2007a).

As stated earlier, the closing of inefficient enterprises meant not only the loss of jobs, but also loss of the benefits provided by the work unit. When the old welfare system was dismantled, a new system had not yet been established. The socialization of welfare made the lives of those who lost their jobs even worse.

The extent to which the closing of state-owned, inefficient enterprises affected Chinese people can be extrapolated from the changing components of the Chinese economy. Once predominantly state controlled, less than one-third of all enterprises are now state-owned. As of 2005, the private sector was responsible for approximately 70 percent of China's gross domestic product (GDP), while the state ran about 200 large state enterprises, mostly utilities, heavy industries, and energy resources (China Industry, 2008).

The pattern of change in the employment rate reflects the tremendous effect of economic reform on urban Chinese residents. China's official unemployment rate has remained at between two or five percent for the last two decades. Even in the late 1990s and early 2000s, when the effects of economic reform and SOE restructuring were at their most intense, the rate barely exceeded four percent (China Labor Bulletin, 2007). However, the official unemployment statistics only include urban residents who have registered as unemployed. Neither the rural unemployed nor urban employees who have been laid off are included, as these latter retain an "employment relationship" with their former employer. Unemployment is more severe in the poorer western and central regions and the northeastern provinces that had a high concentration of SOEs. In 2005, the highest official unemployment rate was five percent in the northeastern province of Liaoning (China Labor Bulletin, 2007a). Enterprises in the southeastern coastal areas, such as Guangdong and Shanghai, which opened up to foreign investment much earlier, were far more capable of providing employment opportunities to workers.

Thus, the cessation of the Iron Rice Bowl and the closing of unprofit-able state-owned factories resulted in millions of unemployed laborers in urban areas. Along with surplus laborers from rural areas, these urban workers migrated from poor, undeveloped state-enterprise-ridden areas to relatively rich, developed, private-enterprise-ridden areas. The creation of Special Economic Zones (SEZ) in the southeast coastal areas became a magnet for these migrants and they constituted what is referred to as a "floating population," i.e., temporary migrants without local household registration.

Unequal Economic Development Motivating People to Migrate

As the economy boomed and public welfare improved, China began to witness a large-scale migration of people, both within and beyond its borders. Economic reform strategies resulted not only in high rates of unemployment, but also in an unequal pace of economic development. In order to attract international investments, the government designed a variety of favorable economic policies and applied them to southeastern cities. The financial development in these areas is greatly responsible for China's economic boom since the 1980s. Although economic growth in China was dramatic, it was also highly uneven, generating vast inequali-ties of living standards and opportunities between those at the hub of economic growth and those at its margins. Average rural incomes in China remained less than half of those enjoyed by city dwellers, and earnings from agriculture continued to stagnate (Davidson, 2001). The income gap between rural and urban areas prompted people to move eastward for a better life. These inequalities have triggered this migra-tion (AMC, 2000).

According to most recent statistics, the migrant population has increased from less than 2 million at the beginning of the Economic Reform, to 140 million in 2007. This figure accounts for 10 percent of the total population, with farmers constituting the main portion of the migrant population (*Legal Daily*, 2007). Experts estimate that from now until 2015, at least 250 million rural laborers will move to urban areas, swelling the migrant population to approximately 400 million (*Legal Daily*, 2007).

A popular phrase, borrowed from the title of an ancient Chinese novel, aptly describes the regional pattern of migration in the 1980s: Peacocks flying southeast. Because three of the first four special eco-nomic zones (Shenzhen, Zhuhai, and Shantou) are located in Guangdong, the province has witnessed an economic boom, with a large amount of foreign investment and a prominent migrant presence. Although it has less than 7 percent of China's population, Guangdong accounted for 27 percent of China's floating population in 2000 (Liang and Ma, 2004). The cheap labor afforded by these migrant workers is the fuel that powers Guangdong's thriving economy, which accounts for half of China's gross domestic product (Rosenthal, 2002).

The scale of internal migration in China is so phenomenal that the population in destination cities becomes really huge, compared to what it was before the economic reform. This can be demonstrated by the population changes in one of the SEZs, namely Shenzhen. In 1979, the year before Shenzhen was decreed an SEZ, it was a small border town with less than 40,000 calling it home (Hobson and Heung, 1998). The population of the 1953-square-kilometer region boomed to 10 million people in 2005, 31 times the number recorded 25 years ago, according to an official newspaper (Xinhua News Agency, 2005), making it the largest migrant city in China. Several government employees interviewed for this study say that the registered permanent population in Shenzhen has reached three million, while the registered temporary population is seven million. Adding to these figures the unregistered people living there, the total population of Shenzhen is about 14-15 million, with some sources even estimating it to be as high as 18 million.

The new residents come from a variety of backgrounds: educated and uneducated, skilled and unskilled. Many people who are unemployed in the region they are originally from, desperately migrate to other cities because opportunities for unskilled workers are greater there than in their home villages. Their lives change following migration.

Farmers constitute the main part of the migrant population (*Legal Daily*, 2007), and like most migrants, are politically marginalized and economically disadvantaged (Davidson, 2001). They are unskilled, have limited education, and may have lived in poverty before migration. More than 80 percent have no education beyond middle school and 70 percent have no training. Their age ranges from 16-40. Some of the new dwellers are children of the first migrant generation (*Legal Daily*, 2007). It is reported that in some mountain areas in Sichuan Province, no one between the ages of 15 to 40 can be found at home; everyone moves out after finishing middle school. Almost half of the area's young adults live in two places, Foshan and Dongguan-gray satellite cities just outside Guangzhou and Shenzhen (Rosenthal, 2002).

After moving into developed cities, most migrant workers have a limited choice between physically demanding occupations, such as construction, renovation, and manufacture (*Legal Daily*, 2007). They have few rights, and are blamed for every social ill, from crime to pornography. By migrating, they may solve the employment problem, but they encounter other problems including a high cost of living, children's education, and conflicts of culture and values. Some of them may not be able to make enough money to support themselves, let alone send remittances back to their families. In addition, not all migrants can find a job. For women and girls, the sex industry provides a convenient option (Ren, 2000) and is a major receptor of female migrants (Davidson, 2001).

Resurgence of Prostitution

Prostitution in History

Prostitution has existed in China for more than 2,000 years (Ren, 1993; Gil and Anderson, 1998; Zhou, 2006). It is difficult to determine when and how the practice originated, but it is possible to speculate about the development of government-owned brothels. Some researchers believe that China's first brothels were established in the seventh century B.C. by the famous statesman and philosopher, Guan Zhong, who used them as a means of increasing the state income (Ruan, 1991). Institutionalized prostitution in China began in the Han dynasty (256 B.C.-A.D. 220), when the famous monarch, Emperor Wu, recruited female camp followers for his armies. These women were called "ying-chi" (camp prostitutes) (Ruan, 1991). In the Han dynasty, the prostitution business also began to segregate into two systems—officially run brothels and privately owned prostitutes (Ren, 1993). The institution of government-run prostitution reached its peak in the Tang (A.D.618-905) and Song dynasties (A.D. 960-1279), whereas private, commercial prostitution became most highly developed during the Ming (1368-1644) and Qing (1644-1911) dynasties (Ruan, 1991).

In fact, the history of prostitution in China was so rich, that it became the theme of many famous works of Chinese fiction, such as Jin Ping Mei and Du Shi Niang. Famous ancient poets in feudal societies, such as Li Bai, have depicted prostitutes. Some courtesans in Chinese history have become very well known, for example Chao Fei-yan who became a queen, Hsueh Tao who composed sophisticated poetry, or Li Shih-shih, who was much admired by a most enamored emperor on account of her beauty and sexual techniques (Ruan, 1991).

The commercial sex industry in China was enhanced by state agencies specifically created for the sex industry. The Ming Dynasty (1368-1644) established a ministry to regulate and manage prostitution (Ren, 1993). It was not until the Qing dynasty (1644-1911) that the government began to abolish state-owned brothels (Ren, 1993; Ruan, 1991). Nevertheless, in ancient China, prostitution was always regarded a privilege for upper-class men (Ren, 1993; Zhou, 2006).

Prostitution did not reach its highest point of proliferation until the second half of the nineteenth century when China was force to open its door to the rest of the world (Zhou, 2006). The business of prostitution was highly organized, and prostitutes fell into different categories within the hierarchical structure (Hershatter, 1997). A high-ranking prostitute was trained to be skilled in many different arts such as singing, painting, writing poetry and playing musical instruments (Zhou, 2006). In 1920, there were 60,141 registered prostitutes in Shanghai, and 3,550 in Beijing. It is estimated there were 7,000 unregistered in 1917 (Ruan, 1991). By 1935, prostitutes, either licensed or unlicensed, constituted 2.3 percent of the total population of Shanghai (Zhou, 2006).

Prostitution was so rampant before the Communist Party took power, that the government launched a series of intense campaigns against it, such as shutting down brothels; arresting brothel owners, procurers, and pimps and providing educational and vocational training to prostitutes (Ren, 1993; Ruan, 1991). Prostitution was purportedly eradicated by the Communist government soon after the Communist Party came to power in 1949 (Barry, 1995; Jeffreys, 2004a; Ren, 1993; Ruan, 1991). As a symbol of its success, the Communist Party closed research institutes for venereal diseases in 1964 (Evan, 1997). Although some studies demonstrate that the disappearance of prostitution was far from total (Hershatter, 1997; Ruan, 1991), at least prostitution did not exist as the object of serious governmental concern for almost three decades. It was not until the 1980s when it was revived and became increasingly visible in China that prostitution, along with other social problems such as drug use and increasing crime rates became a priority on the government's agenda and a major concern of the public and law enforcement authorities.

A Rampant Phenomenon

Though technically illegal, commercial sex is omnipresent in contemporary Chinese life and a very popular theme in media reports (e.g., French, 2006a and 2006b; Lynch, 2003; Goodman, 2003; Sunday, 2007), with some describing it as the fastest-growing industry in the country (French, 2006a). Since the economic reform, China has recognized the recurrence and growth of prostitution, which was ostensibly abolished when the country operated in relative isolation (Ruan, 1991). Beginning in 1982, however, the rate of prostitution increased every year (Zhou, 2006). Between 1986 and 1990, the number of those engaged in prostitution increased fourfold when compared to the previous five years, despite repeated crackdowns and police raids. Since 1987, 183 new educational detention centers were built exclusively for those arrested for prostitution (Zhu Xudong, 2001). Analysis of official data on the arrests of prostitutes and their clients in Mainland China suggests that between 1982 and 1997, some 2 million cases related to prostitution were processed by the Public Security Department (Pan, 2000). Since this figure refers only to those who have been arrested for prostitution-related offenses, it constitutes only a fraction of the number engaged in prostitution, and tells us little about the actual extent of the sex industry in China (Hershatter, 1997; Pan, 2000).

There is no reliable data about China's sex trade. Estimates of the number of prostitutes vary widely from one million who earn their primary income from sex, to eight or ten times that figure, including people who sometimes accept money, gifts or rent in exchange for sex (Sunday, 2007). Chinese officials estimate three million prostitutes nationwide, the U.S. State Department reports as many as ten million (French, 2006a), while several other sources say the number is closer to four million (i.e., Agence France Presse, 2000; Ren, 2000; *The Economist*, 2000).

Police report that prostitution arrests account for only 25 to 30 percent of all actual infractions; some experts estimate that the number is only 10 percent while others think it is lower than 5 percent (Zhu Xudong, 2001). Whatever the number, prostitution is rampant in China. While acknowledging the methodological limits of comparison, Gil et al. (1994) illuminated the prevalence of prostitution in China by comparing it with incidents of prostitution within the United States, which is not as heavily populated as China. In 1990, there were 91,093 arrests for prostitution and commercialized sex in the United States. During 1992, Chinese public security forces made approximately 200,000 prostitution arrests nationwide.

The rapid growth of prostitution can be evidenced by the following facts. In the 1980s, flourishing prostitution businesses were especially visible in the Special Economic Zones and other eastern, coastal cities (Wong, 1992; Jeffreys, 2004a). But now it has become so prevalent that "sellers of sex can be found throughout present-day China." (Jeffreys, 2004b: 83). It is scarcely possible to walk for 10 minutes in any big Chinese city without coming across the sex trade in one of its many guises (French, 2006a).

The prevalence of the practice is evident—prostitutes solicit customers openly in public places. No longer limited to well-known bars, or a growing number of karaoke parlors, prostitutes are everywhere in China, and they come from all walks of life: college students looking to pay tuition, uneducated women at private residential compounds, those who approach customers via mobile phone networks (Sunday, 2007), and so on. Although specialized brothels no longer exist in contemporary China, sex services are provided at a variety of facilities, including hotels, restaurants, rented apartments, roadside stores, hair salons, coffee houses, dance halls, sauna lounges, teahouses and other entertainment facilities. This is one of the most striking features of prostitution in today's China (Hershatter, 1997). It is reported that in Ningxia, a northwestern, backward, autonomous region of China, prostitution is used to lure motorists to more than 1,000 gas stations. Motorists have to buy a tank of gas before they may purchase sexual services (Reuters, 1998a).

The variety of people involved in selling sex includes farmers, workers, unemployed persons, private business operators, corporate employees, and state-employed staff (Zhu Xudong, 2001). "In the past, prostitutes came principally from the unemployed and the poorly educated; a few were foreign. But now, employees of state, collective and private enterprises, party and state cadres, intellectuals, science and technology personnel, and even university students and researchers are becoming prostitutes" (Quanguo Renda, 1991: 12). Their clients used to come from outside of mainland China; now, they represent all walks of life, including celebrities, high class party or government officials (Zhu Xudong, 2001).

The thriving resurgence of prostitution in China coincides with significant economic reform strategies (Ren, 1999 and 2000) and the influx of the labor force into cities (Gil et al., 1994; Ren, 2000). More rural women among the migrant population means more of them in the sex trade. In a study surveying 2,057 women prostitutes, Gil et al. (1994) found that most prostitutes were from rural areas. Before 1985, only about 3 percent of women arrested for prostitution came from rural areas. But this increased to 62 percent in a 1999 survey (Xu, 1999). The impact of urban reform strategies (especially the cessation of the "Iron Rice-Bowl" employment system and the closure of ineffective state-owned enterprises) on Chinese women's lives can be exemplified by changes in the ages of women detained for prostitution. Two surveys found that the maximum upper age of women prostitutes increased from 37 in 1991 to 54 in 1999 (Ren, 2000). Tens of thousands of workers were laid off due to the reform measures. Women, especially those in their late 30s, or those over 40, bear the brunt of these measures as evidenced by demographic changes in prostitution.

Prostitution and Human Trafficking

With prostitution thriving in China, an important aspect of this issue—the connection between human trafficking and prostitution—is largely ignored by the government, law enforcement authorities, academics, and the public. Rapid economic development along China's east coast, along with the unemployed laborers in undeveloped and underdeveloped parts of China, has resulted in massive internal migration. This mass movement has seemingly created opportunities for traffickers to lure women and girls who are desperate for well-paying jobs. They can become easy prey for sex traders, who offer jobs that do not materialize except for prostitution (Gil et al., 1994).

It is claimed that China is a source, transit, and destination country for human trafficking; the majority of which is internal trafficking (Human Trafficking, 2008); it has a significant amount of internal trafficking of children and women for sexual and labor exploitation (The U.S. Department of State, 2006). Three purposes of trafficking in women in contemporary China can be identified, namely, prostitution, forced labor, and marriage (Lee, 2005; Lu et al., 2006).

Selling children, especially young girls, was a prevalent practice in poor families seeking to solve their financial problems in patriarchal, feudalist China. Selling and buying women to be wives was largely accepted in some regions, and often triggered kidnapping or abduction. However, with the development of the economy, of communication and information networks, and the improvement in women's education and status, human trafficking for marriage purposes is not as prevalent as it used to be. This is evidenced by the falling rates of kidnapping and abduction. Over the past ten years or so, the rate of kidnapping and abduction has shown a generally decreasing trend, from the initial rate of 2.29 per 100,000 in 1991, to a rate of 0.44 per 100,000 in 2002 (Lu et al., 2006). Due to limitations of the statistics, it is not clear how many women were kidnapped or abducted for the purposes of prostitution. To the best of my knowledge, the data covers only those who were kidnapped or abducted by obvious force or deception; not those who were coerced or coaxed to leave their hometown. Due to the fact that forms of force have changed, and include many subtle, impalpable methods, as outlined in the UN definition of human trafficking (Human Trafficking, 2007), very few women trafficked for sexual or labor exploitation are included in this data. Therefore, the decrease in these crimes may be attributed to a reduction in women being trafficked for marriage purposes.

According to a Chinese leading newspaper, *China Daily*, an official for the Public Security Ministry said that the traditional crime of human trafficking for the purpose of marriage has gradually been controlled and the number of selling women and children has been dropping 20 to 30 percent a year. However, human trafficking takes two new forms-forced labor and sexual exploitation and the number of such cases is rising (Wang, 2007).

The Ministry of Public Security estimates that 10,000 women and children are being abducted and sold each year; in addition, it reported about 2,500 trafficking cases during 2008 (U.S. Department of State, 2008). From 2001 to 2005, in a remote southwest province in China from where many women are trafficked, 1,794 cases involving trafficking of women and children have been exposed, and more than 2,000 victims have been rescued (Xinhuanet, 2005).

These statistics, nevertheless, still do not provide any information about how many women are trafficked for sexual exploitation, or whether sexual trafficking is a more serious problem compared to trafficking for other purposes. The exact extent of women forced into prostitution is unknown due to lack of data. Statistics indicate that tens of thousands of women are sold every year (Gil and Anderson, 1998). The question of whether those women in the sex trade are forced, deceived, or co-erced into the sex trade has never been a priority of research concerning prostitution in China.

The trade of human beings in China goes back a long way. Histori-cally, it refers to the practice of traffickers abducting and selling women and girls to be wives. Sometimes, especially in cases of poverty, the women and girls are sold by their own families. The result is the com-modification of human beings, especially women. Under current cir-cumstances in China, the trafficking of human beings may take on new forms for different purposes, such as for sexual exploitation. However, due to the fact that prostitution was purportedly eradicated in China for almost 30 years, there is little research on prostitution in relation to sex trafficking. A handful of studies on Chinese prostitution focus heavily on the abolition of prostitution by the Communist government in the 1950s, the socio-cultural factors that contributed to the resurgence of prostitution, the current legal response and the limited effect of police campaigns against it (e.g., Anderson and Gil, 1994; Evans, 1997; Gil and Anderson, 1998; Ren, 1999; Zhang, 2006; Zhou, 2006). There have been rare attempts to explore whether the sex industry is related to sex trafficking; how these women migrate to their destination cities and end up in prostitution; whether or not they are victims of trafficking; and the nature and extent of sexual trafficking in China. My research is intended to shed light on these issues. It will represent one of the few attempts to examine sex trafficking in China in the context of the development of prostitution in general.

Research Site

This study was conducted in Shenzhen, China. Shenzhen, one of the thriving sex industry centers, was a small fishing village in the Pearl River delta. Due to its proximity to Hong Kong, the Chinese Government decreed it as one of the four Special Economic Zones in 1980. It is located in the very south of Guangdong province. It is just 25 kilometers away from the center of Hong Kong. Overlooking Hong Kong to its south, this area is commonly referred to as Hong Kong's "backyard."

Since the 1980s, Shenzhen is China's best-known boomtown. Few cities anywhere have created wealth faster than Shenzhen; the city has grown at an annual rate of 28 percent since it was decreed a Special Economic Zone, albeit this rate slowed to 15 percent in 2005 (French, 2006a). Since the 1980s, Shenzhen is renowned throughout the country for its economic growth, high salaries, modern fashions, and adherence to so-called "bourgeois" morals. It is an open secret that economic progress has brought with it the seedy side of the free market: prostitution, corruption, drug trafficking (Wudunn, 1991).

Greater contact with Hong Kong and Taiwan businessmen has cultivated a booming prostitution industry in Shenzhen. Many sex establishments involving internal migrants have been set up in the forms of massage parlors, nightclubs, karaoke lounges, beauty salons, and brothels. Prostitution, usually disguised in karaoke lounges and massage parlors, ranks as one of the biggest industries in Shenzhen (French, 2006a), which is referred to as the "den of vice" (Cody, 2006). In Shenzhen, there are an estimated 200,000 women working in the sex business (Hughes, 2002; Wudunn, 1991). According to one government employee's estimate, however, there are about 700,000 prostitutes in this city whose population is nearly 15 million yuan (1 US dollar is worth about 7 yuan) (conversation with a government employee).

Prostitution is widespread in Shenzhen, and brothels and saunas attract many men from Hong Kong just across the border (Reuters, 1998b). Over the past few years, the number of trips made by citizens of Hong Kong to mainland China has shown a constant annual increase of 10 percent or more (Lau et al., 2002). It was reported that citizens of Hong Kong made more than 50 million trips to mainland China in 2000 (Department of Census and Statistics, 2001). Furthermore, it was reported by Lau and Thomas (2001) that approximately one-third of the surveyed adult male travelers in their study reported having sex with one or more prostitutes during the previous six months while traveling in mainland China. A government employee estimated that even today, there are about 50,000 Hong Kong citizens per day (mainly on weekends) who come over to Shenzhen with the purpose of seeking sex services. Each person spends 400 yuan; thus, the daily expenditure is 20 million yuan (conversation with a government employee).

Overview of Research Methods

The aim of this research is to discover the socio-economic factors, individual backgrounds, current circumstances and situational factors that drive Chinese women to migrate and enter into the sex industry. Along with other kinds of qualitative work, ethnography is the preferred method of achieving this goal. It is a powerful tool for accessing women's lives and it allows a process of representation for those who often have little voice (Sanders, 2004). It has become a popular approach to social research. Through ethnographic fieldwork, methods such as field observations and in-depth interviews, we can understand how and why women migrate and enter into commercial sex work.

Data Sources

The data of this study was collected though field observations at commercial sex establishments in Shenzhen, and through in-depth interviews with women practicing prostitution. Interviews were also conducted with sex ring operators, and law enforcement officers. Field observation and interviews are both independent methods of collecting information. However, they are also interdependent. Interviewing is an extremely important and valuable source of data (Hammersley and Atkinson,

1995; Maxwell, 1996). It is a way of gaining a description of actions and events and of obtaining the perspectives of the participants. Most importantly, it is the only way to learn about events that took place in the past, or those to which access cannot otherwise be obtained (Maxwell, 1996). Observation and interviews can provide additional or missing information, and can each be used to check the accuracy of the other. The triangulation of observations and interviews can provide a more complete and accurate ax`ccount than either one alone. There are, thus, distinct advantages in combining participant observation with interviews. In particular, the data obtained from each method can be used to illuminate data obtained from the other (Hammersley and Atkinson, 1995: 131). Through interviews and observation, a description of behavior and events, and the perspectives of actors can be obtained.

This study also draws upon secondary data sources such as official statistics, government documents, legislation, policies on trafficking and prostitution, books, articles in journals, research reports and media accounts. It is worth commenting on the official data regarding arrests of women and their customers in one district police bureau of Shenzhen. The data in question represents most of the arrests related to prostitution made by the district police bureau during the period of January 1, 2007 to May 30, 2008. Due to the rigid evidence requirements regarding prostitution-related arrests, police cannot arrest prostitutes and their customers unless 1) they are caught in the act; or 2) a condom is found at the scene that can prove that sexual behavior occurred; or 3) there is proof of a monetary transaction (conversation with a police officer). As a result of these requirements, usually both prostitutes and their customers are arrested during police raids. Consequently, 37 cases found that a total of 43 women and 43 men were arrested. Information obtained from this official data mainly consists of demographic characteristics of arrested prostitutes and customers, i.e., age, source provinces, marital status, education, etc. and incident information, such as when these incidents happened (timing), where they happened (venues), prices of the trade, and punishments imposed. Because of the limited information provided by this data source, police statistics were included in the current study only to serve one purpose, i.e., to illustrate the representativeness of women recruited in this study in terms of their demographic characteristics. As shown in Chapter 4, demographic data of both arrested women and interviewed women was compiled and compared, which evidenced high representativeness of women participating in this study. Inclusion of the police data allowed a general profile of prostitutes in Shenzhen developed.

Sampling Objectives

Research in the field of prostitution is difficult for many reasons. The most challenging factor is that the research population constitutes a so-called "hidden population" (Heckathorn, 1997). Prostitution also involves stigmatization and illegal behavior, leading individuals to refuse to cooperate, or give unreliable answers to protect their privacy. Random sampling of sex workers is impossible. Based on his own research experience, Weitzer (2005a) noted that in order to compensate for the weakness of non-random sampling, prostitutes in different types of venues should be included, and the sampling and interviews should be carried out in a rigorous and impartial manner.

Research questions in this study focus on a) describing women's differing paths to prostitution, b) exploring socio-economic and individualistic factors that motivate women involved in commercial sex, and c) identifying trafficking victims among women working in the commercial sex industry. The best and most efficient way to explore these research questions was to set the sampling frame to include individuals who are a) active prostitutes as opposed to incarcerated samples; b) working in varied sex venues. To achieve a diverse and representative sample, therefore, women in different sex venues were included in this study. Specifically, women in the following sex venues were included: 1) streetwalkers; 2) hair salons; 3) massage parlors/sauna; 4) nightclubs and karaoke lounges.

A total of forty formal interviews with prostituted women were conducted; nine with operators or managers of sex establishments, including nightclubs/karaoke bars, hair salons, massage parlors, and those involved with street prostitution. Fifteen interviews were also conducted with law enforcement officers. I intended to include interviews with representatives of non-government organizations (NGOs) to enrich the sources of data for this study. Unfortunately, I had to give up this idea after exhaustive efforts had been made to contact several local agencies of the All-China Women's Federation in Shenzhen. None of them agreed to participate in this study because they did not possess any information about women in the sex industry. No victims related to prostitution have tried to seek help from them.

Snowball Sampling

A snowball sampling method was employed to obtain participants for both formal and informal interviews. The most difficult aspect of research using snowball sampling techniques is finding the initial subject who then refers the researcher to other subjects (Maxfield and Babble, 2001; Wright and Decker, 1994). Hammersley and Atkinson (1995) suggest that the initial access may be focused on "gatekeepers" who can grant or withhold permission. Therefore, the priority is to find out who has the power to open up or block off access. In the case of the present study, the following people were determined as potentially having the authority to grant or refuse such permission: the prostitutes themselves or their friends/colleagues/bosses who could either be owners, managers, or supervisors of entertainment facilities.

My intention was to use my *guanxi* or social connections. I had relatives and friends living and working in Shenzhen and they could help me locate such gatekeepers. These relatives or friends had either direct or indirect relationships with people who were managers or owners of entertainment facilities, or they knew people who were regular users of commercial sex and maintained a friendly relationship with the women or with the madams. These friends and relatives, in turn, asked other friends and relatives to help me contact the subjects. In short, I began with direct personal contacts, and then asked those acquaintances to refer me to other middlemen, and so on, to eventually locate subjects and produce informative and insightful data. I employed the snowball chain until a suitable sample had been obtained. One benefit brought about by these social connections was that I was able to gain the trust and confidence of the research participants, a factor that was extremely important for the gathering of truthful and accurate information.

People who act as the first middlemen between the researcher and potential subjects are referred to as intermediaries. A number of potential intermediaries were contacted, and eventually, a total of four intermediaries were involved in this study. Each of them introduced me to others who would be able to refer me to gatekeepers working in commercial sex. The gatekeepers then referred me to prostitutes. In this way, three middlemen were usually involved before the potential subjects were reached (See the following graphs).

Intermediary 1 →Community officers→owner or manager of hair salons→subjects.

Intermediary 2→manager/John→Mami→subjects.
Intermediary 3→owner of the venue→Manager→subjects.
Intermediary 4→owner of the venue→Manager→subjects.

Obtaining a sampling of streetwalkers involves a different process from the one described above. Initial contact with streetwalkers was undertaken directly by the researcher. The first streetwalker was located directly in this way and led to two other subjects being referred to the researcher. Three other streetwalkers were reached via their pimps.

Researcher→subject→subjects

Researcher→street pimp→subjects

Intermediaries also played an important role in providing me with general information about Shenzhen, the development and magnitude of the sex industry in this bustling city, its principal sex service venues, the hot spots for streetwalkers, etc. Preparation for fieldwork began even before I went back to China. A number of phone calls to my friends provided me with some information about this city I had never visited, and built up my confidence, even though I had no idea if any women would be willing to participate in this study and whether I would be able to accomplish my proposed research. These friends later became intermediaries who referred me to their acquaintances, colleagues or friends. Without their help, it would have been impossible for me to accomplish this study. Within a very short time, I was able to obtain knowledge about the component districts in Shenzhen: the area with a high concentration of entertainment facilities, the hot spots and main venues of prostitution, etc.

Wright and Decker (1994) suggested that an alternative means to contact potential subjects involves "frequenting locales favored by criminals" (1994: 17). Applying this to my study, I devoted an extraordinary amount of time visiting a variety of sex establishments to initiate the snowball chain. This, however, proved impractical. On two occasions, I visited karaoke lounges, intending to talk to potential subjects. I did not tell the women the real purpose of my visit because I wanted to test how much information I could get by talking with them as a regular customer would, without them being aware of my real purpose. On another occasion, I told hostesses about my research intentions and wanted to find out if it was possible to interview the women in their natural environment. These efforts proved not to be viable for several reasons. Firstly, I felt uncomfortable and awkward asking the women questions such as how much they earned, or how they ended up in commercial sex. Secondly, some questions aroused their suspicion, or made them unpleasant, since it is unusual for regular customers to ask such questions. Thirdly, even when I told them the true purpose of my visit, they would not admit that they provided sex services. Finally, the noisy environment, with people drinking, singing and playing games was not really conducive to conducting interviews. I realized very soon that interviews could not be completed in a natural business environment and there was no way for me to locate subjects without help from a third party (except in the case of streetwalkers).

In my search of women practicing prostitution, I intentionally avoided seeking referrals directly from law enforcement officials, although some of my intermediaries are indeed police officers. Nor did I interview women currently detained or arrested for prostitution. For practical and methodological reasons, Wright and Decker (1994) think that referrals by law enforcement officials would "arouse the suspicions of offenders that research was the front for a sting operation" (1994: 17). Due to the difficulty of locating women in the prostitution industry, some research projects rely on gaining information from women in custody or those detained at the border. Interviewing someone at a detention facility is not an ideal situation because individuals are constrained and influenced by the environment, and this affects what they say and how much they are willing to talk (Kelly, 2002). Furthermore, a sample obtained in this manner might be highly unrepresentative of active prostitutes. Such a sample might include a disproportionate number of prostitutes who work on the street or at hair salon (police date shows that women working at these two venues are disproportionately arrested), but exclude those who work in an invisible way (such as women working in karaoke lounges).

Interview Setting and Rapport Relationship

In order to conduct interviews in an ideal context and to enable subjects to talk to me without any constraint, I intentionally arranged for interviews to occur in contexts that are conducive to disclosure. Therefore, upon obtaining the subjects' consent to be interviewed, I would ask them to choose a convenient place where they felt safe, and allowed them to decide the best time for the interview.

I have learned from experience working as a research assistant for a project on prostitution that these women can refuse at any time to talk to you even if they had agreed in advance to be interviewed. Thus, in order to seize all opportunities, I conducted the interviews immediately upon obtaining their consent. Most interviews were conducted during the subjects' working hours.

The research relationship established between interviewers and interviewees is the means whereby the research gets done. This relationship affects factors such as whether subjects participate in your study and how much information they would like to share with you (Maxwell, 1996). One of the greatest challenges is establishing trust (Dalla, 2006). Potential participants are more concerned with what kind of person the researcher is than with the research itself. It is irrelevant whether or not they have knowledge of social research, or what their attitude is as regards the study itself (Hammersley and Atkinson, 1995). This implies that a good rapport between interviewer and interviewee is of paramount important in ethnographical research.

One salient consideration in shaping a relationship with the people studied is personal appearance (Hammersley and Atkinson, 1995). Investigators must dress and behave in an appropriate way, in harmony with the research setting, otherwise, the establishment of trust may be jeopardized. By way of illustration, in response to a friend's spontaneous invitation one day, I went to a nightclub directly after conducting an interview. I did not get a chance to change my clothes. I was dressed casually, in a T-shirt and blue jeans, attire that is definitely incompatible with a nightclub setting. I became aware of this very shortly, from the expression of the mammies, in which curiosity and suspicion were apparent. On other occasions, however, especially when I conducted interviews, dressing casually and neatly was helpful in developing a good rapport and reducing the psychological distance between interviewees and myself. The tricky part is to present oneself as a non-threatening, easy-going person, as well as a well-educated classy woman attractive to your subjects. In this way, voluntary participation and information-rich data can be obtained.

All interviews were conducted privately, with only the interviewer and interviewee being present, although, on several occasions some subjects said that they would like to be interviewed together. Under such one-on-one interview circumstances, interviewees were willing to divulge information and express opinions that they would not have done in front of others. All interviews were conducted after acquainting subjects with the purpose of the conversation. Otherwise, subjects would not have spoken openly and freely.

Interviews occurred at different places, including my hotels, the subject's work place, a community office, restaurants, and in a friend's car. Interviews with women working at hair salons were conducted at a community office that is located on the third floor of an apartment building in a residential area. A number of convenience stores and hair salons line a narrow alley. This place was chosen because many young women work in hair salons in this residential area. When the interviews were conducted, no third party was involved except the interviewer and subjects.

Interviews with women working at nightclub/karaoke lounges and sauna/massage parlors were conducted either in my hotel room or at the places where they worked. Helped by a prostitution client, the manager of a club, and the owner of sauna/massage parlors, I waited for the subjects in my hotel. Interviewing subjects at their workplace, however, is a better strategy for it allows them to relax much more than they would in less familiar surroundings (Hammersley and Atkinson, 1995). Therefore, I didn't object when subjects preferred to be interviewed at their work-place. Interviews with women from karaoke lounges and massage parlors were conducted at their work places. Street workers with their pimps were also interviewed in a room or lounge in a hotel. One independent street worker was interviewed in my friend's car, and two others were interviewed in restaurants (see Table 1.1).

Subjects are very cautious, even when they are willing to participate in this study. One subject working at a sauna parlor wore sunglasses during the entire interview even though the interview was conducted at night. Another subject working in a karaoke lounge kept asking me not to record information about her children, although I had repeatedly assured her that I would not record any identifiable information.

Field Observations

Field observation in my research project refers to the collection of data by visiting sex venues and observing, reflecting upon, and interpreting the actions of the individuals being studied. Whereas participant observation involves assuming some kind of a role in a social group or its fringes (Jupp, 1989), the field observation that I conducted was confined to observing the working conditions of the groups under study, and the social interactions among them in their natural surroundings and with minimum disturbance.

A total of eight field observations were conducted over a two-month period at four different commercial sex venues in Shenzhen. Three of these were carried out at nightclubs/karaoke lounges, one at a massage

Table 1.1   Interviews

Subject	Time	Minutes	Interview Place
Hair salon			
Xiao Xiu	4-5 p.m.	60	Community office
Sha Sha	3:30-4:40 p.m.	60	Community office
Ah Lian	5-6 p.m.	60	Community office
Ah Hong	11:50 p.m.-1 a.m.	70	Community office
Li Xue	5:10-6:30 p.m.	80	Community office
Xiao Yu	6:35-7:30 p.m.	55	Community office
Ah Rong	7:40-8:40 p.m.	60	Community office
Chen Hong	9-9:50 p.m.	50	Community office
Xiao Hui	6-7:10 p.m.	70	Community office
Ah Mei	8-9 p.m.	60	Community office
Nightclub/Karaoke lounge			
Lily	9:10-10 p.m.	50	Hotel
Li Na	10:30-11:20 p.m.	50	Hotel
Ah Ying	1:50-2:30 p.m.	40	Hotel
Nan Nan	5-6 p.m.	60	Hotel
Xiao Ke	6:30-7:15 p.m.	45	Hotel
Li Fei	9:40-10:30 p.m.	50	Hotel
Wang Mei	12:45-2 p.m.	75	Hotel
Na Na	7:55-9 p.m.	65	Booth
Li Ying	9:10-10 p.m.	50	Booth
Wang Xia	11:30-12:10 a.m.	40	Booth
Li Ying	10-11:10 p.m.	70	Booth
Massage parlor/Leisure Center			
Ah Wen	2:45-3:40 p.m.	55	Hotel
Yan Yan	10:30-11:30 p.m.	60	Hotel
Xiao Ya	4:15-5:10 p.m.	55	Hotel
Liu Yan	7:50-9 p.m.	70	Manager's office
Fei Fei	9-9:50 p.m.	50	Manager's office
An An	9:55-10:55 p.m.	60	Manager's office
Ah Xiang	6:20-7:15 p.m.	55	Manager's office
Lan Lan	7:20-8:10 p.m.	50	Manager's office
Mei Fang	7-7:50 p.m.	50	Technician lounge
Le Le	8-9:10 p.m.	70	Technician lounge
Wang Hong	9:25-10:15 p.m.	50	Technician lounge
Xiu Xiu	6:30-7:15 p.m.	45	Booth
Hong Mei	7:15-7:45 p.m.	30	Booth
Street			
Ding Ding	1:30-2:40 a.m.	70	Hotel
Xiao Fang	9:20-10:50 p.m.	90	Hotel
Lin Dan	11:30-12:30 a.m.	60	Hotel Lobby
Lin Yan	9-9:50 p.m.	50	Car
Xiao Ju	5:30-6:20 p.m.	50	Restaurant
Wen Wen	7:20-8:10 p.m.	50	Restaurant

parlor, one at a hair salon, and three on the streets where streetwalkers solicited customers. All the observations at off-street sex venues were made by the researcher and her friends visiting these venues as regular customers. Due to the fact of gender, I could not approach streetwalkers as a regular customer. On three occasions, I went to streets that were frequented by streetwalkers, and at one point, I met a woman who became one of the subjects. Most observations were conducted at night, between 8:00 p.m. and 12:00 a.m., except the one in the massage parlor, which occurred in the afternoon. The length of each observation varied. On an average, approximately two hours were spent per observation, as longer periods of time become quite unmanageable (Hammersley and Atkinson, 1995)

Throughout the observations, I paid particular attention to the working conditions, individual behavior and social interaction among the prostitutes, patrons, and operators of the venue (such as mammies, bosses, and owners). Whenever possible, I also engaged in informal conversations with the above-mentioned actors. These informal conversations served two purposes: (1) they could lead to potential participants becoming actual subjects of this research, rendering the sample more representative, and (2) they could provide information about the operation of the commercial sex trade, as well as about the interactions among the above mentioned actors. Although no subject was recruited directly from off-street field observations, these did provide me with valuable information about how the business was operated, how these women worked and how they were treated by mammies and managers, and so on.

Table 1.2   Field Observations

# of Observation	Venue	Time	Minutes
1	Nightclub/Karaoke	10-12 p.m.	120
2	Nightclub/Karaoke	8-10 p.m.	120
3	Nightclub/Karaoke	9-11 p.m.	120
4	Hair Salon	8:30-10:30 p.m.	120
5	Massage Parlor	3-5 p.m.	120
6	Street	9-10 p.m.	60
7	Street	9:30-10:30 p.m.	60
8	Street	11-12 p.m.	60

Street observations offered me a distinctive way to study how street-walkers go about their business, and how their solicitation activities are frequently disrupted by police patrols. In addition, conversations with residents of areas where streetwalkers plied their trade provided me with an understanding of local people's attitudes toward street prostitutes.

Limitations and Strengths of This Study

Strengths

Research that examines the effects of both structural and individual factors on women's involvement in sex work is scarce indeed. Anti-trafficking literature emphasizes the role of structural factors, such as poverty, inequality in social and economic life, and political turmoil. These structural factors make women vulnerable to trafficking and/or prostitution. Studies on prostitution place emphasis on the effects of childhood experiences on women's involvement in prostitution. Very little knowledge exists about the role played by individual circumstances or immediate events that prompt the women to migrate and end up in the sex industry. Additionally, there remains the question of how structural factors, combined with immediate events such as unemployment, divorce, illness, urgent need of money, victimization, etc. motivate women to decide to get involved in prostitution and put their future in the hands of alleged traffickers. In addition, prior research has omitted to examine the distinctive characteristics that make these women different from other women who, under similar circumstances, did not choose the same life path. Little, thus, is known about the manner in which these women make the decisions to migrate and get involved in sex work in relation to 1) their immediate circumstances, and 2) other options (if any) available to them.

Furthermore, very little academic research—particularly research that is empirically based—has been conducted on prostitution and traf-ficking within China, and published in academic outlets. While some research has indeed been published on prostitution, and on trafficking to and within other parts of the world, research specific to China is lacking, particularly so with respect to sex trafficking. Through its focus on ethnographic interviews with the women, this study intends to help address this gap. Through face-to-face interviews of women working in various sex venues, this study intends to discover 1) the differing paths to prostitution, 2) the structural factors, individual characteristics and immediate circumstances contributing to their involvement in the sex trade, and 3) the extent to which they are forced, deceived, or coerced into sex work.

The second major strength of this study is derived from the methodological approach it employs.

Criminologists have recognized the importance of field studies of active offenders (Wright et al., 2006), and have a long history of interviewing those engaged in illicit behaviors in order to gain insights into the nature of crime and criminality (Copes, 2003; Copes and Hochstetler, 2006). The offenders' perspective is crucial to understanding the criminal decision making process, because they are in the unique position of being able to describe their motives, the causes of crime, criminal calculus, and the perceived deterrence of crime control strategies (Miether and McCorkle, 2001). The offender is viewed as an impartial narrator of events and qualitative research is seen as the most appropriate way to gauge criminal motives (Copes and Hochstetler, 2006).

The offender's perspective can be obtained by conducting interviews with individuals known to law enforcement authorities—e.g., those who are incarcerated (e.g., Wright et al., 2005; Shover and Honaker, 1992) or active offenders (e.g., Bennett and Wright, 1984; Cromwell et al., 1991; Jocobs et al., 2003). There are fundamental qualitative differences between the two types (Jacobs, 2006). Institutionalized offenders are not the same as active offenders in terms of their sophistication, skills in evading arrest, or the extent to which they are concerned about being arrested (Jacobs, 2006).

It has been argued that data obtained by interviewing active offenders has greater reliability and validity than data obtained from incarcerated offenders. One reason is that incarcerated offenders are "unsuccessful criminals" (McCall, 1978) which calls into question the extent to which a sample obtained through official sources is representative of the total population of offenders (Copes, 2003; Jacobs et al., 2003; Wright et al., 2006). The other reason is that offenders do not behave "naturally" in a prison setting (Wright and Decker, 1994), and therefore may not be honest with investigators for fear of repercussions from criminal justice agencies and personnel (Copes, 2003). In addition, their account of past activities may be distorted by the passage of time, the prison environment, and a host of other factors (Wright and Decker, 1994). A full understanding of criminal behavior requires that criminologists incorporate field studies of active offenders into their research agendas. Without such studies, both the representativeness and the validity of research based on offenders identified through criminal justice channels will remain problematic (Wright et al., 2006). Research focusing on active offenders provides a better possibility of obtaining accurate and reliable data (Cromwell et al., 1991; Jacobs et al., 2003).

Informed by the aforementioned research on offender interviews, this study sets a sample frame that includes only those women who were practicing prostitutes at the time of interview. This sample frame excluded those identified by authorities or NGOs as trafficking victims, and those incarcerated for prostitution. According to Tyldum and Brunovskis (2005), due to the fact that the ratio of cases identified by law enforcement entities or NGOs to the total number of trafficking cases remains unknown, it is difficult to determine to what extent the identified cases are representative of the universe of trafficking cases. Cases identified by the police are likely to be influenced by the ability of law enforcement agents to recognize trafficking, and the willingness of victims to contact law enforcement agencies. In particular, victims of trafficking who were aware they were going to work in the sex industry, or those that had prior prostitution experience are likely to be underrepresented in data on victims identified through NGOs or law enforcement authorities. Similarly, prostitutes incarcerated by authorities are not representative of the whole population of prostitutes; visible prostitutes in the lower end of the class-stratified occupation usually tend to be overrepresented (Weitzer, 2005a). Thus, it would be methodologically biased to study prostitution and sex trafficking subjects by setting a sample frame that included only those women brought to the attention of law enforcement authorities and NGOs.

Most research on prostitution has been carried out on the least prevalent type of prostitute, namely streetwalkers. Streetwalkers constitute only a minority among prostitutes, yet they have received the lion's share of attention. The larger population of indoor sex workers, such as those who work in brothels, bars, and massage parlors are overlooked (Weitzer, 2005b). This study includes women in various sex venues. As a result, it includes the following three distinctive features that are rarely characteristic of previous studies: 1) the subjects are women who are active prostitutes, 2) they work at diverse venues, 3) they constitute a population within which victims of trafficking make up a subpopulation. By setting such a sample frame, it is possible to reach current trafficking victims, even if some of them might be reluctant to provide information susceptible of placing them in jeopardy. There is also an added likelihood of coming across past trafficking victims. Through the experiences recounted by the interviewees, a general picture of the background characteristics of this subpopulation can be formed, and the proportion of prostitutes who are victims of trafficking can be inferred. Understanding the stories of previous trafficking victims could help us identify the factors that result in their becoming prey to traffickers. The sample in this study is better representative of the trafficked population than the statistics provided by law enforcement agencies and NGOs who do not cover more than a small proportion of the total population of trafficking victims.

Weaknesses

Although, as subjects of ethnographic studies, active offenders have some advantages over offenders known to criminal justice agencies or officials, exploring the offender's perspective presents researchers with numerous difficulties, due to the nature of their behavior and the fact that their identities are hidden. For the same reasons, migrant commercial sex workers are difficult groups with whom to conduct interviews, and results can be problematic for several reasons. Conclusions from this study may have limited validity, either external or internal, due to reasons of methodology or the nature of the information.

First of all, all interviews were conducted through snowball sampling, a method that calls into question the reliability of this study. Active offenders are generally hard to locate (Irwin, 1972) and danger is inherent in fieldwork with active offenders (Jacobs, 2006). The difficulty and dangerous involved in collecting information from active offenders has been well documented by practitioners of this approach (see Jacobs, 2006; Wright et al., 2006). As a result, the nature of samples of many studies on active offenders, including active prostitutes, is of opportunity and convenience (e.g., Sharpe, 1998). This is the case of the current study. Participants in this study either knew my intermediaries or met me by coincidence as they worked on the street. Therefore, the samples cannot be considered representative of the entire population of prostitutes.

Sample bias may also be introduced by the fact that voluntary participants probably "are more reflective, intelligent, and well-spoken than the typical street offender" and the researcher's writing relies heavily upon those interviews (Copes and Hochstetler, 2006: 25). Respondents in the current study are generally more accessible and more willing to talk, thus implying that they are not under the strict control of their employer, pimps, or recruiters. Moreover, because the number of participants in qualitative studies tends to be small, such samples are less representative of the larger population from which the sample is drawn. Therefore, findings from this study may not be able to be generalized to other countries, or even to other areas in China. For example, the high percentage of rural migrant women in this study cannot be generalized to other areas of China, such as the northeastern areas. Indeed, some studies (Huang and Pan, 2003) have found that in their sample, almost all women involved in prostitution are from urban areas.

The second limitation lies in the nature of the data collected during the interview, namely, self-reported information.

Data obtained by interviewing active offenders should reflect what is going on in the offender's mind with considerable accuracy (Wright and Bennett, 1990). However, some criminologists have voiced concerns about the extent to which subjects are telling the truth (Glassner and Carpenter, 1985; Irwin, 1972). Due to the illegality of activities in which offenders are involved, fieldworkers are assumed by active offenders as suspicious, and "acting undercover in some capacity with a real mission to expose them" (Sharpe, 1998: 17). They are also considered "spies of some sort" (Jacobs, 2006: 12) or the interview may be viewed as the frontline of a sting operation (Wright and Decker, 1994.) As a result, it is reasonable to suspect that offenders may not tell the truth even if they agree to participate in the study.

Problems with self-reported information mainly include issues of honesty and memory relapse. These are the most serious threats to the accuracy of the data. When discussing illegal behavior such as prostitution and drug use, individuals tend to conceal or exaggerate information (Graham and Bowling, 1995). This study found that some respondents had difficulty remembering how long they had been practicing prostitution, how often they committed acts of prostitution, or details about the economic aspects of these activities. The women may only answer those questions which they are willing to answer, and may provide inaccurate answers to sensitive questions, such as the amount of money they earned, or details about the first time they provided sex services. One subject, for example, told me that she worked in a foot massage parlor for almost two years without providing sex services. With the money she earned, her parents bought a house. However, the money she earned was not enough and she therefore came to Shenzhen and started to work as a prostitute. Based on my field observation and conversations with actual foot masseuses, I had learned that masseuses who provide actual massages end up developing very big and visible calluses on their knuckles; in some cases, their fingers even become deformed. During my conversation with the subject under discussion, I observed that she did not have the telltale callous, leading me to doubt that she answered that specific question honestly.

Nevertheless, face-to-face data collection is among the most accurate self-report designs (Huizinga and Elliott, 1986). It is the most practical and accurate way of gaining information about behavior that one cannot detect, or that is not observable. Such information may relate to an individual's feelings, the meaning of their personal experiences, such as being raped, or being in urgent need of money, living in poverty, losing jobs, getting divorced, and so on. Though street criminals have a stereotypical image of lying, or avoiding the truth, there is little evidence to support this claim (Maher, 1997). This is not to say that offenders' reports are immune to lies, distortion, or memory relapse. Rather, they appear to be less susceptible to inaccuracy than some might think (Jacobs and Wright, 1999).

Copes and Hochstetler (2006) have noted that offenders are often quite willing to discuss their lives and criminal careers in great detail. It has been empirically proved by numerous researchers that once subjects have been persuaded to participate in a study, they often demonstrate a willingness to tell the interviewer their life experiences in greater detail than the researcher expected (see Jacobs 1996, 2000; Jacobs and Wright, 1999; Shover, 1985, 1996). This is understandable because the secrecy of criminal work "means that offenders have few opportunities to discuss their activities with anyone besides associates" (Wright and Decker, 1994: 26). However, once a relationship of trust and rapport is established between subjects and the interviewer, offenders seemed to enjoy talking "straight" to someone about their life experiences and deviant behavior. This was confirmed in the current study by the fact that some of the subjects told me after the interview that they felt relieved and comfortable after talking with me.

The third threat to the validity of this study arises from what Maxwell (1996: 89) refers to as the "threat to valid description." I did not record interviews or observations either on audio- or videotape, and this poses a potentially serious threat to the validity of this study. Where observations are concerned, it is difficult to accurately transcribe what one has observed, since what information is relevant to this study is dependent on the observer's judgment. Furthermore, not recording an interview may entail the loss of some of the information provided by the subjects or information may be recorded inaccurately during the transcription process. In order to rule out these validity threats, I employed a number of strategies. I ensured that the expanded notes I made were detailed and complete enough to provide a full and revealing picture of what I observed. I transcribed the interviews verbatim, rather than simply writing down what I believed was significant.

Sharpe (1998) has noted that relying on interviews and field observation does raise questions of reliability and validity; it is difficulty for the researcher to gauge how typical the participants are and how reliable the information is. However, the data in this study relies on the perspectives of the women subjects, law enforcement officials and sex ring operators; the data sources include in-depth interviews, official statistics, and field observations. This strategy of a triangulation of perspectives may "enable a comprehensive, unique and realistic picture of female prostitution to be presented and analyzed" (Sharpe, 1998: 26).

2

Human Trafficking and Feminist Debates

Prostitution, in one form or another, has existed in many, if not all, societies. Generally, it refers to the act of providing sexual services in exchange for money. It is so deeply rooted in social, political, and economic life that it is impervious to legal control and public condemnation, and it adapts to any changes in society. It has been argued that there is a certain "inevitability" regarding the existence of prostitution (Selfe and Burke, 2001). If this is true, why then does the public denounce prostitutes; and why do the authorities, at least superficially, try to eradicate this "inevitable" phenomenon? "Much of the concern over prostitution is due to it being regarded as a moral problem and vice which is either anti-social or in some way bothersome to others" (Sharpe, 1998: 1).

Historically, prostitutes have been praised, tolerated or vilified (Sharpe, 1998), in large part due to differing perspectives on prostitution. As regards human trafficking, however, all governments and organizations agree that the trafficking of human beings for sexual exploitation is heinous. It is a crime that severely violates human rights and one, therefore, that should be combated and eradicated.

The subject of human trafficking has received increased international attention since the 1980s due to globalization, improved transportation and communication networks, and growth of the sex industry (Coontz and Grebel, 2004; Outshoorn, 2005). The complexities of the phenomenon and opposing views regarding prostitutes have resulted in numerous controversial debates on human trafficking. The origin of these debates dates back to the end of the nineteenth century when "white slavery" aroused public outrage and became a top priority of international organizations. "White slavery" refers to the abduction and transport of white women for prostitution. The first international agreement on human trafficking—i.e., the International Agreement for the Suppression of the White Slave Trade—addressed the fraudulent, forced and abusive recruitment of women for sexual exploitation in another country. The agreement did not equate "white slavery" with prostitution (Gozdziak and Collett, 2005). Human trafficking reappeared on the agendas of international organizations and conventions in the 1980s. However, a definition of human trafficking did not emerge until 2000, with the signing of the United Nations Protocol to Prevent, Suppress, and Punish Trafficking in Persons (hereafter referred to as the UN Protocol). The UN Protocol is a result of negotiations between two camps: one views prostitution as legitimate labor, while the other regards all prostitution as violence against women (Doezema, 2002). In either case, the debate about what constitutes human trafficking did not end with the signing of the Protocol.

Definition of Human Trafficking

The United Nations Protocol defines trafficking in persons as:

> "The recruitment, transportation, transfer, harbouring or receipt of persons, by means of the threat or use of force or other forms of coercion, of abduction, of fraud, of deception, of abuse of power or of a position of vulnerability or of the giving or receiving of payments or benefits to achieve the consent of a person having control over another person, for the purpose of exploitation."

> "Exploitation shall include, at a minimum, the exploitation of the prostitution of others or other forms of sexual exploitation, forced labor or services, slavery or practices similar to slavery, servitude or the removal of organs."

> "The consent of a victim of trafficking in persons to the intended exploitation ... shall be irrelevant where any of the ...fore-mentioned means... have been used" (United Nations, 2000).

The UN Protocol defined trafficking as a crime against humanity, characterized by the intent to exploit (Raymond et al., 2002). Three categories of exploitation are identified: sexual exploitation, labor exploitation, and removal of organs. The definition also includes a wide range of means utilized for trafficking; generally containing the elements of force, fraud, or coercion. The consent of the trafficked individual is irrelevant when these elements are present. The definition also encompasses every stage of the trafficking cycle; it targets all people involved in trafficking, and addresses a spectrum of violations at every segment of the chain.

According to the UN Protocol, trafficking can operate on two separate levels: the process of recruitment and the context of work or services. The reason for this is that recruitment can be a matter of choice, while the context of work could involve the application of force (McDonald et al., 2000).

This definition makes a distinction between human trafficking and human smuggling. Human smuggling is "the facilitation, transportation, attempted transportation or illegal entry of a person(s) across an international border.... Human smuggling is generally with the consent of the person(s) being smuggled, who often pay large sums of money and once in the country of their final destination will generally be left to their own devices" (U.S. Department of the State, 2005: 1). The person being smuggled is generally cooperative, and thus there is no actual or implied coercion or exploitation involved. Persons being smuggled are complicit in the crime. They may have a "contract" with the smugglers to work off a smuggling debt, but when the debt is paid, they are free to leave (U.S. Department of the State, 2005). Trafficking involves recruiting as well as exploiting, and must contain the elements of force, fraud, or coercion. Unlike smuggling, trafficking does not require crossing an international border. It is also possible that a person being smuggled may at some point become a trafficking victim when an element of force, fraud, or coercion is introduced.

The legislative definition of human trafficking may seem clear, but in reality, the scope of how human trafficking should be defined is still open to debate, largely due to the differing interpretations of what constitutes coercion, and of terms such as "position of vulnerability" and/or "exploitation." Raymond et al. (2002) argued that any definition of trafficking must be broad and inclusive enough to represent the reality of what happens to all women who are trafficked—either internationally or domestically, with or without their consent, and by means of force, fraud, deception, abuse of the vulnerability of a victim, etc. Therefore, they asserted that when a determination about whether these women are victims of trafficking is made, not only should "palpable force and coercions" (2002: 124) used in the course of movement, and within the institution into which women are trafficked, be taken into account, but also "the context of consent—including inducement, vulnerability, and other subtle pressures" (2002: 124) caused by the interaction of socio-economic and political determinants. Such an interpretation leads to the following conflations.

1) *Conflation of human trafficking and human smuggling*: Human smuggling and human trafficking are usually a result of similar circumstances, such as poverty, lack of economic opportunities, civil unrest, and political uncertainty (U.S. Department of the State, 2005). Smuggled people may consent to be transported, and pay a huge smuggling fee under the same induced or vulnerable context as trafficked people. As a result, women migrating and working in the sex industry are often regarded as trafficked victims in anti-trafficking discourse, and some regard all migrant women practicing prostitution as trafficked victims. However, regardless of the institutions that a migrant works for (legitimate or illegitimate), if a smuggled person works twelve or more hours a day, seven days a week, to pay off a smuggling fee,

does it not constitute "exploitation"? Is he or she coerced to work under a condition of slavery? If the answers to these questions are yes, how can we make distinctions between smuggling and trafficking?

2) *Conflation of sex trafficking and sex exploitation*: Regarding the relationship between sex trafficking and sexual exploitation, Hughes (2002) recognizes that sexual exploitation is not always indicative of trafficking; while Raymond (2002) argues that "trafficking and sexual exploitation are intrinsically connected and should not be separated merely because there are other forms of trafficking; or because some countries have legalized/regulated prostitution..." (2002: 499).

The underlying reasons for these conflicting interpretations of the definition of human trafficking lies in: 1) a radical feminist ideology which equates prostitution with trafficking. Raymond (2001) argues that the definition of prostitution and trafficking cannot be separated due to the fact that much trafficking is for prostitution and other forms of sexual exploitation. 2) an anti-trafficking discourse that overemphasizes pressures caused by structural factors which contribute to an environment encouraging both human smuggling and trafficking. These factors include poverty, economic and social inequality, political unrest, etc. In a nutshell, due to the vagueness of the UN Protocol definition, some anti-trafficking researchers equate trafficking in women with human smuggling, while others conflate victims of human trafficking with women working in the sex sector (Lazaridis, 2001).

People generally agree that the worst case of human trafficking—where an innocent woman is kidnapped, forced to provide sexual services, and cannot escape—rarely occurs. Many women are willing to migrate, and some know in advance that they will work in sex sectors. Yet, they are indiscriminately regarded as victims of trafficking in some studies because they are assisted by a third party. These studies fail to examine whether or not the necessary elements of "force, deception, or coercion" are involved in the process of recruitment and transport, or identifiable in the institutions the women work for. This is exemplified in the following excerpt from Raymond et al. (2002):

> Nu does not fit the stereotype of the "naïve and innocent, virgin girl" kidnapped for prostitution. Rather, a cumulative experience of structural deprivation, and a culture of violence and battle for survival beginning in babyhood and persisting throughout her life, rendered her vulnerable to prostitution. These factors induced her to migrate.... Her decisions at all points were products and manifestations of a structurally-mediated force of circumstances, common to although differing in degree for the other respondents in this study, and masses of women in prostitution (2002: 132).

Feminist Debates on Human Trafficking

The confusion in the interpretation of the definition of human trafficking is a consequence of opposing feminist views on prostitution. It is both a new, as well as an old crime. Although related to the "white slavery" of the nineteenth century, human trafficking today bears little resemblance to its historical counterpart (Doezema, 2000), and is more complex than it was in the nineteenth century. This becomes apparent when we examine anti-human trafficking discourse during these two distinct historical periods.

During the first wave of feminism in the second half of the nineteenth century, the image of a human trafficking victim was "a young and naive innocent women lured or deceived by evil traffickers into a life of sordid horror from which escape is nearly impossible" (Doezema, 2000: 24). Therefore, in the campaign against "white slavery," most feminists agreed to the abolitionist goal of ending state regulation of brothels and deploying state power to stop all prostitution (Outshoorn, 2005).

The modern feminist's anti-trafficking campaign however, is split along ideological lines in keeping with their views of prostitution, and the relationship between prostitution and human trafficking (Doezema, 2000; Outshoorn, 2005). During the second wave of feminism, discourse against human trafficking developed along two camps, each reflecting its own distinctive views on prostitution. These two competing and contradictory views are those of the "regulationists" as opposed to those of the "abolitionists" (Doezema, 2000). "Neo-abolitionism" is compatible with the traditional abolitionism that originated in radical feminist thought; "regulationism" is the new discourse which frames prostitution as sex work, and has developed out of liberal and socialist feminist thought (Outshoorn, 2005).

Neo-abolitionists view prostitution as violence against women, defining it as sexual exploitation. They believe that prostitution is sexual slavery and an extreme expression of sexual violence against women. It is therefore essential that it be abolished, and that all those profiting from sexual exploitation be penalized, with the exception of the prostitute herself. The term "trafficking," thus, should include all forms of recruitment and transportation relating to prostitution. Violence is intrinsic to prostitution, so whether or not force or deception takes place is irrelevant (CATW, 1999). Regulationists view prostitution as a form of work, and a possible option of survival chosen by women, which should be respected (Bell 1994; Chapkis, 1997). In cases where prostitution is an option, the force or deception that are necessary components in the definition of human trafficking may not be present.

This violence v. work debate between abolitionists and regulationists brings into focus the burning question, namely, whether adopting a career in prostitution can be a choice. Abolitionists reject the notion of voluntary prostitution, maintaining that that no woman would prostitute herself by choice or free will (see Outshoorn, 2005). To abolitionists, women's consent to sex work is meaningless. Regulationists, on the other hand, distinguish between voluntary and forced prostitution, believing that the vast majority of trafficked women are migrant laborers who should be protected by labor legislation. Women have the right to sexual self-determination and to work as prostitutes. They should be able to work under decent labor conditions and migrate to do sex work. Prostitution itself is therefore not the problem. The critical, problematic issue is the context within which women get involved in trafficking and prostitution, forced or not. Trafficking exists only when force, deception, or coercion occurs during the course of recruitment, transportation, control, and in the institution to which they are trafficked. The Coalition against Trafficking in Women (CATW) is the main exponent of abolitionism, and their platform regards all prostitution (voluntary or forced) as a violation of human rights and believes that all migrant sex workers are victims of trafficking (Coontz and Griebel, 2004; Outshoorn, 2005). The primary exponent of regulationism is the Global Alliance against Trafficking in Women (GAATW). In the view of regulationists, women can be victims of sex trafficking, but not all women sex workers are victims of forced prostitution. Much of what is referred to as trafficking is actually the smuggling of human beings (Wijers, 2001).

The experience of migrant women working in the sex industry is, in fact, more complex than that expressed by the "forced vs. voluntary" debate (Agustin, 2005). Some studies that focused on the perspectives of migrant women working in the sex industry have found that women are aware that they will be working as prostitutes (Agustin, 2005; Brunovskis and Tyldum, 2004). Many migrants doing sexual work do not describe themselves as 'being forced' into it, or as having no other options in life (Agustin, 2005). Agustin (2000, 2005) asserts that choices are made when these women migrate, because even among the poorest migrants, not everyone opts for sex work, just as not everyone opts to migrate from places of poverty.

The human trafficking discourse conflating migration that involves selling sex with "trafficking" has been the subject of numerous critiques (e.g., Doezema, 2000; Pickup, 1998). Many authors have attempted to distinguish between the concepts of "trafficking" and migration of people who sell sex (Alexander, 1996; Skrobanek, 1997; Agustin, 2003 and 2006).

Studies on human trafficking indicate that rarely has a woman who never thought of doing sexual work while contemplating migration, been given false information about a job, and eventually forced to provide sex services. In most cases, migrant women knew about the nature of their work in destination countries. In some cases, people start out doing legitimate work, but feel compelled to sell sex because of the differential in pay (Agustin, 2005). Regardless of the different degrees of force or coercion, CATW conflates all "facilitated" migration with trafficking (Agustin, 2005).

Factors Contributing to Prostitution/Migration and Human Trafficking

Prostitution and human trafficking are both related to migration. Although migration is not a required factor in defining cases of human trafficking, it is generally agreed that prostitutes are not natives of the places where they practice prostitution. Women who are living in poverty, or looking for a better life, tend to migrate for economic, social, or political reasons, in search of better opportunities.

Many studies on prostitution and human trafficking have focused on factors that motivate women into prostitution, or render them vulnerable to trafficking during the migration process (e.g., Gil et al., 1994; Ren, 1999; Davidson, 2001; Hughes, 2002; McDonald et al., 2000; Vocks and Nijboer, 2000; Raymond and Hughes, 2001; Raymond et al., 2002; Sharpe, 1998; Skeldon, 2000; etc.). These studies examine how women from Asia, the former Soviet Union, Eastern Europe, and South America migrated and ended up in the sex industry. A variety of factors, both macro and micro, have been found to contribute to the growth of prostitution, migration, and human trafficking. These factors generally fall into one of two categories: structural factors and individual characteristics. Structural factors may be economic, political, patriarchal, or cultural and may include poverty (Ren, 1999; Raymond et al., 2002), high unemployment rates (Hughes, 2002; Ren, 1999; Vocks and Nijboer, 2000), economic deprivation (Hughes, 2002), economic and social inequality (Hughes, 2002; Vocks and Nijboer, 2000), patriarchal family structure (Vocks and Nijboer, 2000), demise of social welfare and health care systems (Hughes, 2002; Vocks and Nijboer, 2000), sexual liberation

(Gil et al., 1994; Ren, 1999; WHO, 2001), massive migration (WHO, 2001), cultural factors where women assume family responsibilities (Raymond et al., 2002), or old values whereby women are regarded as commodities (Gil et al., 1994). Among these factors, economic motives were decisive (Voicks and Nijboer, 2000). For example, Hughes (2002) found that unemployment has been a significant factor contributing to the trafficking of women. Women in the sex industry find it irresistible to earn a considerable amount of money in a short period of time (Vocks and Nijboer, 2000), and therefore prostitution is an alternative form of employment for many women in poverty (Ren, 2000).

It is also agreed that a variety of "complex socio-economic, political, ideological 'push and pull' factors interact in a certain configuration to prompt women to migrate and render them trafficked" (Raymond et al., 2002: 32). According to Hughes (2002), Russian women are involved in the sex trade due to economic deterioration. After the Soviet Union collapsed, many people were suffering on account of the fall in economic production, the high unemployment rates, and the demise of social welfare and health care systems. All these factors result in economic instability and newly impoverished populations. Due to economic inequality, women bear the brunt and make up 60-80 percent, or even 90 percent of the registered unemployed. Numerous women in the sex sector of Russia and abroad have cited the need to support children as the principal reason for being involved in prostitution. Similarly, Vocks and Nijboer (2000) found that a variety of factors have driven more women from Central and Eastern Europe into prostitution. Among these factors are patriarchal family structures, inequality in the job market resulting in more unemployment among women, the breakdown of existing social security facilities, and high inflation rates.

In Asia, most people who sell sex do so because of few alternative opportunities, and the responsibility of daughters to sacrifice themselves as a means of supporting their families. Entry into the sex sector is an attempt to help families escape poverty rather than an occurrence forced upon them by unscrupulous traffickers (Caouette and Saito, 1999). In Asia's patriarchal society, women have less access to education than men, and therefore they have fewer employment opportunities. They are, nevertheless, expected to assume the responsibilities of supporting their families and raising their children. Sex work provides many uneducated and unskilled women with an income that far exceeds what they would earn in any other occupation (WHO, 2001).

Poverty, the most cited factor contributing to women's involvement in prostitution and their vulnerability to human trafficking, can be relative or absolute. Some studies highlighted the effect of relative poverty on women's involvement in prostitution. Many people are selling sex because of relative deprivation rather than absolute poverty. For example, an undocumented number of young women from Asia's middle classes are now selling sex (often on a part-time basis) to supplement their incomes as they pursue their education (WHO, 2001). Sex workers may be poor, uneducated women in difficult financial circumstances, but they may also be well-educated women who choose to sell sex because of the high monetary reward (Evans, 1997). Gil et al. (1994) found that these women do not come solely from low-income households. In one sample from their study, 76 percent of prostitutes come from middle or high-income families. In another sample, only 53 percent are from low-income families. Ethnographic interviews from the same study also found that some prostitutes stay in the sex industry to maintain a luxurious lifestyle, one that enables them to buy expensive clothes, makeup or other products.

Based on the evidence that increasing numbers of educated and upwardly mobile young women are joining the sex trade, Evans (1997) believes that "prostitution is no longer represented as the response of impoverished and uneducated young women at the bottom of the urban and rural social hierarchy to the difficulties of making a livelihood" (1997: 176). It is more lucrative than the relatively meager incomes afforded by other professions. Raymond et al. (2002) notice that Filipino victims of trafficking migrate to "earn what women thought would be *a decent livelihood*" (2002: 55, emphasis added). In the meantime, Raymond et al. (2002) maintain that migration is *the only viable option* to earn that decent livelihood.

Studies on human trafficking also shed light on some individual backgrounds relating to women's vulnerability to prostitution and sex trafficking (e.g., Raymond and Hughes, 2001; Raymond et al., 2002; Vocks and Nijboer, 2000). These factors include a history of sexual abuse, limited education, broken families, mistreatment or other domestic problems (such as violence, divorce, alcoholic fathers or brothers), desire for economic independence from partners or families, or the desire to maintain competitive lifestyles, etc.

Who Are the Traffickers?

Many studies on sex trafficking found that traffickers and victims often know each other and sometimes have close relationships (McDonald et al., 2000; Vocks and Nijboer, 2000). The origins of sex workers tend to be based on connections, suggesting the importance of family and friend-ship networks with regard to their entry into prostitution (Skeldon, 2000). In most cases, recruiting was done by friends, acquaintances, or even family members (Caldwell et al., 1997; IOM, 1995; Vocks and Nijboer, 2000). For example, ten out of forty women in Raymond and Hughes's (2001) study were recruited by their spouses/partners into the sex industry. Boonchalaski and Guest (1998) examined two sectors of the sex industry in Thailand—brothels and massage parlors—and only 13.5 percent and 7.4 percent respectively had been introduced to the sector by agents or middlemen. Introductions by friends or self-arranged introductions were the most prevalent modes of entry. Only 13.5 percent of those in the brothels reported that they had been forced into the industry, and not a single girl in massage parlors reported the use of force.

Differing Paths to Prostitution

Women in the sex industry take varying routes into prostitution. Some are offered legitimate jobs and then tricked into prostitution; while others know they will work in the sex sector but are deceived as to the work conditions (Caldwell et al., 1997; IOM, 1995; Wijers and Lap-Chew, 1997). Several studies have tried to distinguish among these women based on the extent to which they are forced, deceived, or coerced. There are several models of classification of women in the sex sector as regards their routes to prostitution (see Hughes, 2002; Vocks and Nijboer, 2000; McDonald et al., 2000; Lazaridis, 2001). Based on the choices women had during the process of mov-ing to the Netherlands and working in the sex sector, Vocks and Nijboer (2000) classified them into three categories: kidnapped or sold women, deceived women, and exploited women. McDonald et al. (2000) classified women in their study into four categories: purely trafficked, semi-trafficked, unintentional sex trade workers, and oc-casional prostitutes.

A review of studies on prostitution and human trafficking suggests that migrant women in the sex industry may fall into one of the follow-ing five categories.

1) *Involuntary migration.* Women falling into this category are ab-ducted, kidnapped, or in other words, forced to migrate. They never have any chance to make their own decisions about migration or their involvement in prostitution. There is no doubt that they are trafficked for sexual exploitation.

2) *Voluntary migration, seeking to work in the legitimate sector, ending up in the sex industry against their will.* Women falling into this category generally live under poor financial circumstances or want to make more out their lives, and are not afraid to take risks. They migrate to improve their own financial circumstances or to help their families. They are promised jobs in the legitimate sector (e.g., as models, waitresses, domestic workers, secretaries, etc). Upon arrival at the destination, they find themselves "trapped into a hopeless situation, heavily in debt to traffickers" (Lazaridis, 2001: 81).

3) *Voluntary migration, knowing in advance that they will be involved in sex work.* These women are lied to regarding working conditions, the extent of debt, and the length of their involvement. They may be charged more money than others, business may not be as good as promised, or they may not get as much money as they were led to expect. In addition, they may not have been aware that they could be controlled by a third party in one way or another, such as by not being allowed to leave the premises, or not being allowed to possess identity documents.

4) *Willing Prostitutes.* These women agree to work in the sex industry prior to migration. They may have previous experience in prostitution. Some who do not have a history of prostitution may be from dysfunctional families, or have little, if any, education. They may have to divide money they earn with sex ring operators (madams, pimps, etc.) or they may keep all the money they earn, depending on the establishments they work for.

5) *Drifting Prostitutes.* Some women cannot find jobs in their destinations, or the jobs available to them do not provide the income they desire. So they drift into prostitution after being at their destination for a while. They are independent, and do not owe any debts because of sex work. They may give part of their income to sex ring operators, depending on the type of sex venue. Furthermore, they may enter into prostitution due to peer pressure, or to supplement income they may earn from legitimate sectors. They do not get involved in sex work immediately upon arrival. Meaker (2002) refers to them as resident migrant sex workers.

In their sample, Vocks and Nijboer (2000) found an order of frequency in the categories into which the women are divided. Least frequent are the cases where women are abducted and transported to work in the sex industry, followed next by women who are deceived by recruiters concerning the nature of their occupation. Women who know about the nature of their occupation but not about the circumstances, constitute the largest category of victims. According to the Ministry of

Internal Affairs in the Russian Federation, more than half the women who engaged in prostitution in foreign countries knew they would be involved in prostitution before they left Russia (Hughes, 2002). It is not necessary for a third party to use force to recruit women and girls into the sex industry/migration because rural young women and girls are generally eager to migrate for employment opportunities. The supply of labor for the sex industry does not rest entirely upon trickery, for it is also possible to openly recruit women and girls into prostitution (Davidson, 2001). Brunovskis and Tyldum (2004) found that it is very rare that women who become victims of trafficking are taken out of their countries against their will. Those who have studied the various sectors are virtually unanimous in their assessment that the majority of these women entered the sex industry voluntarily (Skeldon, 2000). The vast majority chooses to migrate, and some are aware that they will work as prostitutes.

Equating trafficked victims with women working in the sex industry or other conditions of sexual exploitation overlooks the complex and diverse experiences of migrant women and their motivation for entering prostitution. These different paths suggest that the issue of prostitution, migration and human trafficking is more complicated than the dichotomy of forced/voluntary prostitution suggests.

Limitations of Prior Studies

Since human trafficking returned to the international agenda in the 1980s, it has been one of the major concerns among governments, international agencies, and NGOs. Enormous attention and academic interest have been devoted to the topic of human trafficking. However, our knowledge of this subject is still relatively poor (Gozdziak and Collett, 2005). There is a lack of accurate statistics on sex work (WHO, 2001). The vast majority of European countries are unable to provide reliable data as to the number of cases, victims and their characteristics and perpetrators (IOM, 2001). The numbers that are commonly cited have little basis in reality. Due to the lack of quantitative data and the enormous difficulties of producing accurate assessments of trafficking, many commentators repeat statistics that are often extrapolated from unverified numbers (Raymond et al., 2002). But these numbers have been repeated so often that they have become accepted as fact (WHO, 2001), and statistics on human trafficking need to be treated with caution (Wijers and Lap-Chew, 1997; WHO, 2001).

A review of studies on human trafficking suggests that several factors contribute to the limited knowledge base: methodological problems, ideological problems, and limited research on human trafficking.

Methodological Problems

The development of research methods on trafficking remains in its infancy (Salt and Howgarth, 2000). Some research draws information from newspaper reports and media investigations to compile a picture of trafficking (Gozdziak and Collett, 2005). Others base their studies on data from intermediaries, such as social service providers, NGOs, counselors, law enforcement officers, victim advocates, and others working with trafficking victims (Gozdziak and Collett, 2005; Salt and Howgarth, 2000). The methods used to produce estimates of the scope of trafficking are not very transparent (Gozdziak and Collett, 2005). The methodological weakness has produced slippery data on the number of trafficking cases and has resulted in limited knowledge about victims and perpetrators of human trafficking.

The assumption that human trafficking and prostitution may be connected to organized crime and violence restrains attempts to access women in the sex industry and the alleged trafficking perpetrators. Some researchers may use covert methods as their way of obtaining information about trafficking; others depend on trafficking victims themselves to obtain information on traffickers. Even when researchers have made direct contact with traffickers, the latter tend to be small-scale operators, lacking representation (Kelly, 2000). In addition, controlling measures used by traffickers or exploiters, fear of reprisals, and "whore stigmas" attached to those plying the commercial sex trade deter these women from participating in studies. Even when they do participate, their fear of traffickers and of law enforcement and immigration officials discourages the women from telling their stories truthfully.

When access to victims is possible, few studies specify which kind of establishments these women work for. Skeldon (2000) noted the complexity of the sex sector, which is divided into many sub-sectors, each catering to different markets, and having differing prices and organizations. Women who work in differing sex venues not only have varied backgrounds, but have also followed distinctive paths into prostitution. Therefore, the extent to which they are forced, deceived, or coerced varies. To obtain a comprehensive understanding and knowledge of sex trafficking, it is necessary to study women in various sex venues.

Language barriers constitute another difficulty when access to victims is possible (Kelly, 2002). In most international trafficking situations, the women do not speak the local language and researchers must rely on interpreters. The presence of a second stranger creates two problems. First, women may be more unwilling to talk to researchers and second, the details of their experiences may be lost in the translation process. Furthermore, many research activities take place in contexts that are not conducive to disclosure (Kelly, 2000). For example, interviewing women in detention centers or prisons is not ideal from a research point of view. Individuals are constrained and influenced by their surroundings, and this will affect the amount of information they are willing to divulge.

Ideological Problems

Human trafficking research must distinguish between human trafficking and human smuggling; as well as between trafficked women, migrant women in the sex industry and sexually exploited women. While it may be easy to do so in theory and in legislation, the definitions often overlap in reality, leading some researchers to simplify the situation by equating trafficked women with smuggled women or migrant women working in the sex industry.

Anti-trafficking discourse regards prostitution as violence against women; violence is intrinsic to prostitution. Proponents of this discourse, therefore, oppose all forms of prostitution, and regard all women in prostitution as victims of trafficking. This results in inaccurate data on human trafficking, as well as exaggerated estimates of the scope and extent of human trafficking. For example, figures produced by anti-trafficking NGOs are inaccurate in that they probably overestimate the number of trafficking victims (WHO, 2001) due to the differing concepts of prostitution.

Conflation of migrant abuse, trafficking, and prostitution seems to be common in anti-trafficking discourse and counter-trafficking campaigns (Chapkis, 2003). Some studies on the sex industry and on female migration are placed under the heading of "trafficking" (Bindman and Doezema, 1997). Some writings on human trafficking equate trafficked women with prostitution, although voluntary prostitutes are included in their samples (e.g., Raymond and Hughes, 2001; Davis, 2006). In some instances, all transnational or migrant sex workers are defined as trafficking victims without taking into account the abusive conditions of their employment or deception during the recruitment process, thus lumping together all migrant women in the sex industry (e.g., Raymond et al., 2002). When collecting data on human trafficking, governments often mix data related to trafficking, smuggling, and illegal migration (Laczko, 2002). In some accounts, all undocumented migrants who crossed borders with assistance are counted as having been trafficked (Gordy, 2000). As a result, the available data on human trafficking is confusing and unreliable.

Limited Research Topics

Kelly (2002) identified the following sub topics on which previous research on human trafficking for sexual exploitation is concentrated: 1) estimating the scale of the problems; 2) mapping routes and relationships between countries of origin, transit and destination; 3) documenting methods of recruitment; 4) exploring the control mechanisms used and the abuse of human rights involved; and 5) undertaking critical reviews of current legal and policy frameworks and making recommendations for new action. Research on human trafficking for sexual exploitation has not moved much beyond these topics.

Some studies indeed identify structural factors and individual backgrounds that make women vulnerable to prostitution and human trafficking. Rarely, however, have attempts been made to examine whether any immediate events in the women's lives (such as divorce, job loss, meeting someone who has been in the sex industry, etc.) influenced their involvement in prostitution. And if indeed they did, it must be asked how these events, in conjunction with structural factors and individual backgrounds, triggered women to migrate and become involved in the sex industry. In what way did these events push women to take the risk of "putting their future in the hands of traffickers"? If it is true that migration and involvement in the sex industry is the "only viable option" (Raymond et al., 2002) for women living in poverty, how can the fact be explained that "even with the poorest migrants, everyone does not opt for sex work" (Agustin, 2000 and 2005)?

It is obvious that the extent to which women are forced, coerced, and deceived into prostitution varies significantly among sex establishments, and some of the women do not fall into the UN Protocol's definition of human trafficking. Anti-trafficking studies lump them together and count them as trafficked victims, perhaps to heighten the perception of the seriousness of the problem. No attempts have been made to estimate the proportion of women falling into each category. Therefore it is not clear how many women in sex industry are trafficked women, a fact that contributes to the ambiguity surrounding the nature and scope of the problem.

Skeldon (2000) describes the worst forms of trafficking as follows:

> The young girl is sold out of poverty to unscrupulous brokers, or kidnapped from a village and transported to the city, where she is kept in sordid conditions to serve an endless procession of men until she is eventually released to return home to die of AIDS (2000: 17).

This image serves as a powerful driving force to seek the elimination of human trafficking. However, how often happens is much more difficult to assess. It is imperative that research be conducted to provide important insight into the comprehensive picture of women in the sex industry. Rigorous ethnographic and sociological studies based on in-depth interviews with women in the sex sector can provide baseline data on trafficking victims and their characteristics, providing a balanced and comprehensive picture of women working in commercial sex.

3

Explanations of Prostitution and the Rational Choice Perspective

As seen in the previous chapter, prostitution and sex trafficking are related phenomena, yet they are distinct from each other. Women may become victims of trafficking even though their migration and involvement in prostitution may be voluntary. Many trafficking victims continue to work in the sex industry after they are rescued or have freed themselves from traffickers. Most sex trafficking occurs at some point in the process of migration; cases in which women are kidnapped and forced to migrate and work as prostitutes are very rare. Factors contributing to human trafficking and prostitution, such as poverty, unemployment and/or inequality, are often times overlapping. Women may decide to work as prostitutes under the same circumstances as those who are trafficked. The immediate circumstances under which they first embark on this trade vary, and therefore it is necessary to draw a distinction between prostitutes and victims of trafficking.

This chapter will explore a theoretical framework within which to study, understand and explain women's involvement in commercial sex. It will begin with existing explanations of prostitution, followed by theoretical guidelines to accommodate all relevant factors contributing to the occurrence of sex trafficking and prostitution.

Factors Contributing to Prostitution

The literature on prostitution includes research from diverse disciplines, including law, psychology, sociology, medicine, and women's studies. Researchers have tried to identify factors that are responsible for women's entry into prostitution. Previous research has examined the relationship between prostitution and early childhood experiences (Brunschot and Brannigan, 2002; Bullough and Bullough, 1996; James and Meryerding, 1977; Jesson, 1993; Nandon et al., 1998; Seng, 1989; Simons and Whitbeck, 1991); family background (Dalla, 2006; Sharpe,

1998); poverty (Bamgbose, 2002; Brunovskis and Tyldum, 2004; Hoi-gard and Finstad, 1992; Sharpe, 1998); drug use (Dalla, 2006; Graham and Wish, 1994; Potterate et al., 1998); societal factors (Bamgbose, 2002; Brunovskis and Tyldum, 2004; Cusick, 2002; Dalla, 2001; Sharpe, 1998); as well as attitudes toward prostitution (Bamgbose, 2002). However, social research on the biological, psychological, and sociological factors that cause prostitution has been far from impressive. Empirical findings regarding the nature of the relationships mentioned above have failed to provide consistent evidence of a connection between them, and of the nature of the connection (Brunschot and Brannigan, 2002; Dalla, 2006; Gil et al., 1994; Evans, 1997; WHO, 2001). Nevertheless, a review of research on prostitution does offer several explanations for women's involvement in prostitution.

Previous studies have attempted to connect prostitution to early childhood experiences, such as being raised in a dysfunctional family, being subject to sexual or physical abuse, showing patterns of runaway behavior, and other specific events and experiences in an individual's formative years. Although these studies provide valuable information for a better understanding of how the developmental process may influence women's entry into prostitution, they fail to reach a consensus. A case in point is childhood sexual experience. Some studies (James and Meryerding, 1977; Simons and Whitbeck, 1991) support a direct relationship between early sexual abuse and later involvement in prostitution. According to James and Meryerding (1977), a child who is sexually abused is more likely to see herself both as a sexual object and as sexually debased. In a society where women are valued based on sexuality, those who view themselves as debased may perceive prostitution to be a viable alternative. Similarly, those who are rewarded for sexual favors may see their sexuality as a primary means of gaining status. The degree to which women regard their body as their greatest asset is crucial in their decision to adopt prostitution. In contrast, researchers such as Seng (1989) find that the relationship between early sexual experience and prostitution is not direct, but involves runaway behavior as an intervening variable. It is not so much that sexual abuse leads to prostitution as it is that running away leads to prostitution. Such inconsistent and contradictory evidence reveals the complexity of identifying causal paths leading from childhood experiences to adult prostitution.

Studies with no comparison groups tend to emphasize the effects of an "unpleasant and chaotic childhood" (Earls and David, 1989: 16) on involvement in prostitution, while studies involving comparison groups reveal that at least some of these negative life experiences are also found in women not involved in prostitution. Brunschot and Brannigan (2002) examined the effect of childhood mistreatment on those women choosing street prostitution as a career. Using a control sample of students, this study concluded that "those who have been sexually abused are at no greater risk of becoming prostitutes than of becoming students.... These findings suggest that negative sexual experiences do not necessarily manifest themselves in future overt sexual deviance, such as prostitution" (p. 229). Nandon et al. (1998) contend that "when an appropriate comparison group is used, known precursors of prostitution fail to discriminate between the prostitution and nonprostitution groups" (p. 207).

Brunschot and Brannigan (2002) suggest that research in prostitution needs to move beyond preoccupation with the pathological backgrounds of individuals, to establish the wider social circumstances that may mitigate the consequences of childhood experiences. As Jesson (1993) stated, there is a danger in relying too heavily on psychological factors that may emphasize pathological aspects of the individual young person at the expense of recognizing other social and family-based factors that may explain later involvement in prostitution. Many studies have followed Jesson's lead, and there has been a shift from the earlier emphasis on psychological predisposing factors to social and situational factors (i.e., Bamgbose, 2002; Dalla, 2006; Hoigard and Finstad, 1992; Sharpe, 1998).

Poverty is frequently cited as a cause of prostitution (Hardman, 1997; Delacoste and Alexander, 1998). Although no single common factor for prostitution has been identified, there is certainly one common motivator for prostitutes—money. Research finds that not all women who engage in prostitution come from poverty stricken backgrounds (Brunovskis and Tyldum, 2004). Some women start to prostitute themselves to make money to build houses, save for their children's education, pay off debt, or because they have lost their jobs or hate their work. Neither poverty nor economic deprivation can adequately explain what causes prostitution, for both these factors fail to discriminate between impoverished women who become prostitutes and those who do not (Brunovskis and Tyldum, 2004; Delacoste and Alexander, 1998). Many women claimed that they were "forced" into prostitution because of unemployment, because they were underpaid, or because they labored under other desperate economic situations. However, in many cases, the poverty of the women is relative (Brunovskis and Tyldum, 2004; Sharpe, 1998).

Sharpe (1998) found that the majority of women were indeed not able to secure regular employment due to inadequate qualifications or lack of skills. Many of them, however, deliberately wanted to avoid routine work and the rigidity that a legitimate job would entail. The problem is not a lack of jobs, but the low level of salaries. Prostitution thus emerged as a rational occupational choice, affording easy money for little effort (Sharpe, 1998: 55).

While Sharpe's 1998 research reveals that family background and early life experiences do not give clear indications as to why some women go into prostitution, other studies indicate that family member and friends play a significant role in the introduction process (Brunovskis and Tyldum, 2004; Sharpe, 1998).

Moving Beyond a "Single Factor" Model

Whilst many prostitutes have undergone similar life experiences, it is impossible to identify a single factor that is responsible for women turning to prostitution (Brunovskis and Tyldum, 2004; Sharpe, 1998). Information to determine the relative importance of these variables is, at best, insufficient (Earls and David, 1989). Bullough and Bullough (1996) noted, "When all is said and done no single factor stands out as causal in a woman becoming a prostitute" (p. 171). In researching various studies on the subject, Cusick (2002) concluded that authors virtually never argue that any of these variables directly cause prostitution, or that any of these factors are necessary for entry into prostitution. Brunovskis and Tyldum (2004) concur that it is more reasonable to say that the women have been influenced by several factors, all of which served to lower their threshold for entering prostitution or traveling abroad. Bamgbose (2002) maintains that a high unemployment rate, poverty, social values, consumer lifestyle, and the desire to uphold a certain status in a declining economy are all factors contributing to prostitution.

Obviously, the road to prostitution is paved with a wide range of interconnected factors, including childhood experiences, current life circumstances, situational factors, and personality and temperament characteristics (the lust for money and excitement). It is a complex interaction of social, emotional, psychological and economic factors (Sharpe, 1998). Previous studies have documented a correlation between prostitution and various life experiences—childhood mistreatment, poverty, unemployment, running way and drug use, to name a few. Yet, it is clear that many women who are exposed to the same experiences do not adopt the same lifestyle.

Why the Rational Choice Perspective?

Most theoretical approaches have focused on female prostitution in terms of psychological, sociological, and economic explanations (Flowers, 2001). These theories explain prostitution in relation to mental disorders, family, prior sexual victimization, social structure, immorality, financial deprivation, etc. As with any deterministic theories of crime, however, they fail to examine the perspectives of the main actors (i.e., the women involved in commercial sex) and whether these women make decisions or exercise any choice to work in commercial sex. This is probably due to ideological reasons.

Human trafficking discourse centers on the effects of structural factors on sex trafficking. Few studies focus on the women themselves, or ask whether there are any differences between prostitutes and non-prostitutes in terms of their aspirations, values and norms, personal attributes, etc., how social context, personal circumstances and situational factors play a role in their decision to enter prostitution and how women in prostitution react to specific life events or unsatisfactory circumstances. There are some researchers, however, who have pointed out that women make rational choices and that the classic theory of crime could apply to women's involvement in prostitution.

Sharpe (1998) contends that adopting prostitution is "the result of a complex interaction between individual rational choice and the association with, and influence of, female friends or relatives already involved in the business. When further compounded by a multitude of external pressures, of a financial, domestic and personal nature, the combined impact could serve to make the road to prostitution seem like a very reasonable, logical and viable option" (1998: 55). Cusick (2002) does not doubt that young people who become involved in prostitution do not make truly informed choices; they are victimized by predatory adults. He also contends that academic and policy researchers should aim to uncover a fuller typology of entry models, bearing in mind during this process, certain classic sociological explanations of youth deviance.

Jesson (1993) suggested that attention be paid to immediate circumstances and situational factors, such as the existence of a number of prostitutes already working near the area, the presence of pimps or sex establishments such as saunas and massage parlors, and the demand for sex. Although varying social situations may play a significant role in women's entry into prostitution, Earls and David (1989) believe that research must dig deeper in order to discover why some individuals turn to the sex trade while others do not.

As stated in the preceding chapter, feminists are divided along ideological lines on the subject of prostitution. Radical feminists (abolitionists) regard prostitution as the epitome of women's oppression. Prostitution is inherently violent, thus the concept of "forced prostitution" is a pleonasm (see Outshoorn, 2005). Based on this reasoning, all women in commercial sex are forced into it, and therefore, all forms of prostitution should be halted. On the other hand, liberal feminists (regulationists) regard prostitution as a possible work alternative. They distinguish between forced and voluntary prostitution and agree that anti-human trafficking efforts should target the former. They believe the rights of women who consent to work in commercial sex should be acknowledged and protected.

However, "meaningless consent" does not necessarily imply that no choice or decision is involved when women initially undertake migration and/or prostitution. Agustin (2005) claimed that women must make individual choices since not everyone living in poverty decides to migrate. Money aside, according to Agustin, women enter the sex industry because of human desire, a predisposition for risk taking, thirst for adventure, new opportunities and independence. The presence of networks already in place is also a contributing factor (Agustin, 2005).

Empirical studies on human trafficking contend that women in the commercial sex business rarely migrate against their will or because they were tricked into doing so. Rather they are actually eager, sometimes even desperate to relocate, hoping for better opportunities (Davidson, 2001). Most of them know what they are getting into when they relocate, and are aware of other options available to them. The various paths to prostitution suggest that the degree of consent depends on the categories women fall into. Some women are selling sex because of relative, rather than absolute poverty. Even those who are uneducated and live in poverty know that working in commercial sex is not the only option. In addition, not all women are passive and/or ignorant. Most studies worth reading describe migrating women as independent decision-makers who travel abroad, weigh their options, talk to their friends and families and take advantage of opportunities, continually making decisions along the way (Agustin, 2005).

It is safe to claim that most women choose to work in the sex industry because it pays so well (Evans, 1997; WHO, 2001). A large percentage of women involved in commercial sex do make choices. However, it must be recognized that the choices available to them are limited. Furthermore, their decisions are influenced by a variety of factors, including their personal backgrounds and circumstances, situational events, social networks, socio-economic conditions, development of communication and transportation networks, and changes in social norms and values. Economic incentive, undoubtedly, is the decisive factor motivating these women's involvement in sex work (Vocks and Nijboer, 2000). Structural factors predispose individuals to migration and involvement in commercial sex. Studies have also found that recruitment, transport and the overall operation of commercial sex establishments rarely involve criminal organizations. The recruiters are usually relatives or friends (Caldwell et al., 1997; IOM, 1995; Vocks and Nijboer, 2000). Despite its undesirable nature, sex work is an option available to migrant women with limited education or skills.

As previously indicated, prostitution is not a typical solution for most women faced with unemployment or unattractive jobs. The road into prostitution is a long and winding one. Women who consider it an acceptable alternative means of support have a value system and a view of the human body far different from those held by society at large (Hoigard and Finstad, 1992). The development of an individual is the result of the interaction between the person and his/her environment over time. A person's present circumstances cannot be fully understood without examining his/her past history, current situation, social relationships, etc. Certain factors will influence his/her future options and decisions. In other words, individuals are not passive reactors to the environment. Rather, they attempt to actively cope with whatever situations they find themselves in. This suggests that women are not passive reactors to the environment; they perceive and interpret specific situations differently based on their acquired attitudes, beliefs, norms and values.

Drawing upon previous studies, and the wide range of experiences of migrant women in prostitution, we may thus come to the conclusion that prostitution is a result of a variety of interconnected factors appearing in women's lives at different periods of time. Established factors (such as poverty, sexual abuse, drug use, etc.) do not furnish an exhaustive explanation at the individual level. Therefore, any attempt to understand why women get involved in prostitution must be built under a theoretical framework which permits taking into account a variety of factors, ranging from historical events to current circumstances, from social contexts to personal situations, from societal (social) factors to the individual's attributes, temperament, personality and moral norms and values. The

Rational Choice Perspective (RCP) provides a framework of analytical guidance able to accommodate such a requirement.

The Rational Choice Perspective as Theoretical Framework

The Rational Choice Perspective (RCP), put forth by Clarke and Cornish in the 1980s, is based on the free will and choice model of the classical school, as well as the economic model of rational man (Jeffery and Zahm, 1993). The RCP, in contrast to other dispositional theories, applies different assumptions about human nature and the nature of criminal behavior. It assumes that offenders commit crimes for personal benefit. They make choices and decisions; and exhibit a measure of rationality in the process (Clarke, 1995; Cornish and Clarke, 1986). Thus, the RCP views the offender as goal-oriented, deliberate, and rational. It tries to see the world from the offender's perspective.

The RCP acknowledges the effects of a wide range of factors on the occurrence of crime, not only related to "the offender's background and current circumstances but also about the offender's immediate motives and intentions, moods and feelings, moral judgments regarding the act in question, perception of criminal opportunities and ability to take advantage of them or create them, and assessment of the risks of being caught as well as of the likely consequences" (Clarke, 1995: 95). All these diverse factors have varied influence on the occurrence of crime.

In explaining the occurrence of crime, the RCP makes a distinction between crime and criminality. Consequently, it distinguishes between situational factors such as the perceived costs and benefits of crime, opportunities for crime, as well as the influence of motivational variables of traditional theories on the occurrence of crime. While emphasizing the effects of situational inducements and impediments on the occurrence of crime, this theory acknowledges the role of background factors in shaping or determining the values, attitudes and personality traits that predispose the individual to criminal involvement (Clarke and Cornish, 1985; Cornish and Clarke, 1986). "In decision-making context, however, these background influences are less directly criminogenic; instead they have an orienting function-exposing people to particular problems and particular opportunities and leading them to perceive and evaluate these in particular (criminal) ways" (Clarke and Cornish, 1985: 167).

According to the RCP, a wide range of factors are involved in an offender's readiness to commit a specific offense (criminality), encompassing "various and contemporaneous background factors with which traditional criminology has been preoccupied; these have been seen to determine the values, attitudes, and personality traits that dispose the individual to crime. In rational choice context, these factors are reinterpreted as influencing the decisions and judgments that lead to involvement" (Cornish and Clarke, 1986: 4). The occurrence of specific crime events is "influenced by situational factors related to opportunity, effort, and proximal risks" (Cornish and Clarke, 1986: 4). Thus, the decision process involved in the commission of a particular crime is largely dependent upon the immediate circumstances and situation (Clarke and Felson, 1993).

Although the RCP has its origins in recent economic theory (Cook, 1980), it does not represent a wholesale adoption of economic theories of crime (Clarke and Felson, 1993). The most significant modification the RCP has made to the economic model of offenders is that of "limited rationality." It views "free will" as a given, assuming that people have been always making choices in everyday life. However, The RCP does not imply that offenders are free to choose whatever they want. Offenders' choices are constrained by limited time and capacity, and the availability of relevant information (Clarke, 1995). Further, an individual's objective circumstances influence the nature of criminal opportunities available to them (Cook, 1980). They are molded by their family background, race, gender, socio-economic status, previous experiences, etc. For example, most common street thugs could not be successful computer hackers as they have neither the knowledge nor the opportunity to carry out such an activity. Consequently, offenders do not opt for choices that are not open to them (Felson, 1994). The RCP appears to imply "soft" determinism: although options may be limited, some leeway to choose still exists (Clarke and Cornish, 1985).

The proponents of the RCP intentionally use the term "perspective" to indicate that the RCP is not a theory of crime, but rather an organizing perspective from which theories for specific crimes could be developed, or within which existing ones could be usefully located (Clarke and Cornish, 1985; Cornish and Clarke, 1986). The purposes of the RCP are to advance the understanding of criminal behavior and be helpful in crime control. Or, as Clarke and Felson (1993) put it, the RCP was initially developed to deflect criticism of the atheoretical nature of situational crime prevention. However, it is not merely restricted to this goal. The authors regard their efforts as "being directed to the more complete understanding and, ultimately, more efficient control of crime" (Clarke and Felson, 1993: 7).

Enlightened by the RCP, three levels of factors can be identified with respect to women's participation in prostitution, namely, their immediate circumstances at the time of initial involvement in prostitution, socio-economic factors contributing to their circumstances and the situational factors that either induce or impede their involvement in prostitution. The RCP pays relatively little attention to the motivational variables of traditional theories, not because they are unimportant, but because they play a lesser role in the occurrence of crime. The Rational Choice Perspective stresses the roles of current situational variables, such as opportunities, rewards and costs, but it also takes into account the offender's perceptions of these variables, which are determined by a variety of background factors (Clarke and Cornish, 1985). While being guided by the RCP, this study does not intend to judge the relevance of distal or proximal factors in motivating women into prostitution or human trafficking. Rather, it aims to identify those factors at both the social and the individual levels that profoundly affect the lives of Chinese people and give rise to the prevalence of prostitution and human trafficking within the context of a society in transition.

Utilizing the RCP as a guiding theory does not necessarily deny the radical feminist assertion that prostitution constitutes violence against women. It does not suggest that some women are not forced into the sex trade against their will nor imply that prostitution could be a form of work. Most women are driven to commercial sex work by macro-level structural factors including poverty, inequality in economic and social life, the patriarchal system, political unrest, etc. Under these oppressive conditions, women have fewer opportunities than their male counterparts and their choices are made in "a context of structured, politically imposed inequality that ranges from male-female relations to the relationship between Western nations and the Third World" (Barry, 1995: 83). Therefore, most of these women are forced by their "circumstances," rather than by alleged traffickers exerting "force, fraud, or coercion."

Furthermore, using the RCP as a theoretical framework does not suggest that there is no sexual exploitation involved in commercial sex, nor does it advocate the decriminalization or regulation of prostitution. There are, nevertheless, many differences between forced and voluntary participation in the sex trade, based on women's circumstances and motivations. Classifying all women in commercial sex as trafficking victims will produce less informed policies and strategies, making it impossible to stop prostitution, prevent human trafficking, and protect victims effectively. Human trafficking and prostitution are related phenomena, but they are also separate and different. Dealing with them, thus, requires distinctive policies and strategies.

4
Pre-Prostitution Life

Researchers have attached a great deal of importance to the family background, education, childhood experiences, and employment history of women involved in prostitution. Although the ensuing picture is relatively complex, it is generally agreed that women working as prostitutes are usually from lower social classes, or broken families, or have a history of poor performance in school (Hoigard and Finstad, 1992; Sharpe, 1998). In order to understand the entry of these women into prostitution, it is necessary, therefore, to examine their family background, socio-economic status, childhood experiences and education. This chapter aims to present demographic characteristics, highlighting the family background of the women, their education and employment history, all of which are presumably related to their involvement in commercial sex.

Source Areas, Age, Marital Status, and Parents' Occupation

Source Areas

Most studies on prostitution or human trafficking focus on migrant women, either domestically or internationally. This is mostly because prostitution is closely related to both internal and international migration. Prostitutes generally do not engage in the trade in their own hometowns or villages (Lim, 1998; Shaw, 2006). This is also true in China. Most prostitutes in areas such as the Guangdong province are not originally from that province (Gil et al., 1994; Lau et al., 2002). Examination of both police statistics and interview data in this study reveals the same pattern.

No women interviewed or arrested were original residents of Shenzhen. Half of the women interviewed (N=20) came from the provinces of Sichuan, Hunan and Chongqing (Chongqing is one of four provincial-level municipalities; it was a sub-provincial city within Sichuan province until 1997). Guangxi, Guangdong, Yunnan, Fujian, Anhui, and Hubei are also major source provinces, and a total of 16 women came from these provinces. Finally, of the last four subjects in the study, one woman came from each of the following provinces: Shangdong, Jiangxi, Shaanxi, Hainan.

When compared to the interview data, police data, too, shows a similar pattern where source provinces are concerned. The source areas of both data are concentrated in the southwestern (i.e., Sichuan, Chongqing, Yunnan, Guangxi) and southern provinces (i.e., Guangdong, Fujian, Hunan, Hubei, Anhui, Jiangxi). Very few women were from inland northern provinces, such as Shaanxi, Shandong, Henan. Not all source areas are poor, on the contrary, Guangdong and Fujian are generally regarded as developed affluent provinces in China. Three of the interviewed women and one of the arrested are Guangdongnese: however, none of the women are local, that is to say, Shenzhenese. Furthermore, the most striking aspect of the social background of those I interviewed is that most women, i.e., 37 of the 40, were from rural areas. Only three women came from urban areas of which two worked at a nightclub/karaoke lounge and one was a streetwalker. According to police data, 33 women were from rural areas, as opposed to 4 from urban areas.

Table 4.1   Source Provinces

Provinces	Interview Data	Police Data
Sichuan	4	6
Hunan	11	8
Chongqing	5	1
Yunnan	4	4
Guangdong	3	1
Fujian	3	2
Hubei	2	5
Guangxi	2	3
Anhui	2	2
Jiangxi	1	1
Hennan	0	5
Shananxi	1	1
Hainan	1	0
Shangdong	1	0
Unknown	0	2
Total	40	43
Rural or Urban		
Rural	37	33
Urban	3	4
Unknown	0	6

Age and Marriage History

Some research on prostitution has found that women in prostitution are generally young, single and without children (i.e., Gil et al., 1994; Vocks and Nijboer, 2000; Yang et al., 2005). In the current study, the average age of women interviewed was 23.6, ranging from 18 to 39 years of age. Most of them (N=34) fell between 18 and 30 years of age (85 percent). Thirty women were single, five were married and four divorced. One woman cohabited with her husband because that was the condition under which her husband agreed to go through with the divorce. They never separated although they were legally divorced years ago. A very distinctive feature of the ten married women in the group was that five of them were subsequently divorced. Among this group of ten married or divorced women, six had one child and four had two children.

Table 4.2   Demographic Characteristics of the Women

Age	Interview Data (N=40)	Police Data (N=43)
16-20	13	17
21-30	21	16
31-40	6	9
Range	18-39	16-39
Mean	23.6	24.17
Average age		
Hair Salon	20.9	N/A
Massage/Sauna Parlor	23	N/A
Night Club/Karaoke Bar	25.3	N/A
Streetwalkers	26.3	N/A
Marital status		
Single	30	30
Married	5	8
Divorced	4	1
Cohabiting	1	0
Unknown	0	4
Education		
0	0	2
1-6 years	11	18
7-9 years	19	10
10-12 years	10	4
Unknown	0	9
Mean	8.2	7

Some studies (e.g., Brunovskis and Tyldum, 2004) have found large differences, in terms of age and education, between women from different source areas, and those working at varying venues. This pattern is confirmed by women interviewed in this study. The average age of women in the four sex venues varied, with women at hair salons having the minimum average age, and streetwalkers having the maximum average age. Consistent with this pattern, all women working at hair salons were single. With regard to women working at nightclubs or karaoke lounges, eight were single and three were married. Ten of the thirteen women working at massage/ sauna/entertainment centers were single, two were married, and one was divorced. Two of the six streetwalkers were divorced, one cohabited with her ex-husband, two were single, and one was married. The marital status pattern is consistent with the average age of women in each venue. As seen above, the women working at hair salons were the youngest. Police data regarding the women's age and marital status shows a similar pattern: most were predominantly in their later teens and twenties with ages ranging from 16 to 39. The average age was 24.17. Thirty of the forty-three women who had been arrested were single, eight were married and one divorced.

Parents' Occupation

Although 37 of the 40 women interviewed were from rural areas, not all of their parents were farmers. Since the 1980s, when the economic reform policy was implemented, more and more farmers left their land, becoming part of the migrant population seeking work in urban areas. Most participants' parents belonged to the first generation of this floating population. They either worked in factories or other private enterprises or operated small "mom-and-pop" or other family businesses. As a result, only about half of the women's parents were farmers at the time. Nine of the mothers and eight of the fathers were migrant workers. Eight fathers and eight mothers ran private businesses. Most of the participants had at least one sister or brother. The mean number of siblings was 2.16. Most women (N=31) had one to three siblings (not counting the subjects themselves).

Childhood Life, Family Conditions, and Education

Childhood Life and Family Conditions

Most women interviewed (N=37) talked about their childhood life and family conditions. Not all of them fit the traditional stereotype, i.e., that prostitutes come from poor backgrounds and low class families.

Table 4.3 Parents' Occupations

Parents' Occupations	Mother (N=40)	Father (N=40)
Farmer	20	20
Migrant worker	9	8
Teacher	1	1
Private business owner	8	8
Worker	2	1
Public officer	0	1

Approximately half (N=18) categorized their family conditions as poor, some (N=13) as "not bad" or "average," while six women categorized their family conditions as good or affluent.

Most women were from poor rural areas and therefore, it is not surprising that they categorized their family condition as poor. They described various aspects of poverty, and indeed, some of their experiences are really sad and miserable.

Li Xue, a 22-year-old girl who worked at a hair salon, became teary-eyed when I asked her to talk about her childhood life. She told me that her family was very poor and could not afford to send children to school.

I quit school when I was in the 4th grade; my older sister and my two younger brothers quit when they were in 7th grade because my parents could not afford it. I helped my mother to collect recyclable garbage even when I was a small child. We went to towns where we had never been before to pick up garbage. We suffered a lot (Li Xue).

Xiao Fang, 19 years old, was a streetwalker, but she did not solicit customers by herself on the street. Her family was so poor that fellow villagers often made them the butt of jokes.

My parents had three kids—more than other families. My mom grew crops and did chores at home. My father was a carpenter and we depended on him to make money. So my family was poor and, because of this, my parents fought frequently. Villagers looked down upon us. If we borrowed money from them, they would ask whether we would be able to pay it back.... Our villagers said that stone would be able to walk if we became rich (Xiao Fang).

Liu Yan, a mother of one child, who was working at a massage parlor, came from a family where both parents were disabled. One can imagine what this means to a family in rural areas, where family income depends mainly on the labor-intensive agricultural sector.

Table 4.4   Family Conditions

Family conditions	N=40	Percentage (%)
Poor	18	45
Average	13	32.5
Good	6	15
Unknown	3	7.5

My family condition was really bad when I was a child. As far back as I can remember, my mother had always felt dizzy. My father's limbs had gone numb four or five years before I first left the village and he could not do any heavy work (Liu Yan).

Some women were from remote poverty-ridden mountain areas, where infrastructure such as transportation, is undeveloped and the local economy therefore lags far behind. Children have very few opportunities to get an education.

My parents had five daughters. I quit studies when I was in the 5th grade. My younger sister went to school for only one year. We lived in a mountainous area, and it is very poor. Even today, I have to walk 20 kilometers if I want to visit my parents. No public transportation is available (Li Ying).

We live in a remote mountainous area. Now it takes me more than an hour to walk home. My two older sisters never went to school. But my father had to send me to school because all other kids in the village went to school. My family was very poor when I was a kid (Yan Yan).

Because of poverty, some subjects started to work and contribute financially to their families even while they were still in their early teens, in addition to doing chores at home.

I suffered a lot when I was a kid. I had been a housemaid since I was 11 years old (Xiao Ya).

My childhood life was not good. I want to cry when I recall my childhood life. I grew crops, did laundry, and cooked. My parents would not let me eat if I did not work (An An).

Life was very hard when I was a child. I could not even get enough food. I had to feed the cattle after school and would be reprimanded by my parents if they ran away. Thus I could not focus on studying and performed very badly at school (Le Le).

These women were raised in poverty, and as a result, they did not go to school very much. Some of them went to school for no more than six years. Some families tried very hard and made every effort to send their children to school, but the children would have to forgo a college education for economic reasons.

My father passed away when I was 6. I quit studying when I was 13. Although it did not cost a lot of money to go to school, someone needed to do chores at home. One of my sisters was married, and the other sister was going to school. So I quit studying to cook and feed pigs at home (Lin Yan).

My father was disabled and could not grow crops. We had to hire people to grow crops for us. My family borrowed money to support me going to high school. My parents struggled very much so I quit studies and did not take the college entry exam. I did very well in school, but they couldn't afford to send me to college even if I were admitted. Therefore my family felt very sorry about that (Sha Sha).

Some families may not have been as indigent as those described above, but they did not have enough resources to afford sending their children to college, even when their children did well in school. Children's chances of going to school were especially compromised if the family was constrained by a specific financial issue.

During my last year of high school, my father lost money in business. He fell ill and had to be hospitalized. My family was in need of money, and therefore I did not take the college entry exam when I graduated from high school, although I did very well at school (Chen Hong).

I did not pass the college entry exam and planned to take the exam again the following year. But my family conditions became bad. We were fined because my mother violated the family policy, giving birth to my twin brothers. So I came here to work (Ah Wen).

All women, however, were not from poor families. Some described their families as affluent, loaded, or "not bad." However, they did not get very much education because they did not do very well in school, either influenced by peers or affected by their parents' divorce.

Wang Mei did not take the college entry exam because her parents got divorced when she was in middle school, and she could not focus on studies from then on. She started to work after she graduated from high school.

Both my parents are business people. We are very wealthy and we have a house and cars. I learned performance arts, such as singing, dancing, and piano when I was young. My parents divorced when I was in the 8th grade and this affected me very badly. I did not want to study after that (Wang Mei).

Xiao Xiu, a 19-year-old girl working in a hair salon, decided to go out into the work force with her fellow villagers after graduating from middle school, even though her family could afford to send her to school. Her family condition was better than average—her parents ran a Chinese herbal medicine transportation business.

My father wanted me to go to high school, but I did not want to go to school any more because all the other girls in my village were going out to work. My life was good when I was a child. My parents were able to afford whatever other parents bought for their children (Xiao Xiu).

Lan Lan was influenced by her peers who did not do well in school.

My family was affluent when I was a kid. I never struggled. My friends in the same village could not go to school because of poverty. I hung around with them and did not like to study. But my parents wanted me to go to school (Lan Lan).

Na Na, 30 years old, was working at a Karaoke lounge. When she was in high school, her former middle school classmates frequently took her out to dancing halls when they came home from other cities where they were working, making her not want to study.

My father was a public official and my mother worked in a factory. I have two brothers and one sister. They are all older than me and my sister is eight years older than me. My father fell sick very badly before I was born. However, he recovered after I was born. So my father believed that it was because of me (I was a blessing), and therefore he spoiled me. Many of my classmates were jealous of me. When I was still in school, my former classmates who worked far away from my hometown would visit me when they got back, and we frequently went to a dancing hall. Gradually, I did not want to go to school and came out with them (Na Na).

Some subjects said that they did not do well in school although their families were able to afford to send them to school.

I dropped out of school when I was in 9th grade in 2004. It was very hard for me to study and I was frequently truant. I came to Shenzhen with my relatives and worked in factories. My parents would let me go to school if I wished (Ah Hong).

My family condition was good when I was a child. My family could afford to send me to school, but I don't like to study (Ah Mei).

My life was very good when I was young. I did not do very well at school, but both my older brothers go to college (Fei Fei).

A few subjects also told me about their parents' relationship with each other. They also talked about their father's character, and this enhances our understanding of their childhood life and family background.

My mother died in 2006 because life was really hard for her. My father doesn't take any responsibility; he also gambles. My mother struggled too much and died of grief (Li Xue).

Both my parents were migrant workers, but financially we mainly depended on my mother. My father was alcoholic. He would not get up for several days when he was drunk; he also beat my mother sometimes (Xiao Hui).

My father sold a girl when I was eleven or twelve. He then fled and we were fined 5,000 yuan. My family condition became bad since then (Lily).

If my family conditions had been good, I would have liked to study. I did not do badly in school. But I could not focus on studies because my parents fought frequently due to poverty (Xiao Fang).

Education

On account of family poverty, or due to poor performance in school, the average number of years of education of the women interviewed was 8.2 years, ranging from 2 to 12 years. A little over one quarter of the women (11) had no education beyond elementary school. Nineteen had none beyond middle school. Ten of the women attended high school or a technical/vocational school after they graduated from middle school, and seven of them graduated from those educational institutions (see Table 4.2).

Police data shows that the women who had been arrested had a similar level of education as those interviewed, i.e., most of them had no schooling beyond nine years. Nevertheless, the women who were arrested had a lower level of education than those interviewed, largely due to the fact that most of them were streetwalkers, and this group tends to be older than those working at other venues. Their limited schooling can be attributed to their family conditions and was largely a result of the fact that their parents could not afford to send them to school.

The educational level of women in varying venues demonstrates some discrepancies. Women working at hair salons had an average of nine years of education, while women working at the KTV/nightclub and at massage parlors/entertainment centers had 8.7 and 8 years of schooling respectively. Streetwalkers were the least educated, with an average of 7 years of schooling.

Occupations before Prostitution

Most women (N=38) were working in legitimate sectors before getting involved in sex work, with the exception of two women who were housewives. One of them used to work in a factory at her hometown and another woman never worked until she came out with a fellow villager when she was twenty-six, and a mother of two sons. Due to their limited education and skills, jobs available to them were limited and were mainly menial, low-paid, low-status, informal jobs. Twelve women worked in a factory, while eighteen women worked in service sectors that are at the frontline of sex services (hair salons, karaoke lounges, massage parlors, restaurants, bars and hotels). Four of them worked as cashiers, two as sales clerks, and two ran small private businesses (one woman ran a cell phone store, while the other was a street vendor selling ice-cream). Their average monthly income was 1,375 yuan. Thus, they worked in low-income service sectors. Many of them (N=12) had worked in the entertainment sector although they had not yet begun to provide sex services.

Age at the Time of First Employment

Due to family poverty, most women started to work in their teens. The average age at which they began to work was 16.57, the ages ranging, however, from 11 to 26 years. Most of them (N=29) began work for the first time between the ages of 15 to 18, and a little over half of them (54.1 percent) began to work when they turned 16, or even before that age.

Table 4.5   Legitimate Job

Legitimate Job	N=40	Percentage (%)
Legitimate Occupations		
Factory worker	12	30
Karaoke/massage/hair salon	12	30
Cashier	4	10
Restaurant employee	4	10
Sales clerk	2	5
Private business operator	2	5
Housewife	2	5
Hotel employee	1	2.5
Bar employee	1	2.5
Age of first employment		
11-14 years	4	10
15-18 years	29	72.5
19-20 years	3	7.5
Time in legitimate occupations		
Less than 1 year	3	7.5
1 year	11	27.5
2 years	4	10
3 years	8	20
4 to 9 years	8	20
10 or more	4	10
Mean	4 years	

Duration of Work in Legitimate Sectors

Each of these thirty-eight women worked in legitimate sectors for varying periods of time, ranging from 2 days to 20 years. The average years of work before they got involved in prostitution is about four years. The mode is one year (N=11). One woman worked for only two days before entering into prostitution, while another worked for three months. Most women (more than 90 percent) had worked for at least one year before they started to work as prostitutes. They may have worked in many different jobs in several cities before migrating to Shenzhen.

Perceptions of Work in Legitimate Sectors

All interviewed women were asked about their perceptions of previous legitimate jobs. One dominant feature among their perceptions about their legitimate job was that it was grueling and the payment was low, especially in the case of those who worked in factories, or as waitresses or cashiers. Xiao Xiu had started to work in factories with her fellow villagers since she graduated from middle school in 2003. During the ensuing two years, she had worked in two provinces for some time until she came to Shenzhen in 2005.

> I went to Shangdong province with my fellow villagers and worked in a factory in September, 2003. I earned about 400-500 yuan a month. The work was very hard and I could not save any money. After the 2004 Chinese New Year, I worked in a weaving factory in Zhejiang province and earned about 900 yuan a month. I worked 4 days and then had two days off. I also worked in a hotel and made a little more money than when I worked in the factory. Later I didn't like the hotel job and came to Shenzhen with my fellow villagers in June 2005. I worked in another factory and earned about 700-800 yuan and the factory provided lodging and food. In May 2006, I worked in an electronics factory. I went to Internet bars frequently at that time. I met a guy on line and we dated. In August of the same year, we worked in the same factory and I made 1,200 yuan a month, with the factory providing lodging and food (Xiao Xiu).

Le Le, mother of one son, held different legitimate jobs. She sold rice noodles, was a waitress at a restaurant, a hostess at a karaoke lounge, and a sales clerk at different periods of time. What impressed me most when she told me about her previous jobs is her experience while selling rice noodles:

> I sold rice noodles in Guilin City in 1999 and quit that job after two weeks. It was too hard. I got up at 5 a.m., and had to ride a bike to work for half an hour. It was very scary to be riding while it was still dark. If it rained, my shoes would get wet and I could not change them until I got off from work in the evening. I made only 180 yuan a month (Le Le).

Ah Lian and Xiao Hui had worked in factories for some time and both perceive that working in a factory is strenuous and low-paid.

> My father took me to Dongguan after I graduated from middle school and I worked in a factory. Then I worked in a factory in Shenzhen (it was 2003, I was younger than 16). It was too hard to work in a factory. Sometimes you work overtime until midnight and you make only a little over 1,000 yuan (Ah Lian).

> After quitting school in 2000, I went to Fujian to work in a factory because my mother was working there. I helped my mother in her small restaurant one year later. At the beginning of 2004, I went to Shenzhen and worked in a factory because my sister was there. I earned 800-900 yuan a month. The most I earned was 1,500 yuan when I worked overtime (Xiao Hui).

Xiao Ya was 25 at the time of the interview. She had started to work when she was 11. Her mother and two sisters were all migrant workers in Guangdong province. She migrated to Guangdong because of the higher salaries paid there.

> I had been a housemaid since I was 11 years old until I came to Guangdong when I was 15. I went to Guangzhou with my aunt in 1998 and worked in factories. The most I made was just over 2,000 yuan. I came to Shenzhen three years ago and first worked in a shoe factory (Xiao Ya).

Having worked at menial jobs for long periods of time, some women stated how sick they were of these jobs because of the low salaries and high level of strenuousness.

> My aunt worked in a factory, so I worked there for about two years. I worked overtime very frequently; it was very tough. The most I made was a little more than 2,000 yuan; only 1,200 yuan if I did not work overtime. Later I became sick of it and wanted to do something else. I had a friend who works at this nightclub so I went there (Nan Nan).

> I had worked as a waitress at restaurants or hotels in Hubei Province for many years. I made only 600-700 yuan. I became sick of being a waitress and did not want to continue any more (Li Ying).

Some women worked only a short time in legitimate sectors, found it very hard, and quit very soon.

> I was a cashier at an Internet bar. I worked 12 hours a day and it was too hard for me, so I quit the job after two days (Ah Ying).

> I came to Shenzhen with my boyfriend in March 2006. In the beginning I worked in an electronics factory. When I worked in the night shift, I would fall asleep. I could not stand the night shift; I had never struggled in my life. I was fined twice

for sleeping at work—50 yuan each time. I worked for just one week and was fined 100 yuan. I was frustrated and depressed. I quit the job two weeks later, after earning only 500 yuan (Wang Mei).

I came to Shenzhen with my mother and younger sister in February 2008. I worked in a restaurant for over a month. The salary was very low. I made a little over 800 yuan a month. So my sister and I started to look for other jobs one month later, but did not find one we liked (Xiao Fang).

A few of them did not complain about their legitimate jobs, but found them boring or just wanted to leave because of the appeal of high salaries in Shenzhen.

I went to Dongguan with my cousin in 2000 and worked in a factory for two years. I made over 1,000 yuan a month. I went back to my hometown in 2004 and worked in a shoe factory. I also worked in a supermarket as a sales clerk. My life was very boring (Mei Fang).

I worked in a factory after graduation. My job was very good, it was not hard and the factory provided us some stock. But I wanted very much to leave at that time. I came to Shenzhen with two other colleagues after working in a factory for two years (Li Wen).

Conclusions

The possibility that certain developmental factors could play an important role in women's involvement in prostitution led to the examination of family conditions, childhood experience, as well as their education and employment histories. The examination of women's demographic characteristics and their lives during childhood revealed that women in this study fit the stereotype of women in the sex industry in that they were from lower class families and had limited education. Childhood poverty and low family social status were the most prominent characteristics of these women.

Most women participating in this study were from rural areas. Some of them were from poverty-ridden areas and the families of some were indigent when compared to their neighbors. Background variables show that these women did not come solely from low-income households. Almost half of them did not characterize their childhood life as being poverty-stricken. Their parents were predominantly farmers, migrant workers, or operated family businesses. Aside from the two women whose parents divorced, and the two women whose fathers had died when they were children, the women all came from stable family backgrounds and did not demonstrate a negative relationship with their parents.

Due to poverty, some families could not afford to send their children to school. Their priority was survival, over and above education. A total of eleven of the forty women in this sample made it explicit that they had to quit studies due to long-term family poverty or because of specific family financial conditions. Because of family conditions or poor performance in school, the women in this study had a limited education. Most of them did not do very well in school for a variety of reasons, while a few others could not pursue their education due to poverty, or specific family financial conditions. Some of them began contributing to their family's income at ages as young as eleven, working or doing chores at home.

Women working at different sex facilities did not show significant variations in terms of their age, family background and education. However, streetwalkers were relatively older and less educated than prostitutes in other sex venues. Women working at hair salons were relatively younger and more educated. They migrated with the hope of changing their economic status or looking for more opportunities in Shenzhen—a developed city with the largest migrant population in China. All of the women in this study came from areas other than the city in which they worked as prostitutes. This data is consistent with previous studies on prostitution and human trafficking.

Literature on women in the sex industry has demonstrated that many women worked in legitimate sectors before getting involved in prostitution. However, the work available to them consists of low-paid, strenuous and menial jobs (Hoigard and Hinstad, 1992; McDonald et al., 2000; Sharpe, 1998). As far as women in this study are concerned, on account of family poverty, some of them began contributing to their families by working or doing chores after quitting studies at a time when they were merely in their early teens. Most of them had worked at different jobs for varying periods of time. Their jobs were low-paid and strenuous, and were mainly in factories, restaurants and entertainment establishments.

Very few women from urban areas participated in this study. A significant proportion of the floating population consists of women from rural areas. In addition, research has found that the proportion of prostitutes from rural areas has risen dramatically from 3 percent before 1985 to 62 percent in 1999 (Xu, 1999). Police data reveals a similar pattern of source areas. Therefore, it is safe to claim that because of the geographical pattern and social network in the prostitution industry, the population of women in the sex industry consists of more women from rural areas than from urban areas.

In conclusion, participants in this study constitute a group in which most women were young, unmarried and childless. They came from stable families although their parents were poor. No evidence of neglect or negative relationships with their family (especially their parents) was found in this study. Due to poverty and the low socio-economic status of their parents, children's education was not a priority. Thus, even when children did have the chance to go to school, they did not do well scholastically, on account of lack of self-discipline or lack of parental discipline. Most of the women began to work in legitimate sectors when they were teenagers, and prostitution was rarely their first job.

5

Paths to Prostitution

Previous studies demonstrate that women in the sex industry take different paths to prostitution. The extent to which they are willing to be involved in prostitution, and the degree to which they make informed decisions, vary along the voluntary vs. forced continuum. The vast majority chooses to migrate, and some are aware that they will be working as prostitutes. This decision is often born of a wish to improve their economic status. Although the common motivating factor is a need for money, not all the women come from an impoverished background. This chapter explores how and why Chinese migrant women initially get involved in prostitution, and highlights the immediate circumstances under which these women cross the threshold into prostitution.

As stated in Chapter 2, it has been suggested that a variety of factors motivate women into prostitution, or render them vulnerable to trafficking during the migration process. These factors may be structural, and include poverty, inequality, unemployment, and a patriarchal culture. The factors can also be individual, and include specific life events and the influence of friends, acquaintances or relatives. Previous literature also finds that women in the sex industry take varying routes to prostitution. Migrant women in the sex industry have been classified in several ways, based on the characteristics of their migration, and the conditions under which they work. Brunovskis and Tyldum (2004) identified three broad reasons why women wanted to migrate or to work in prostitution, namely, "response to an acute crisis," "long-term poverty," and "wanting more from life." Drawing upon previous studies, and analyzing data from the present study has enabled the establishment of a typology of six different paths by which Chinese women end up in prostitution. Specifically, these categories include: a boyfriend changing their life, specific family or personal events, persuasion by relatives, influence of friends/co-workers, self-initiation, or force/deceit/coercion exerted by others. More than a single factor is involved in women's initial participation in prostitution. This classification is based on proximal events or factors, i.e., those taking place immediately before their first act of prostitution, which, in combination with other factors, prompts or forces them into the sex industry. These events may have occurred in Shenzhen (N=35), the source provinces (N=2) or in the other places where the women had migrated before arriving in Shenzhen (N=3).

A Boyfriend Changing Their Life

Xiao Xiu, 19 years old, shrewd and articulate, met her first boyfriend online. He was often out of work, and she broke up with him. Then she met her second boyfriend, and they hung around together. This boyfriend was not a good worker either. However, she fell in love with him. After a while, she succumbed to his influence, became tired of factory work and quit her job. Penniless, and in urgent need of money, she chose an easy way to make money.

> I met another guy in December 2006 and we began cohabiting. On the eve of the Chinese New Year in 2007, the factory gave me a bonus of about 1,000 yuan. We fooled around and I was responsible for all the expenses. We spent all the money and started to look for a job after the Chinese New Year. In the beginning of March 2007, we worked in a factory. He slept during work and had a high record of unsatisfactory products. He was fired and then I left too. I fell in love with him and believed in him. He did not want to work and played casino games instead. We did not have money so I asked my father to send me some. We planned to go to his hometown in Henan province. On April 3, 2007 we went to the train station to buy tickets. He ran away from the station (I do not know why). I had no money. I called my aunt, but she had no money because she had just paid the rent. I started to look at ads for jobs that provided a salary of more than 10,000 yuan per month, and called the phone numbers in the ads. I knew the nature of the job. What I was thinking at that time is that I would take the job as long as it provided me food and a place to live. I made the call and the boss picked me up. On the way, the boss asked what I wanted to do. I told him that I wanted to be a waitress in a restaurant. Then he started to persuade me. He said that you should make money, as much money as you can once you come out; you have nothing to worry about as long as you have money—even when your husband abandons you. I had decided to take this job when I called him. Therefore I pushed the boat along with the current—I agreed to work for him when he told me about that.

> He and his wife operated the business together. They made money by asking girls to disguise themselves as virgins (girls dip a sponge in pigeon blood, refrigerate it, and put it in their vagina before leaving for work). … They do not control us, but they will complain if we are not accepted by potential customers. They did not ask me to work the first few days, and bought me clothes. I cried for several days when I later recalled telling my friend that I would not do this even if I was beaten to death. I wanted to go home and they sensed that. The man asked me if I wanted to leave. I cried and they started to comfort me, saying "you will succeed once you choose this path. Think how excited your mother will be when you send her money. You can marry a good man once you make a lot of money." On the fourth day, I started to work. My first customer was a man in his 50s. I had one or two customers each day, if any.

Each customer paid me 3,000-5,000 yuan and I gave all the money to my boss. By the end of April 2007, I did not want to work, I wanted to go home. One day, I went to Dongguan. I had a customer in a hotel. I earned 1200 yuan and I bought a ticket with it. My father complained that I did not bring home any money. My boss found my home phone number in my diary and called before I got there. He told my mother that he was my friend and asked for me to call them. When I thought that working in a factory was too hard, I called him and promised him that I would get back to work in a few days. I got back on May 8. Later in July, the female boss became angry with me and she usually used me to vent her anger because she believed that her husband liked me. One time I made 2,000 yuan and left. I wanted to work in the factory again. There was a foot massage parlor recruiting women promising a salary of 5,000 yuan per month (involving hand job). I went there, and for several days, I learned how to massage. One girl told me that her customer almost raped her, so I left. Then I went to Zhengzhou, Henan province and worked as a sales clerk for two months. It is so hard to make money. In October 2007, my mother called and asked me to go home during the Chinese New Year. It is shameful to go home without money. Therefore I started to work at a hair salon in Zhengzhou. The customer pays 100 yuan and I get 70 yuan out of this sum. I made 10,000 yuan per month. A little more than a month later, I worked at a sauna center and made 12,000 yuan per month. I told my mother that I was learning facial care in Shenzhen—that I was very busy and would not go home during the Chinese New Year. I went home for seven days after the New Year, gave Mom 3500 yuan and returned to Zhengzhou four days later. But I could not earn as much as I did before the Chinese New Year. So I came here on April 27, 2008 with a girl and worked at a hair salon.

Ah Hong had worked at a factory for more than two years before she met her boyfriend who was a businessman, running a mahjong house and making a lot of money. But her boyfriend liked gambling and used drugs. After being with him for a while, she became a drug addict. She did not tell me this until I had almost wrapped up the interview. Probably because of his addiction to drugs her boyfriend's mahjong house didn't make money and was closed. Since then, she has been working in a hair salon and supporting their drug habits.

> I met my boyfriend who operated a mahjong club around here. He could make 10,000-20,000 yuan a month when business was good. But he gambled frequently, and lost a lot of money. I went to disco dancing clubs with him frequently and I became a "bad girl" since then (she means that she started to use drugs). In January 2007, both of us had no money and I asked my mother to give me 1,000 yuan. But we squandered it. My boyfriend asked me to work at his friend's hair salon. I agreed because I had spent some of his money. His friend's girlfriend worked in a hair salon. His friend blamed me for not working and fooling around. I agreed to work in a hair salon because my boyfriend consented, and I was not a virgin any more.

Fei Fei was 18 years old. Her hometown was only two hours away from Shenzhen. Her parents migrated and worked in Shenzhen when she was very young. She grew up with her grandparents. After graduating from middle school in 2006, she came to Shenzhen and worked as a cashier at a supermarket. She also worked at an electronics factory. She dated a guy later. Her father forced her to break up with him because her uncle lost money after she and her boyfriend visited her uncle's family. She hated her father, became rebellious, and ran away from home. But her destiny changed dramatically since then. She met another girl who had run away from her home for the same reasons. Her girlfriend had a boyfriend who was a manager at a sauna parlor, and they started to work there soon after they got to know each other.

> I was a cashier at a supermarket in Futian district, Shenzhen city after I graduated from middle school. I was dating, and my father found out. He did not allow me to date. He said that he would not let me go home if I dated. So I ran away from home. I had only 1,000 yuan and started to look for a job. I worked at a bar for one month. I sensed that they were cheating me so I left. I didn't get paid for that month and I didn't get my deposit back. I knew a girl at the bar. She knew a manager (her boyfriend) at a sauna parlor and suggested that we work over there. I knew that there was sex service involved there. But at that time I had no money and would take the job as long as I got paid. I have worked at a sauna parlor since 2007.

These three girls were not from poor families, and in two of the cases, their parents gave them some money when they were in need. Their lives may have followed a totally different path had they not met their boyfriends, or someone else who influenced them into sex service. Xiao Xiu had been working in a factory for almost four years before she met her boyfriend; then she quit her job when her boyfriend was fired. It appears that she chose prostitution after becoming penniless. However, she had known or heard that her peers worked as prostitutes; she must have noticed the same advertisements before, and knew very well that such work would provide her with quick and immediate money. What struck me is that she could remember the date of some important episodes when she told me the story, underlining that entering into prostitution was a significant event in her life. She hesitated and struggled for some time while working for the husband and wife sex operators, thinking of returning to a factory job. However, when she thought of the hardship of factory work, she resumed working for the couple.

Ah Hong worked in a factory for at least two years before she met her boyfriend. Her boyfriend took her to disco dancing halls and she started to use drugs. It is obvious that a variety of factors were involved when she decided to provide sex services at a hair salon: not being a virgin, having friends who were prostitutes, and the boyfriend's consent. All these factors lowered the threshold for her, and enabled her to enter into prostitution. There is no doubt that her life would have been different had she not met her boyfriend.

Fei Fei had not worked at a legitimate occupation for as long as the two preceding subjects. On account of her boyfriend, she had run away from home and had to earn money to support herself. She used to work in a factory before running away from home, but she didn't look for a factory job. Instead, she started to work in a bar. It is very evident that she made this decision after comparing work in a factory with work at entertainment facilities. She felt insecure working in the bar. By coincidence, in the bar she met a girl who had had a similar experience, and was introduced by her to a sauna parlor.

Specific Family or Personal Events

Some women decided to get involved in prostitution work after a specific life event left them in an urgent situation, or changed their life circumstances in such a way that they were pressured to make big money in a short time.

Sha Sha, a 19-year-old Hunanese girl, went to Dongguan—one hour away from Shenzhen, and worked in a factory after she graduated from high school in 2007. Her family borrowed money to support her going to high school. She didn't take the college entry exam because her family couldn't afford to send her to college even if she were admitted. It is a really sad situation for a girl who did very well in school. Her life became even worse several months later after she began working. This poor girl had never had any sexual experience before entering the sex industry. She had sex with a guy she liked before she started to have sex with her customers, thinking she would regret it all her life if her first sexual experience had been with a customer.

> My father broke a bone and had surgery. My father did not tell me about this, and I did not know until a few months later, in October 2007. My father needed another surgery to take out the metal plate. It was not easy for my parents to bring me up and I wanted to pay my debt of gratitude to them. Therefore I came here from Dongguan after the 2008 Chinese New Year. There was a fellow villager who worked at a hair salon. She asked me if I had made up my mind (to do this). I said yes.

Ah Wen, the same age as Sha Sha, was from Fujian province. Her family was not as poor as Sha Sha's. Both her parents were teachers. She did not pass the college entry exam in 2007. She meant to take the exam the next year. But her family financial situation changed a lot due to the birth of her twin brothers. She worked for a car dealer and made a decent amount of money. But it was not enough to relieve the family's financial burden. So she came to Shenzhen and worked at a massage parlor.

> My father was a teacher in a middle school in the township, and my mother was an elementary school teacher in my village. Both of them were expelled after my twin brothers were born in 2005 and they were fined 56,000 yuan. My twin brothers are only 3 years old. I graduated from high school in 2007. I did not pass the university enrollment exam. Because of the fine, my family could not have afforded to send me to college even if I had passed the exam. I was a waitress and then a car salesperson in my hometown. I did not come here until April 2008. I am a good salesperson. I could sell eight or nine cars in a month. The boss did not want me to leave. I asked him to raise my salary, but he could not raise it too much. So I quit that job and came here on my own. My father makes a little more than 1,000 yuan a month. My family called me and asked for money even before I found a job in Shenzhen (she became teary-eyed). I had no other choice than to take this job.... I intended to be a waitress at this sauna parlor, but they did not need a waitress. After thinking about it for several days, I took the job (Ah Wen).

Ding Ding, a 30-year-old single mother, who was raped at the age of nine, is from Sichuan Province. She divorced in 2003 when her daughter was only one year old because her ex-husband always cheated her. She also told me some things about her boyfriend who she met after her divorce. She came to Guangdong partially because she wanted to get away from her boyfriend who was violent and dishonest. She had worked a lot of different jobs after her divorce, mainly as a waitress at different restaurants. She ran a small shop selling cell phones in Chengdu—the capital of Sichuan Province—before she came to Guangdong Province. She had a heart condition and had had a relapse the previous year. Consequently, she couldn't take care of her business and lost money. In the meantime, she needed money soon to schedule surgery for her heart.

> One of my friends who had been in Guangdong told me that you could make more money in Guangdong than in other places no matter what you did; people would laugh at you if you were poor; if you came out and made a lot of money, nobody knew you were a prostitute. So I went to Guangzhou first. A friend of my friend introduced me to a sauna center in a hotel. I could not accept it even when I was in training. There were a variety of services offered. I wanted to leave, but they would not let me go. They said that I had to pay them a lot of money because they had spent a lot on my lodging, food and training. I said: "Are you a gang (secret society) member? I have no money. I will call the police if you do not let me go." I knew a manager of the hotel so I called him. He said that if I did not want to do that, I could be a hostess and may be promoted later. Other people also persuaded me. They said that it was not very difficult and I would know how to do it. But I was still reluctant

to do that job. Then they introduced me to Shenzhen. They also told me how much I could make in Shenzhen. I knew there were sex services involved. What I thought at that time is that I needed money for heart surgery or I would die, and my priority was to save my life.

Lin Lin was 39 years old—the oldest subject, but she looked much younger than her age. Her co-worker at a factory asked her to work at a sauna parlor. She resisted working there when she found out that she had to provide sex services although both her friend and the owner nagged her. Some time later, her daughter became sick and she had to borrow money from the neighbors. Her neighbors looked down upon her afterwards and she began to vacillate. Finally, after hesitating for a year and a half, this woman—who had been working in a factory for almost 20 years, to the point where her fingers had become deformed from all the weaving work—decided to take the job.

The distinctive feature of these four cases is that three of them involve people falling sick—a parent, a child, or the woman herself. Without health insurance, medical costs are such a big burden that even people from rich families can be overwhelmed. Having to pay a huge fine has the same consequence on people involved. Three of the four women had friends who worked as prostitutes. Ding Ding was influenced by her friends; Lin Lin was persuaded by her co-worker; and Sha Sha's friend acted as a role model and a companion who downplayed the perceived risk. Ah Wen said that she had no friends or relatives working in the sex industry, but she had known about the sauna parlor she was working before she went to work there.

Another woman in this category has a unique story: Li Xue, a pretty 22-year-old girl, told me a most tragic and lengthy tale. She started to provide sex services after being raped by a customer. Desiring to be independent from her parents, she stopped collecting garbage with her mother. She traveled with her peers who paid for her ticket, following which she had to divide the money she made with them. She had worked at a hair salon and a KTV lounge for some time before providing sex services. There were a lot of risks when she worked at these establishments: her friend wanted to sleep with her, and her customers wanted her to provide sex services. She refused to have sex with any of them and managed to sneak away. After that, she worked downtown in her home county at a hair salon, and later on at a hotel providing massage services. One day she was raped by a customer and from that time on she began to provide sex services.

In the summer of 1999, I went to Zhuhai with some friends. They told me that they had a friend who was running a hair salon. I liked that kind of work, so I went with them. But I did not find a job, so they gave me money and let me go home. After arriving in my hometown, I worked in a hair salon, washing hair. I made several hundred a month. My girlfriend's boyfriend and another man wanted to take us to Changsha to zuotai. I went with them. The other man wanted to have sex with me on several occasions, but I refused. I worked more than 10 days, zuotai two times and made several hundred. I gave them half of what I earned (we made this agreement before we left). I wanted to leave because I realized that they were using me, taking advantage of me, and wanted to sleep with me. They would not let me go. One time a customer paid me 100 yuan more and I hid it. I bought a ticket with that money. I had no money left after I went back to Huaihua, my hometown. I met a woman who zuotai in Changsha, and she gave me some money. Then I washed hair at a hair salon. A woman at the hair salon also took me to a hotel and I did massages for customers. One day a drunken customer raped me. I told him that I was still a virgin, but he did not believe me. I felt ashamed and dared not report him to the police. In addition, the hotel was close to where my family lived, and I was afraid that my family would be affected and would lose face. That man paid me 50 yuan more and I left that hotel the next day. I became psychologically negative after that—smashing a pot to pieces just because it was cracked. I started to work at a restaurant where I made 20 yuan by zuotai and 100 yuan for "fast food" (quick sex)… Two months later I went home for the Chinese New Year. My uncle's wife asked me what I was doing. I told her that I was learning hair design. She told me that one of her relatives had an entertainment center in another town. Then I went to there to wash hair and do massages. When I was asked if I was open (to providing sex services), I said that I would do whatever was requested as long as I got paid. I wanted to help out my family at that time. But I had no education, what could I do? Only this job.

Persuasion by Relatives

Some previous studies have found that a prominent role is played by relatives, friends and peers in women's involvement in prostitution (Brunovskis and Tyldum, 2004; Raymond et al., 2002; Sharpe, 1998; Vocks and Nijboer, 2000). The present study corroborates these findings. Most women (N=33) had either friends (N=30) or relatives (N=3) who worked in sex establishments. These friends or relatives had a direct or indirect influence on their initial involvement in commercial sex. Direct influence refers to situations where women were reluctant or refused to work as prostitutes, but eventually gave in on account of nagging and persuasion by others. In other words, others not only brought up the idea in the first place; they also kept persuading the women until they agreed to take up prostitution work. No force, deception, or coercion was involved. Without these other people, some of these women may not have got involved in prostitution.

Indirect influence refers to situations such as self-initiation, or situations in which women are willing to work in the sex industry although this may be the result of the influence of friends and/or colleagues. The high incomes they see them earning induces or tempts the women into sex work. The friends provide positive information or point out the advantages of prostitution. They make the women feel confident or comfortable about undertaking this kind of work. To distinguish between the two different modes, namely, direct and indirect, we should examine whether subjects were pushed by others or whether they themselves decided to begin providing sex services. Such a judgment must be made based on the experiences of the subjects, their narrative, and an interpretation of the process by which they got involved in prostitution, their age at the time they initially got involved (a factor affecting their capacity to make informed decisions), etc. It involves, on my part, making a personal judgment as to who exerted the larger influence on their decision to get involved in prostitution—the subjects themselves or their friends and/or relatives.

Ah Rong decided to come out with her aunt and cousin to work because her father lost money in business. She worked at a hair salon. She didn't start to provide hand jobs until more than a year later, during which time her aunt kept nagging her to get on with it.

> My life was very good when I was a child, and we had a nice house. My father bought a boat for his business and lost more than 300,000 yuan in 2003. He also had 120,000 yuan of debt. Creditors came to my home asking for the money, but my parents had nothing to pay them. They asked my mother why they let their daughter stay at home doing nothing. I was upstairs and overheard this. So I told my mother that I wanted to work. My parents did not agree, but eventually I came out with my cousin. We washed hair at a hair salon in Futian District, Shenzhen. No sex services were involved. This happened in the summer of 2003, and I made a little more than 700 yuan a month. Later, my cousin's mother took us to work at another hair salon where we provided massages for customers for 25 yuan per hour, with no sex service. I made about 1,000 yuan a month. I did not do hand jobs until the second half of 2004 when my aunt persuaded me to. I then made between 2,000 and 3,000 yuan. I did not want to do that. I wanted to be a hair designer.

Lily, 25 years old, had been working in this industry for about ten years. She bought a house for her family in the downtown area of her home county. When she was only 15 years old and worked in a restaurant, her aunt proposed the idea of taking her out to work at a nightclub by pointing out the huge disparity of salaries between restaurant work and nightclub work. Lily agreed with her, and accepted the offer. However, she was only 15 years old when this happened, and it is therefore reasonable to assume that her aunt had a direct influence on her involvement in prostitution.

I worked in a restaurant after quitting school when I was in 7th grade. My cousin ran a hair salon opposite the restaurant. I knew what kind of business they were doing at the hair salon. Later my aunt said: "How much can you make in a restaurant? Your family is poor, why don't you come out with me? It is definitely better than working at home." I thought that she was right, so I went out with her. I made only 150 yuan a month at the restaurant. I worked at a nightclub in a town near my home. I was only 15. I knew before I went that there was sex involved, but I did not think it was illegal, or whether or not I could do this work. But I knew that my aunt wouldn't hurt me. In the beginning, I just drank and danced. One day the boss took me to the office of the mayor of the town and told me he was wealthy, and that I should be nice to him. That was the first time I provided sex service. I was still a virgin. He paid me 200 yuan. I did not leave until he paid me 500 yuan. I was inexperienced and knew nothing. I worked at the nightclub for more than one year. I had another aunt who zuotai at the center of the county. She asked me to work there. The price for zuotai is 25 yuan, and chutai is 200-300 yuan. I rarely chutai. I do not know why. Then I did not work for a year or two. I had a problem with my ear and I had to spend more than 10,000 yuan to see a doctor. I ran out of money, so I came out and worked again.

Ah Rong's involvement in providing hand jobs was a gradual process, beginning with washing hair at a hair salon, moving on to providing regular massages and eventually ending up giving hand jobs. This was a direct result of her aunt's persuading and nagging her. She didn't specify what her aunt said when she tried to talk her into this job, but what her aunt said is presumably the same as what Lily's aunt said when she persuaded Lily to start this trade. The income disparity was an irresistible enticement for Lily, who was only 15 when this happened. It may appear that Lily's aunt didn't do much persuading before Lily accepted her "advice." Given her age when this occurred, however, the effects of her aunt's influence on Lily's adoption of prostitution cannot be over emphasized. When she told me her story, she did not demonstrate any remorse. Instead, she regretted that she had got only 500 yuan for her virginity, and this is why she thought that she was inexperienced.

Influenced by Friends, Peers or Co-workers

Women falling into this category can be sub-classified into two categories based on whether or not they had worked in entertainment facilities before providing sex services. Some women (N=11) worked in legitimate sectors and were influenced by their friends who were prostitutes. Their friends' high incomes appealed to them and made them want to follow in their footsteps. Their friends may have provided them with suggestions, advice, or information about sex service jobs that strengthened their resolve and determination, confirmed their intent, or made them confident and comfortable with the trade. Friends also acted as role models, appealing to these women to follow in their path.

Chen Hong, a high school graduate, was a cashier at a supermarket in Changsha—the capital city of Hunan Province. She didn't take the college entrance exam because her father fell sick. She was impressed by her former middle school classmates when they came home from Shenzhen for the 2006 Chinese New Year because they were all loaded. She didn't come to Shenzhen until May 2007 because of her father's heath condition. She was not satisfied with living permanently in her hometown. As a result, when her friend described Shenzhen, she became more determined to leave her impoverished hometown.

> When my classmates came home during the 2007 Chinese New Year, I told one of them that I could not make a lot of money at home. She told me that Shenzhen was a good place. So I went out with her. I knew what they were doing in Shenzhen. I did not think about whether or not I could do it at that time, but how well I could do it. My hometown is very poor. I was thinking at that time that I must leave. I do not want to get married and settle down over there. I do not think it is shameful. One of my classmates is doing this. She is loaded. My family had no money at that time, so I wanted to do this job. She asked whether I had thought it over. I said yes.

Xiao Ya, as the oldest child in her family, began to work when she was only 11. In 1998, when she was 15, she came to Guangzhou and worked in a factory. She came to Shenzhen three years ago and worked in a factory. She was 25 years old and her parents wanted her to go home and get married. She did not want to get married at that time, she wanted to make money. Although she claimed that she wouldn't be working there if she had not known the friend who helped her, in Xiao Ya's case, the desire to make more money came first. Her friend's introduction provided a convenient way for her to enter into prostitution.

> I came to Shenzhen three years ago and first worked in a shoe factory. I have worked at this parlor for less than one month. I am a foot masseuse. One of my friends said that I could make over 1000 yuan by working here. I would not be here without her introduction. I met her and we became good friends when I worked in the factory. I work here just because I want to make more money—no other reasons.

Ah Xiang, who used to work in a restaurant as a waitress, entered prostitution at the beginning of 2007. Her parents were migrant workers and she and her younger brother and sister were raised by her grandparents. She had a lot of friends who had been involved in the business. As a result, she did not regard it as a big deal when she first took the job.

> I was a waitress at a restaurant and made several hundred a month. I started to do this in the beginning of 2007. My friends who do hand jobs talk about their income

very frequently. They make several thousand a month. I know they do hand jobs—no sexual intercourse. I did not feel scared when I initially decided to do this job because many of my friends and classmates were doing this job.

Wang Hong, one of a few divorced subjects, learned dressmaking after graduation from middle school. She didn't use that skill to make a living. Instead, she worked in a factory for four years and was a cashier in a hotel for one year in Dongguan-one hour away from Shenzhen. She then got married in 2005 and her son was born the next year. She proposed divorce in January 2007 when her son was only about four months old, because life was not good, depending solely on her husband's salary. A woman who used to be her co-worker when she worked in a hotel had got involved in the sex trade some time earlier. This friend relieved her of any concerns. As a result, Wang Hong asserts that she would not have done it without knowing the friend. Being discontented with her economic situation stimulated her to get a divorce and the friend working as a prostitute provided a role model.

> I was in a bad mood after the divorce and a woman invited me to go to Shenzhen for a vacation in March 2007. Then I went home. I started to do this work in May 2007. I had decided to work at a foot massage parlor before I came here. I worried whether or not I could do it because I am slender. My friend said that I could do the job—many people like me did this work; it was easy to make over 2,000 yuan a month. I hesitated for a long time and did not start this job until six months after my friend started. My mother is not healthy. I do not have money for her and I feel guilty about this. I started to do foot massage in May 2007 and have been working at this sauna place since October 2007. What I am doing has nothing to do with my divorce.

Li Ying, a mother of two daughters, started this job after working in a supermarket for one or two months in 2006. She is the subject who is originally from a mountainous area without any transportation service to her parents' home. She is one of the two women in this study residing with their husband or boyfriend who knew the nature of the job they were doing. She kept asking me not to write down her daughters' ages because she was afraid of being exposed to the public. Long time poverty and the desire to provide a good life for her daughters motivated her to work in the sex industry.

> A fellow villager picked me up when I came here. I worked at a supermarket for over one month and earned 900 yuan a month. One of my fellow villagers was working at this KTV and I came. My fellow villager said that it is always better to work here than in a factory, because you are able to save some money every month. You cannot save money if you work somewhere else. I can save at least 1,000 yuan each month.

Xiu Xiu's father died when she was 7. Her brother, the only sibling, is also working in Shenzhen. Her boyfriend is in their hometown and doesn't know the nature of her job. She came to Shenzhen in 2003 after graduating from middle school. Two fellow villagers who had been working in a factory in Dongguan brought her and twelve other girls to work in an electronics factory. They came to Shenzhen and worked in a factory one year later. Her peers around her made a lot of money and she was enticed by that.

> I worked in a factory and made about 1200 yuan a month. Some girls who worked in an entertainment center lived in the factory dorm. When we hung out together, they said that they made over 3000 yuan a month and the work was easy. I wrote down their phone number. I quit the factory job in the beginning of 2008 and went home for the Chinese New Year. I called them after I got back. We were trained for one week—there was no sex service included in the training. Then we started working. Several days later, we were told that we could not make a lot of money by just doing formal massage. Then they taught us hand job for four or five days.

Nan Nan worked in a factory before she first worked at a nightclub. Her parents were migrant workers. Her father sent her to work in a factory in Dongguan in 2006—where her aunt worked. She knew a friend who worked at the same nightclub, but she said that she worked there just because she could make more money than in a factory; it had nothing to do with the friend, it was her own decision. She is kind of conservative; in the beginning, she didn't even dare to wear the uniform, which reveals more than it covers. Even now, when she zuotai, she rarely talks to customers.

> When I worked in a factory, I worked overtime very frequently, it was very tough. The most I made was a little more than 2,000 yuan; only 1,200 yuan if I did not work overtime. Later I became sick of it and wanted to do something else. I have a friend who worked at this nightclub so I came in March 2008.

Wang Xia was a housewife when a fellow villager approached her and told her how much she made as a hostess at a dancing hall. She used to work in a factory in her hometown for a while and the salary was really low. She had never left her hometown before she went out with her fellow villager.

> I knew a fellow villager who was trying to desist from drug use in my hometown. She introduced me to work at a dancing hall at Dongguan in 2005. I had never left my hometown at that time. She told me that I could make several thousand a month by accompanying customers to dancing halls. It was also possible to be someone's mistress. So I went there. A customer chose me as a mistress less than one week after I went.

The following two subjects seemed to have entered the business by accident. When they applied for the job, they didn't know that it involved sex service. In fact, they did not know exactly what was involved. But eventually they took the job, either because they ran out of money, or because they desired to make more money. An An was a very independent girl who earned her own tuition when she went to a vocational school to major in hotel administration. She is from Zhanjiang, Guangdong Province. Her childhood life was not good. She didn't know the nature of the job until she was trained. She was very scared even when she was trained. The trainer not only taught them the "technique," but also tried to enlighten them. Therefore she took the job. When explaining her involvement in this work, she also complained about her relatives who did not help her family. Her family was not rich and their relatives did not loan them money to build a house, or support her brothers so they could go to college.

> I came to Shenzhen at the beginning of last year. I worked as an administrative employee in the beginning and was then promoted to supervisor. I worked ten hours a day and it was very tough. I applied for an administrative position at a hotel where one of my friends worked. But the hotel was recruiting "technicians" (euphemism for prostitutes at massage parlors), there were no administrative positions vacant. My friend's sister was a prostitute. She just told me that I couldn't take that job if I had never dated. I didn't even know the meaning of "attacking the plane" and I asked my classmates what it meant (this doesn't imply that she did not know that sex service was involved in this job). We were trained for two months. It was very scary when we were taught how to give a hand job. But the trainer persuaded us. She said that some people bought a BMW or Mercedes-Benz after working several years; if you worked hard for two or three years, you would make more than what people made in their lifetime; then you could go home and run a business, and nobody knew what you were doing if you did not tell them. I cried for the first few days, thinking why so many relatives don't help my family; I also wanted to buy a house in the city.

Xiao Ke's parents were migrant workers in Shenzhen when she graduated from middle school, and she therefore came to Shenzhen in 2005. She worked in a factory for almost three years before she worked at a KTV lounge in 2008. She didn't know that there might be sex service involved when she applied for the job.

> I worked in a factory in the beginning of 2005. I made 400-500 yuan in the beginning and a little more than 1,000 yuan later. I was a clerk and quality inspector in the factory. I was always under pressure and I felt very tired, so I quit the job. I wanted to go to another factory, but I was not hired because I was several months younger than their age requirement. I did not work for several months and I ran out of money. I had a friend who was a prostitute at this KTV lounge. I did not know

until the first day I worked there that there was sex service involved in this job. I only had to zuotai, so I took it.

Xiao Ju, a 26-year-old mother of two boys, had been in Shenzhen for just eleven days. She came there with a fellow villager who was also one of my subjects. Her fellow villager told her what she was doing in Shenzhen. Xiao Ju asked to go with her. She had only three years schooling; her family was poor and she didn't want to study. She had always been working at home after quitting studies—doing chores and growing crops. She is the only woman in this study who migrated and prostituted herself not just for money, but also for companionship.

> My husband is a truck driver. He likes gambling and committing adultery. He doesn't give me money even when my kids fall ill. We have rarely lived together in the past three years. He treats me very badly, we rarely have sex. He also doesn't take care of the kids. I just wanted to make more money to raise the kids. It will cost a lot of money when the kids go to school. Also, I wanted companionship. I felt very lonely when I was home, there was no one to talk to. Furthermore, I had no money. I did not want to go back.

These women had never worked in entertainment establishments before they started the trade. All of them had friends whose job involved sex services. They were not content with their current financial situations, either because they were residing in underdeveloped areas, or because they had migrated and worked in the legitimate sector but made little money which could only cover their daily expenses. They were tempted by the high salary prostitution that pays. They wanted to make more money to help either their families or themselves. To some extent, the idea of working at sex venues had been accepted even before they actually started the trade. Their friends/peers acted as informants whose experiences as prostitutes and knowledge of the job were important information sources based on which they took their final step toward prostitution. This information reduced the perceived risks associated with being a prostitute. Their friends also acted as role models from whose experience the women could picture what their life would be like if they adopted this line of work.

Yet another group includes women who had been working in entertainment establishments before they began to provide sex services. They did not mean to provide sex services to begin with. However, they were influenced, encouraged, or persuaded by co-workers and gradually they accepted sex Work. The duration of time between when they began to work at entertainment facilities and when they began to provide sex services varies, ranging from one week to almost one year (N=5).

Ah Lian, a pretty 21-year-old girl, did not work at a hair salon until after having worked for four years in factories. Her girlfriend advised her to work at a hair salon when she had just quit her strenuous job in a factory. Under the influence of other colleagues and the boss, she started to provide sex services one week later.

> I did not work in a hair salon until September 2007. I quit my job in the factory and looked for another job. One of my girlfriends asked me to work as a hair washer in her friend's hair salon. She said that you could make more than 1,000 yuan in a month. So I started to work there. Some customers asked me for sex service, I refused. But I was influenced by others. In addition, the boss said that other people wanted to do this, but could not—how can you refuse to do this? I started to provide sex service one week after working in that salon.

Wang Mei, whose parents divorced when she was in eighth grade, is one of the few subjects with a high school diploma. She worked in an air conditioning store as a sales clerk and her salary was high compared to that of local workers. She and her younger brother couldn't get along with their stepmother. She had a fight with her stepmother one day and her stepmother told her that Wang Mei was grown up and her father wouldn't raise her all her life. Due to this long-term tension between them, Wang Mei didn't want to live there any more. Partly due to the pressure from her stepmother, she decided to migrate to Shenzhen with her boyfriend. After arriving in Shenzhen, she became frustrated and anxious due to the hard work a factory job entails. Also, her boyfriend had a new girlfriend. She thought about working in the sex industry, but she didn't take up the first offer as she was afraid of being deceived. One day, after breaking up with her boyfriend, she became determined to work at an entertainment establishment as a waitress. Then, under the influence of her colleagues, she gradually began to work as a prostitute.

> With his uncle's help, my boyfriend was hired by a company, but he met another woman and dated her. My heart was really broken and I had only 1,000 yuan left. I saw an ad for an entertainment center. The monthly income was in the ten thousand range, with a minimum of 5,000. I made the call and a woman answered the phone. She told me that she could provide lodging and waive the entrance fee, and I would make 200-300 yuan a day. I was afraid of being deceived so I did not take that offer. One day, I fought with my boyfriend and we finally broke up. Then I worked at the Buffalo Entertainment Company. I was a waitress. The salary was 2,000-3,000 yuan a month. With tips, I made 4,000-5,000 yuan a month. There was no sex service involved. I got to know many women who zuotai. They told me that I was good looking and had a good temperament, and that I would have a lot of customers if I zuotai. They also said that even as a waitress, I was often touched by customers, so why didn't I zuotai? I started to zuotai three months later.

Lan Lan is from a wealthy family. She had been working in a factory and as a waitress in a hotel and sauna parlor from the time she quit studies in 2002. She finally embarked on the prostitution business in the beginning of 2007, enticed by the high salaries of prostitutes, and their luxurious lifestyle.

> I came to Shenzhen in 2005. My cousin is a supervisor in a factory and I worked there for two years, making 700 or 800 yuan a month. The work was very hard. I was a waitress in a big restaurant starting in January 2007. I made 1,000 yuan a month. I quit that job five months later. Then I was a waitress in a sauna parlor for several months. I wanted to be a technician (euphemism for prostitute) when I saw other technicians making over 10,000 yuan a month, eating well and dressing well. Gradually I accepted it. At the end of 2007, I ran out of money again and started to look for a job at a sauna parlor. There are so many women who do this job now. Many women work in factories and then transfer to this line of work.

Le Le, the mother of a son, was the oldest of four children in her family. Her husband's household was registered in Guangzhou, and she and her husband wanted to buy an apartment there, so that their son's household in turn could be registered in Guangzhou—otherwise, they would have to spend a lot of money for their son to go to school there. This was the main incentive underlying her decision to work at a sauna parlor in Shenzhen after hearing about it from her friends. Although her siblings were working, they still asked her sometimes for money. Thus, she had a double financial burden. She suffered a lot when she was selling rice noodles in her home city, and she had done a number of jobs thereafter.

> My cousin's friend took us to Hunan in 2003. She told us that we would work as waitresses at a teahouse. She bought us travel tickets. As a matter of fact, her brother had just opened an entertainment venue and was recruiting people. We provided formal massage service for over one month at the teahouse. Then my cousin's friend took us to zuotai and cheated people. We accompanied customers talking and drinking, trying to figure out whether they had brought a lot of money. If they did, we told the cashier and the cashier would overcharge them. I worked there for one year and came to Shenzhen in 2004. I was a sales clerk in a shoe store, and made 700 yuan a month. I also worked in a restaurant and earned no more than 1,000 yuan. Later I switched to selling shoes again and made over 1400 yuan. I have been doing this for just two months. I have friends who are in this line of work. They said that if I was so desperate for money, I should make a lot of it while I was still young. So I looked for these types of venues by myself. I was too conservative and did not make money when I zuotai in Hunan. Now I have straightened out my thinking, but I am older and it is too late.

Na Na is the only woman in this study claiming to have been spoiled by her parents. She has a good family background. She came out because she believed that she couldn't grow up being taken care of by her parents.

I came out to Shenzhen with my friend in 1998. I was a hostess at a karaoke place at Xiaomeisha. There were a lot of customers from Hong Kong and many women wanted to become their concubines. But customers were very nice to me and other women became jealous. I felt wronged. My friends told me that the job was flexible and nobody disciplined you, so I started to zuotai. Since then, I have always been in this line of work. I have also worked at a nightclub because I wanted to make more money.

These women had the experience of working at entertainment establishments before they started to provide sex services. It is not clear whether they had thought about providing sex services when they accepted their jobs at the entertainment establishments. It is possible that they accepted the jobs considering these venues as "buffer" zones, i.e., zones from which they could either go forward or step back, depending on further observation and the information they could gather while working at these establishments. Upon seeing their co-workers' luxurious lifestyles or feeling embarrassed about their own low salary and austere lifestyle, they cannot resist friends' influence and peer pressure. Add to the enticement of money, these women are ready to cross the line to bring in larger amounts of money.

Self-Initiated

The term "self-initiated" does not necessarily imply that these women got involved in prostitution without any external influence. However, the women in this group do not explicitly demonstrate that any of their friends or co-workers persuaded, encouraged, or advised them to provide sex services. These women may have worked at entertainment establishments before providing sex services, or they may have never worked at these facilities. However, the women who had worked in entertainment institutions before they began to provide sex services had witnessed a lot of the goings on at these establishments. Their co-workers did not appear to exert any obvious influence on them. They were subject to temptation, enticed by the high salary and drifted into the sex industry.

Li Na, a 21-year-old girl, started to work in a factory when she was about 15, and later worked at a foot massage parlor. Her family bought a house in the center of the town with the money she earned. She came to Shenzhen to work at a nightclub because they needed more money to pay off the house.

I started working in a factory in 2002 when I was 15 years old. I worked there for more than three years. I got back home and learned computer work in 2005. I had a classmate who was a foot masseuse in the town. I went to computer class in the morning and worked as a foot masseuse in the afternoon and evening, with no sex service involved. I made two or three thousand a month. The most I could make was four thousand. It was very hard. I didn't do this until I came to Shenzhen after the 2007 Chinese New Year. I had worked at entertainment establishments for a long time and seen a lot. My parents do not know what I am doing. I have a friend who is a manager here. She gave me the address and phone number and I came by myself.

Li Fei worked in a factory from 1998 until the end of 2004, when she first began working at a foot massage parlor. She did not provide sex services at that time, because she was the mistress of a married man who gave her a lot of money every month. On some account, she broke up with her married boyfriend and came to Shenzhen, working at a nightclub.

I worked in a factory in 1998 after graduation from elementary school. My salary increased from several hundred to fourteen hundred. But I had a lot of economic pressure because my sister needed money to go to school and my family built a house. I first worked at a foot massage parlor in Dongguan at the end of 2004, making 3,000-4,000 yuan per month. No sex service was involved. Later, I worked at several different venues. One day, a customer was drunk and asked me to massage his belly. He called me names when I refused; I talked back by calling him names. Then he beat me and gave me black-eyes. I was aggravated and said: "If you remain here, I will kill you." He remained there. I called up my gang friends. They came, hit him, and left him disabled. I left Dongguan then. My friends also asked my boss to delete my records, or else they would run him out of business. I hung out for several months and came here in August 2007. I used to have a married boyfriend who gave me 7,000-8,000 yuan each month. He also gave me some money after I had this trouble.

Yan Yan, a 20-year-old girl from Yunnan Province, started to work at home since 1999 after she quit studies when she was only in the fourth grade. She worked in a factory, and then was a waitress at a karaoke lounge in Hunan Province. She didn't come to Shenzhen until the 2008 Chinese New Year.

I came out and worked in a factory in Hunan province because one of my sisters lived there after she got married. I also worked in a karaoke lounge as a waitress since April 2007, and made 700 yuan a month. I came here after the 2008 Chinese New Year. I had a friend who worked in a factory in Shenzhen. I saw her during the Chinese New Year and she asked me to work in the factory with her. She got back to Shenzhen first after the Chinese New Year. I had thought of working at entertainment venues before I came here because my family condition was not good, and I also wanted to make more money. I went to the factory and knew that you have to work eight hours a day, and four more hours overtime. I did not want to work in a factory.

Lin Dan helped her parents run their family business from the time she quit studies in fourth grade until she went to Guangdong to work in a factory when she was 16. She started to help her parents do chores when she was only six or seven, because her parents operated a small business in the center of the county. She fed pigs, chickens and ducks at home and this left a lot of scars on her hands. She worked at a shoe factory in Dongguan from 2003 to 2006 and then, with the help of her parents, she operated a small clothing shop, but quit that business in the same year. Thereafter, she never worked in a factory.

> Later I knew a friend who worked in a beer factory, and I promoted the sale of beer at a karaoke lounge. Two months later, the boss asked me to work for him because I was good at communication (I was articulate), diligent, and sometimes brought customers in. Later I was promoted to supervisor. I worked for one year and made over 2,000 yuan a month.

> At the end of 2007, I met my boyfriend who was a businessman and had some money. We fooled around frequently and eventually ran out of money. His friend's girlfriend was doing this. My family was so poor when I was a child and I am very afraid of being poor. I just wanted to have some money. I told my boyfriend that I wanted to do this. He disagreed. I reasoned with him and he agreed later. We came to Shenzhen in the beginning of 2008 and I provide sex services in hotels.

A few subjects (N=3) seem not to have been influenced by others, nor had they worked at entertainment facilities before beginning to provide sex services. They did not indicate that they knew anyone working in the sex industry when they first began considering the idea of going into sex work.

Ah Ying came to Shenzhen right after she graduated from a vocational school. Her parents were migrant workers in Shenzhen. She and her brother were raised by their grandmother in their hometown. Now she visits her parents only on festivals although they live in the same city.

> I came here after graduation from school because my parents were working here. They wanted me to find a job by myself. I did not tell them what I was doing. I told them that I was a cashier at an Internet bar. I worked at the bar 12 hours a day and it was too hard for me, so I quit the job after working only two days. I found this karaoke lounge by myself. There was an advertisement at the front entrance. I do this because it is quick money. I have no friends or relatives doing this.

Xiao Fang had been in Shenzhen for only three months when I interviewed her. She has one younger brother and one younger sister. Her family was very poor, compared to her neighbors and they made fun of them sometimes. She had a boyfriend in her hometown. But her father didn't like him and asked her to move and work in Shenzhen. Later she realized that her boyfriend didn't treat her very well and decided to migrate to Shenzhen where her aunt had migrated.

I came to Shenzhen with my mother and younger sister in February 2008. I worked in a restaurant for over a month. The salary was very low. I made a little over 800 yuan a month. So my sister and I started to look for other jobs, but did not find any we liked. Later we saw a lot of ads at the bus station. I wrote down the phone numbers and called them on a public phone. They instructed me to go to somewhere to see a man. This man told me that I could make over 2000 yuan a day if I was lucky. He introduced me to a madam. My sister worked in a factory for three months and made a total of 2,000 yuan. She just started working here a few days ago.

Lin Yan is the mother of a 7-year-old daughter. Her father passed away when she was six. She quit studies when she was 13 because her family needed one of the children to do chores at home. She met her husband later when she worked at a restaurant in Kunming—the capital city of Yunnan province. She got married when she was 22, and divorced one month later because her in-laws didn't like her from the very beginning. But her husband refused to go ahead with the divorce unless she agreed to continue to live with him after the divorce. Then their daughter was born, and they moved to Lin Yan's hometown—a rural area in Yunnan Province. She raised fish and ran a small ice cream business until 2005. They also tried to run a transportation business.

I borrowed money from my relatives and bought a truck for him to do business. We did not make any money. On the other hand, we lost tens of thousands. I came to Shenzhen just wanting to make money. We need money for my daughter when she goes to school, and we do not have a house yet.

I came here with my friend. We intended to work at a factory, but there are only a few factories in Shenzhen. Then we worked at a hair salon and we only provided hand jobs. But we could not make much money. I made only 500 yuan in over 10 days. One woman from the hair salon brought us to work here. I have been here since the second half of 2005.

When they decided to work at sex venues for the first time, these three women did not have any friends or relatives working in the sex industry. Two of them had jobs in the regular sector, but they only kept them for two days and one month respectively. They quit these jobs because they were too strenuous for them. Lin Yan tried to find work at a factory, but could not, and so she went straight to a hair salon. Having no friend working in the sex industry was not a barrier for them. Advertisements could be found at bus station, sex facilities, or other public places. Hair salons and other entertainment facilities are prominently present in Shenzhen. Like other women, these women, too, realized that working in legitimate sectors was physically demanding and low paying.

In the case of women who had been working at entertainment establishments before providing sex services, the effect of friends/coworkers on their involvement in sex services is ambiguous, and not as straightforward as in the case of those who never worked at such facilities before being involved in sex services. Some of them were influenced by their co-workers, while others appear not to have been thus influenced. Working at these facilities provided women with opportunities to witness how much money prostitutes can make, how the business was done, who the customers were, and so on. They had gathered sufficient information to make their own decision. Therefore, these women, unlike their counterparts who had never worked at entertainment facilities, did not show as much hesitation, concern, lack of confidence or anxiety when they decided to get involved in the sex industry. This may explain why their friends' influence on their decision to go into prostitution is not as obvious as in other cases. Regardless, the common feature they shared with others is that they were tempted by the high income. They wanted to make more money.

Force, Deception, or Coercion

Six women in the study were identified as entering into prostitution against their will. In other words, they were victims of human trafficking. Some women of them were willing to work in the sex industry. However, sex trafficking can occur not merely during the various stages of recruitment or transportation, or upon initiation into prostitution. It is likely that they were victims of trafficking because of the context of work. In other words, it was not the woman herself who could decide when, where, or to whom to provide sex services. She may have some externally imposed "quotas"—either the number of days she must work, or the number of customers she must service. Based on examination of all the stages during which trafficking may take place, the following six women in the study fall into this category.

Xiao Hui is a pretty woman who looks like a famous Chinese actress. Her tragic story epitomizes the worst form of trafficking: she was kidnapped, beaten, threatened, raped, and escape was impossible. She was the youngest of four siblings and her parents wanted her to have more education than her other siblings—all of whom had quit studies after graduation from middle school. So she went to a vocational school after she graduated from middle school. But she didn't do very well in school. Not wanting to waste her parent's money, she quit studies in 2000 after attending that school for two years. Then she worked in Fujian Province because her mother was working there. Later, because her sister worked in Shenzhen, she worked in a factory there from the beginning of 2004 until August 2006. In 2005, she met a man online. Her destiny changed dramatically the day she met him in person in 2006.

> I originally met my boyfriend online in 2005. One day in 2006, we met online again and he invited me to go to his place. I told him to come over if he wanted to meet me. We met each other once in a while since then. One day, he and his friend came over to my place and he invited me to go to his place. I thought that he couldn't hurt me when his friend was there. So I went to his place with them. He did not allow me to go home, taking away my resident ID and money. He threatened to kill my parents if I left; he also said that his friend would have beaten me had I not been a fellow villager of his (we are from the same county). I was scared so did not leave, and I regret that. I was afraid of being beaten—who would know if I were beaten to death? I also worried that he would say bad things about me and these rumors would reach my hometown and affect my reputation. I had too many concerns and this is why I suffered. I wanted to run away, so I deceived him by saying that I needed to use the internet. But he followed me when I went to the Internet bar. He stood at the entrance when I went to the bathroom. I did not leave his room for seven or eight days—he always kept an eye on me. On the first night, he wanted to have sex, but I refused and bit him. At midnight, he wanted to have sex again. I did not resist this time because there was no way I could flee.

> More than ten days later, he asked me to work somewhere where I could make several hundred a day and he could deduct a percentage. He took me to a hair salon and he lived in an inn nearby and kept watching me. He and the boss had an agreement—the boss would give all the money I earned directly to him. The boss also helped him supervise me. He would run over to me if I walked away. I averaged 600 yuan a day and worked about 20 days a month. All this happened around August and September of 2006. As time went by, I got to know his personality. He would beat me severely if I was passive, but dared not if I fought with him. One day I took a kitchen knife and threatened to attack him with it when we fought. He hasn't beaten me since then, and I haven't given him all the money I made. Later he took me to work in Zhejiang Province. He thought that I could make more money there. We spent all the money I earned when we traveled around. We got back to Shenzhen in September, 2007 and I have worked at this hair salon since then.

I asked her whether she was free to leave her boyfriend now. She said yes, but she didn't because it was an easy way to make money:

> I have been in the game, so I just want to make more money and then retreat. I have thought about alternatives. But it is not worth it if I leave without earning a lot of money.

Ah Mei quit studies when she was in eighth grade. She did not like to study although her family could afford to send her to school. It seems to me that she was somewhat of a spoiled girl; her family condition was not bad. She did not need to tell her parents each time she went out to work with her peers. She never gave money to her family, and her family did not need her money. Sometimes, she fooled around without working, borrowing money from her friends and squandering it. She was a victim of trafficking on two occasions. The first was an attempted trafficking incident—when she was with four other women. They resisted and escaped. On the second occasion, she was lied to as the nature of the job, i.e., she was not told that she would have to do hand jobs until she arrived at the destination city. As on a previous occasion, she did not have any money on her when she traveled, but she was alone this time and she accepted the job.

> I went to work in a factory for two months after quitting studies (eighth grade) when I was 15. Then I went to Hangzhou, Zhejiang province with my friends. A couple (a man and a woman) brought three girls there. They told me that we would wash hair and make one or two thousand a month. The owner of the hair salon provided lodging and food. This appealed to me so I went with them (this couple did not deceive us intentionally—they did not know the truth either). The couple paid traveling expenses for us and we repaid them by working. The boss at the hair salon asked us to provide sex services. We refused and he locked the five of us up on the second floor. We tried to run away by sliding down from the window. Someone saw us and called the police. Finally we left the hair salon and we took a taxi to Ningbo, Zhejiang province. The couple had a relative over there. We worked at a hair salon for about two months and then we went home. I fooled around at home for a long time before I went to Dongguan, Guangdong province. I went with a married couple. My family did not know every time I came out. The couple bought me a train ticket and told me that I would wash hair and provide massage service, with no sex involved. But after arrival, the husband told me that I needed to touch customers (i.e. give them hand jobs). I had no money, could not leave, so I had to stay and work. I made 30 yuan an hour. The boss of the hair salon got 15, I kept 11, and the husband and wife got 4. The husband later took me to other places in Guangdong. All my work was providing hand jobs at hair salons. Some time later, I borrowed a total of 9,000 yuan from him. Then I did not want to follow him. I worked with all my might to pay off the debt and then left him.

Ah Mei was a girl who never thought about tomorrow as long as she had money today. Her family did not need her money, but she liked traveling and fooling around without working. After paying off the money she borrowed from her friend, she left him. But she did not leave the sex trade. Instead, she went to Shanghai and worked at a karaoke lounge sometime later.

> I went to Shanghai after the 2007 Chinese New Year. I worked at a karaoke lounge in Shanghai until the Duanwu Festival and went home (about four months). I fooled around when I had money and got back to work when I ran out of money. Then I went back to Shanghai and worked until the 2008 Chinese New Year. During the second half of 2007, I stayed in Shanghai and rarely worked. I felt ashamed to ask my parents for money, so I borrowed from my friends, a total of 7,000 yuan. They came to my home before the Chinese New Year and asked me to pay off the debt. My parents asked me how much I owed, saying they would like to help me out if it

was not very much. But it was too much—I did not want them to pay it for me. So I came out secretly. A fellow villager was in Shenzhen. So I came here and worked at a hair salon. I worked with all my might and paid off the debt several days after the Chinese New Year. I was very pleased. I still had several thousand left over, so I went to Anhui for a vacation. I went to Shanghai this month for a reunion with Internet friends, and just got back on the 12th.

If I worked in a factory, I couldn't earn enough money. I am very extravagant, wasting a lot of money. I don't want to do it, but I have no choice; there are no other ways to make quick money. I am lazy, I don't like strenuous work. It is easy to make money by doing this.

Li Xue started to provide sex services after being raped. But she was also trafficked twice later. On each occasion, she traveled with her peers who bought her tickets and provided lodging at their destination. She worked as a prostitute and divided the money with them. When she couldn't make as much as they required, they would threaten to sell or beat her. She worked at an entertainment center after the 2000 Chinese New Year.

There is a woman at the entertainment center. We call her sister Ping. She and her husband took me and another girl to Ningbo, Zhejiang province. She has a relative who provides sex services at a hotel. I dared not knock on the customer's door, so they sent me to work at a hair salon instead. My business was not satisfactory and they complained that I was a burden to them, i.e. not good at making money. All of them were mean. One day, I had a fight with them and left. I came home very late. They threatened to sell me to a drug addict for 2,000 yuan. Their purpose was to have me earn as much money for them as I could. I gave them all the money I made. Then they sent me to another hair salon. There was a woman at that hair salon who invited me to her home. Her husband was very lusty. I wanted to flee away at that time. I thought that I may be able to hide at her home if I had a good relationship with her. One day I called Sister Ping and lied, saying that I was arrested. I hid at this girl's home. One day, when she went out to buy food, her husband raped me. I tried to leave, he beat me. Eventually I left. A man followed me. He seemed to like me. I was pleased when we talked. He rented a room for me at an inn and wanted to live with me. I refused and said that I had just been raped by the other man, and now it was you again. He left upon hearing this. I had no money at that time. He paid for me to stay at the inn for one night. I called my mother after he left and told her that I had been deceived. She borrowed 300 yuan and deposited it in my bank account. I had intentionally opened an account before I left, just in case. I worked at a hair salon after going home. It is very hard to turn around once you get involved in this line of work. I do not know what I should do. This is the only job that I can do, where I can make several thousand a month.

Two men took me to Shenzhen around Christmas 2000. They paid my travel expenses and bought me clothes, and I gave them 50 out of every 100 yuan I made. I zuotai and made 200 yuan per table. I gave each of two madams 50, and then divided the other 100 yuan with the two men. I did not have much left after paying for food and cosmetics. There was another woman who came with us. Her appearance was better than mine and she made more money than me, so the two men threatened to sell me. They also took me to Shazui (a very famous red light district in Shenzhen) and showed me how chicken-heads beat other women. I saw them beat women and burn them with cigarettes. I was really scared. There are a lot of men bringing women here. They live off women. But there are so many pretty women. I am short and cannot compete with them. Then they sent me to Shekou (a district in Shenzhen) and I became a streetwalker. One day I had an opportunity to run away. I had only 20 yuan that day. I kept walking until I arrived at a hair salon, but I did not know where it was. I worked over there and did not want to get involved in sex service. A customer asked me to take off my clothes on the first day I worked. I refused. I offended several customers. The boss consoled me, telling me that I would get used to it. She asked me to do hand jobs from the outset. Then I worked at several other hair salons.

Li Xue's family, including her father and two brothers, depended on her and she could not ignore them.

I want to quit this job, but I cannot. My family is counting on me to pay off debt. How could I do this if I worked in a factory? My brothers do not have a house for marriage yet. I give my father 500-1000 yuan each month and save the rest. I am helping my little brother learn how to cut hair. I will arrange my other brother's life after he is released from prison.

Both Ah Mei and Li Xue had to depend on a third party to take them out because they did not have information or financial resources. They did not have the money to buy tickets, nor did they have social connections at the destination city. They had never been to the city where their friends took them, and they had to depend on their friends to find a job. They relied on the recruiter and the recruiter's networks when they traveled to other cities. Consequently, when they arrived at the destination, they were often in an extremely vulnerable position, one in which they were totally dependent on recruiters and their networks. This vulnerability is often exploited by recruiters in the sex industry.

Liu Yan is the mother of a 20-month-old daughter. Both her parents had health conditions, and her childhood life was not happy. Both she and her brother quit studies when they were in middle school. She was the only woman in the study who was deceived by a relative, in this case by a cousin. She was told that she would work in a factory. When she refused to provide sex services, her salary was withdrawn, or else she was beaten. After being trafficked twice, and later, working voluntarily at a karaoke lounge, she got married, and gave birth to her daughter. Then she worked in a factory for about a year, and she had just begun working at the sauna place a month before I interviewed her.

My cousin brought me to Guangdong when I was 15 years old. My cousin told my mother that I could make 1,000 yuan if I worked in a toy factory in Guangdong. So I went to Shantou, Guangdong province with her. She took me to a hair salon, told me the owner was her friend and I would stay there for several days. I washed hair thereafter. About one week later, the boss asked whether I would like to sell my virginity, and then I knew that I was supposed to provide sex services. I cried for a week. I just washed hair the first month. I asked the boss for my salary one month later. She told me that my cousin had taken my salary. I told my cousin that I wanted to go home. She did not want me to go and I did not have money to buy a ticket. She persuaded me. She said, "You are young, and your family condition is not good. I won't take the money you earn. I just want you to help your family." Other sex workers also persuaded me. Eventually I reluctantly agreed when I realized that my family condition was bad and I could not afford transportation expenses if I went home. All this happened ten years ago, and I still hate my cousin. I worked at that hair salon for over two months and then went home. I made 1,000 yuan by selling my virginity and the boss got 1,000 yuan. I still remember the first customer. He was nice to me and came to see me again.

My neighbor took me to the town center after I stayed home for a year, and I became a waitress at a restaurant. One month later I found that there was sex service there. The mayor of the township liked me. He took me to dinner, sightseeing and also gave me money. I did not have sex with him until two months later. Then I worked as a waitress at a big restaurant and met my boyfriend, who was a chef. One month later, he offered to take me to Dongguan. He said that the salaries were high and I would work in a factory. One of my girlfriends and one of his boyfriends went also. The four of us arrived at his friend's home in Dongguan. His friend's girlfriend could make over one thousand every day and she intentionally showed off in front of us. My boyfriend asked us to do that. Both of us cried. We refused to work and they started to beat us. I still have a scar near my eye. We did not have money and reluctantly worked at a hotel. We turned over all the money we earned. I hid some money in a bottle. They found it and beat me. Two months later in 1999, my boyfriend took me to Guangzhou and separated me from my girlfriend. I worked at a hair salon. The owner and I were from the same area. I told him that I was deceived and he helped me. I asked him to save part of my earnings. My boyfriend liked gambling and we fought everyday (he had sex with me only one time before we came out). I talked to him, saying that I wanted to end our relationship by paying him money. He asked for 10,000 yuan. I told him that I did not have that much. Eventually we agreed that I would pay him 4000 yuan. The owner of the hair salon had saved 2,000 for me and he loaned me the other 2,000 yuan. I worked at the hair salon for two years. After paying off a 20,000 yuan debt (due to that fact that my parents built a house), I went home in 2001.

Liu Yan wanted to make more money for her own family because her husband could not do so.

For a long while after I got married, I did not work. I gave birth to my daughter. The condition of both my family and my husband's was not good. My life was very tough when I was a child, and I did not want my daughter to have a hard life like the one I had. I wanted to make more money while I was still young, so that I could run a small business and give my daughter a good life in the future.

I used to have regrets, but I no longer do. I just wanted to make more money. Some girls are used to luxury lives; they cannot make a living by working in a factory.

I could work in a factory and I am not afraid of hard work. But my husband was working in a factory. He was almost good for nothing and I could not count on him to support the family. My kid will need a lot of money when she grows up. What I am doing is good for myself, my kid, and my family.

Mei Fang's parents were business people, so her childhood life was very good. But she didn't do very well in school. She worked in a factory in Dongguan in 2000 after quitting studies. In 2002, she eloped with her boyfriend because her parents didn't like him. But eventually she broke up with him and then worked at a factory in her hometown. One of her best friends conspired to entrap her in the prostitution business just because she wanted her company.

I went back to my hometown in 2004 and worked in a shoe factory. I also worked in a supermarket as a sales clerk. My life was very boring. One of my good friends told me that there were a lot of opportunities in Shenzhen. She sold wine and could make over 2,000 yuan a month. She kept encouraging me to come out. I went to Shenzhen in the later half of 2005. I brought 1,200 yuan with me. After arriving, she took me to have my hair done, and to buy clothes. I told her that I wanted to work. She said that I was out of date—I needed to dress up and buy some cosmetics. I borrowed over 2,000 yuan from her. She told me the truth after I hung out with her for awhile. She did not sell wine; she was a masseuse, and she provided sex services. I told her that I wanted to work in a factory. She said that there were no factories there, and also asked me to return her money. She said, "I brought you here because I regard you as my friend. Why are you so 'behind the times?' You are not a virgin." I asked her, "Aren't you afraid that people will know what you are doing?" She said, "As long as you do this work, we are both in the same boat and you will not tell anyone (that I am a prostitute)." I considered for a long time and asked whether only massage (i.e. hand-job) was involved. She said yes. So I started to do massage. We are very good friends and are both pretty. She did not want to make money off me. She just wanted to have company. Gradually, I stopped thinking that chastity mattered. Furthermore, your reputation is already bad if you are a masseuse (whether or not sexual intercourse is involved), so why not make an all-out effort? There were also some people who persuaded me. Seeing other people make a lot of money, I wanted to do the same, make a lot of money, and then go home to do business. Therefore, I started to do full-service half a year later. Then I became a concubine. He gave me 10,000 yuan a month and I fooled around everyday. We broke up eight months later and I started to do massage again. I just did hand-jobs until October 2007. I came here to do full service because business became slow.

Mei Fang continued in this line of work because:

I told myself from the first day I took this job that I would not go home to grow crops, I would not be a "working-sister" (i.e. migrant girls working in a factory or other legitimate sectors), I would operate a private business, and would not let others look down upon me.

Xiao Yu was born in 1984 and adopted when she was four. Her adoptive parents were very nice to her. She was a waitress at a karaoke lounge downtown in her home county after she graduated from middle school. Her story of unwilling involvement in prostitution is simpler than that of others. Her boyfriend sent her to Shenzhen and promised to marry her after she made a lot of money. However, before she left, they did not discuss how she was to make money or what she would do in Shenzhen. She had to take the job after he left because she had no money to run away.

> I was a waitress at a karaoke in my hometown after middle school—there was no sex service involved. I dated a man who was married. I did not know this until six months later. I broke up with him and lost faith in men afterwards. But I fell in love with him, so we reconciled six months later. His wife was in Shenzhen so he asked me to work there. He told me that we would get married after making a lot of money. He had a female friend who was a prostitute at Shangsha (a red-light district in Shenzhen). He turned me over to her and left Shenzhen two or three days later. I had no money and dared not run away. This woman had a relative who had a hair salon. She took me there and I worked over there. All this happened in the beginning of 2003. I do not know whether my boyfriend got money.

It was an easy way to make a lot of money, so she kept working at the hair salon since then.

> What else could I do? Several hundred or one thousand a month was not enough. I became lazy after working in this line of work over time. We are not well-educated.

All these stories describe experiences that happened two to eleven years ago. None of the women were under someone else's control or deprived of freedom at the time of the interview. Four of the nine experiences happened in Shenzhen, two in Dongguan, one in Shantou and two in Zhejiang province (Ningbo and Hangzhou). These six women got involved in sex work against their will on nine occasions (including one attempt) and it happened twice to three of them. Only one case involved a woman (Xiao Hui) who was already in Shenzhen when it happened. All other cases involved women who voluntarily migrated to Shenzhen or other big cities in the hope of making more money than they could in their hometowns.

A wide range of methods were used in the process of recruitment and imposition of work conditions to force these women to work in sex venues. These methods included force (kidnapping, locking up, attacking, rape), deceit (not telling the subjects about the nature of the work until their arrival at the destination, lying to the subjects about the nature of the work), coercion (threats that the women's families would be informed they were prostitutes, threats that their families would be killed, threats that the women would be sold), taking advantage of their vulnerability (they did not have the resources to travel, no money to enable them to run away), taking away their salary and ID, ensnaring and persuading them. On five occasions, three subjects (Ah Mei, Liu Yan, and Mei Fang) were told lies about the nature of the job. They were told they would work in a factory or at other jobs where no sex service was involved. They did not know until their arrival, or some time after arrival, that sex services would be involved. When the women refused to comply, they were either subjected to violence, their salary was withheld, or they were coerced. The women reluctantly accepted their fate because they did not have the money required to run away or to live on their own. On two occasions involving one subject (Li Xue), there was an agreement between the victim and the perpetrators regarding how to divide the money she earned. But when she could not make as much as the perpetrators would have liked, they subjected her to violence or threatened to sell her. One woman (Xiao Yu) and her boyfriend did not discuss the nature of the work she would do before they left for Shenzhen. She told me that she was free to leave, but she took the job because she had no money to go away with—there was no force or deception involved. One woman (Xiao Hui) had been in Shenzhen before the tragedy took place. Her experience represents the worst example of sex trafficking, in which the subject is kidnapped, locked up, raped, and forced to provide sex services. She was under the control of the traffickers, she did not have freedom of movement, escape was impossible, her boyfriend took away her ID, she was threatened, and had to surrender all the money she made.

None of them were rescued from forced sex work through police raids. They managed to leave their recruiters by fleeing (N=3), or by redemption (N=1). In most cases, the recruiters just left them alone after they began working at these jobs (N=5).

The people who forced the women into prostitution included boyfriends in three cases, peers/acquaintances in four cases, a relative in one case and the owner of a hair salon in another. None of them were gang members or were involved in organized crime. Usually there was no co-conspirator involved, especially in cases where the boyfriends were the recruiters. Sometimes two people were involved; they were either husband and wife or just two accomplices.

All traffickers did not make money out of the women. Mei Fang's girlfriend just wanted someone for company and so she deceived Mei Fang into getting involved in this trade. Liu Yan's cousin withheld her money in order to force her to work, but she did not take her money after Liu Yan began to work at the hair salon. Xiao Yu said that she did not know whether her boyfriend made money out of her, but she earned as much as other prostitutes did from each customer. Two women (Ah Mei and Li Xue) had agreements with their recruiters about dividing up the money they earned.

Conclusion

This chapter concentrated on the circumstances present in the women's lives at the time when they initially began to provide sex services. The paths to prostitution are diverse and no single model has emerged from this study. This study did not uncover any obvious relationship between prostitution and domestic violence, prostitution and abuse or prostitution and negative relationships with parents. Although many women had lived hard lives before they migrated, and a few of the fathers were alcoholic or irresponsible, the women all grew up in relatively stable families. Two women mentioned that their fathers were irresponsible, gamblers, or alcoholic; two other women mentioned that their parents fought a lot when they were young. Two subjects' parents divorced when the girls were in their early teens, but neither of them stated that their parents' divorce had any direct effect on their involvement in prostitution. One woman was distracted from studying by her parents' divorce and this was the main reason why she did not pursue further education after high school. A negative relationship with her stepmother drove her to leave home and go to Shenzhen with her boyfriend. What happened after arriving in Shenzhen motivated her to get involved in prostitution. It is obvious that her parents' divorce had no direct effect on her involvement in prostitution.

The literature on prostitution and human trafficking reveals high levels of sexual abuse in the backgrounds of women who end up in the sex industry (Raymond and Hughes, 2001; Davis, 2006). However, previous studies have not reached any consistent conclusion. Simons and Whiteback (1991) suggest that early sexual abuse may affect the probability of prostitution in a direct way, because the experience of child sexual abuse fosters attitudes about oneself and the act of sex that facilitate the selling of sexual favors. However, this was not confirmed consistently by the present study. Three subjects were raped when they were 6, 9, and 15 years old respectively. Wang Xia was raped when she was 6. She proclaimed that entering into prostitution had nothing to do with that incident; she would not have adopted prostitution had a fellow villager not introduced her to it. Ah Lian was raped by her neighbor when she was 15. She did not want to go to school after that happened, and she could not verbalize the feeling of being raped. She said that she may not have worked at a hair salon if that had never happened. Ding Ding told me that she was raped when she was 9. She had never told anyone, not even her family. She has hated all men since then, including her ex-boyfriend who abused her very badly. Examining her life circumstances at the time she initially began prostitution, however, it appears that there were many other strongly motivating factors underlying her involvement in prostitution. At the very least, she became a prostitute for money, not for revenge. In cases where there was sexual assault in childhood, this study shows no clear-cut indication of its effect on the adoption of prostitution.

It is obvious that in combination with other factors, being raped can trigger a woman to go into prostitution. Li Xue's experience confirms this. Being raped by a customer affected the development of her self-identity. She may be viewing herself as sexually debased. Such a loss of status constitutes "an important step in the process by which a woman comes to identify with a deviant lifestyle such as prostitution and thus begins to see it as a viable alternative" (James and Meyerding, 1977: 1383).

This study finds that factors related to women's involvement in prostitution vary, and the relevance of each factor to women's involvement in the sex trade is different. In terms of proximal factors, some women get involved in this trade because of specific events. However, this does not imply a causal relationship between the event that occurred and prostitution. The event stands out as an obvious factor in the women's involvement in prostitution because of the time at which it occurred—it happened right before the women's first foray into prostitution, and, in one way or another, was related to their involvement in prostitution.

The effect of friends/relatives/peers on women's involvement in prostitution, and the women's vulnerability to human trafficking cannot be overemphasized. Thirty subjects had friends and three had relatives involved in the sex industry. Five women said that they had no friends or relatives working in this industry. To the extent that the women's adoption of prostitution is related to their friends/relatives/co-workers, the effect of the influence of each of the aforementioned people on the women varies widely. Some women were forced, deceived, or coerced. Some were encouraged or persuaded. Some were influenced by their friends or co-workers who had been involved in prostitution. Some had accepted the idea of prostitution before they turned to their friends for advice or comments.

Prostitution was in no way their first choice. Thirty-nine of the forty women had been working in a variety of legitimate sectors before getting involved in prostitution. For those who adopted prostitution voluntarily, it was not a spontaneous response to a dire economic condition. Some of them had accepted the idea of prostitution long before they actually began the trade, and they did so when the timing was right for them, in other words, when they were in need of money, or had lost a legitimate job. Although eighteen women categorized their childhoods as poverty ridden, most of them were not living in poverty at the time they adopted prostitution. Benefiting from China's economic reform policy, these women were able to leave their rural homes to explore more economic opportunities in other areas. This economy-driven migration had even begun with their parents' generation in the 1980s. Therefore, by going into the sex industry, most women did not make a decision between starvation and prostitution; as a matter of fact, they opted for prostitution because it was easy, quick, and big money.

Money is the reason why most women go into prostitution, although it may not be the only reason. Few women prostitute themselves for reasons other than money. In the case of these women, prostitution is a response to their financial circumstances. Every woman has her unique financial circumstances. They are in need of money for different reasons. Some want to make more money (N=21); some want to relieve their parents' economic burden (N=5); women with children want to save money for their family, children or future (N=6); one woman wanted to save money for her sibling's education (N=1); one woman bought a house for her parents or for herself, and needed money to pay off a loan (N=1); and some just blew up their money in drugs and gambling (N=6).

While many prostitutes in this study had similar life experiences, identifying one or even several factors as responsible for their turning to prostitution is too simplistic. The issue is more complex than that. Undesirable circumstances in the lives of these women constitute one of the factors motivating them into prostitution. Underlying factors include, but are not limited to socio-economic factors, cultural factors, as well as the women's own attitudes toward prostitution. It is a combination of these factors that makes prostitution a desirable option. This will be discussed in Chapter 7.

6
Life on the "Job"

The preceding chapters examined the lives of prostitutes before they got involved in the trade, as well as the paths by which they entered into prostitution. The present chapter will concentrate on their lives following entry into prostitution, and will focus on their working conditions, lifestyles, and concerns. In spite of great media exposure, anecdotes and stories, or even novels of prostitutes at work, little is known about how sex venues are operated, what prostitutes' lifestyles are really like, how they entertain themselves after work, how they perceive and view this work, and so on. This chapter aims to present readers with a profile of their life on the job.

In existing literature on trafficking, relatively little emphasis is placed on the fact that some women, although they may have chosen to work in prostitution, nevertheless end up in situations of forced prostitution and severe exploitation (Brunovskis and Tyldum, 2004). Women who have chosen to work in prostitution but who end up working under conditions that they cannot control or escape from, or who do not receive money for their work, should also be regarded as trafficking victims. Human trafficking may occur not only in stages of recruitment and transportation, but also in establishments of prostitution. A woman's consent to work as a prostitute does not wipe out the possibility that she may be controlled, restricted, or forced to work after she initially agrees to a job in the sex industry. Nor does it mean that she cannot be considered a trafficking victim if she is held under conditions akin to slavery. Forced work and exploitation in establishments of prostitution should also be defined as trafficking. These considerations have led to examination of the conditions under which prostitutes work, the rules of the game, and the manner in which money is divided with third parties.

A prostitute is usually addressed as "miss" (xiaojie) in China. The reason behind this appellation has never been examined. Since the 1980s, waitresses at service facilities such as restaurant, hotels, bars or other entertainment establishments were addressed as "miss," which was considered a form of courtesy. It was in these establishments that prostitution activities reemerged in the 1980s. Since some of the waitresses at these facilities provided sex services, the term "miss" became a euphemism for the term "prostitute." In this study the two terms "miss" and "prostitute" are interchangeable. The four sex venues, namely, hair salons, nightclub/karaoke lounges, massage/sauna parlors, and the street vary significantly in terms of the services they provide, their operation and management, their regulations and prices, etc. and will be discussed separately.

Operation and Management of the Business

Hair Salons

Hair salons are the simplest operations when compared to the other two off-street sex venues in terms of the way the business is run, the employees involved, the services provided, and the magnitude of investment. Operating such a business does not require much investment. Basically, one needs to rent a place, and hire several misses. Usually, these are operated in apartment sized two-story facilities in residential or commercial areas of the city. No hairdressers work at such "hair salons." One will not find any hair cutting tools, or hair clippings on the floor. Such a hair salon is often referred to as a "chicken store" (In Chinese, the terms "chicken" and "prostitute" have a similar sound. Therefore, a prostitute is referred to as a chicken). Usually several misses and an owner are involved in the operation of the business; some owners may not show up at the store. Instead, the owner hires a trusted person to be in charge of the store and act as a supervisor and cashier. Misses usually sit on the first floor waiting for customers. Customers select a miss and the sex services are usually conducted on the second floor. Customers can also take misses to hotels. Based on my field observations, the first floor is relatively bright, clean and spacious, as the owner wants it to be attractive to customers. Mirrors hang on the walls. Some stores even have several hair-styling chairs and shampoo stations for show on the first floor.

The second floor, where sex services are conducted, is unobservable from the outside. I visited one hair salon in a residential area and asked for a massage in order to be able to observe the second floor. Most of the space on the second floor was converted into three small compartments where sex services were provided. These were referred to as "massage rooms." There was a small massage bed and a desk in the room. The light was dim, but this did not prevent me from observing that the bed-sheet and pillow were not clean. I felt reluctant when the miss asked me to lie on the bed. She turned on the air conditioning right after we got into the room, but the room still had not cooled down 30 minutes later when I left. There was a small area in the center, surrounded by the three massage rooms. Two double-decker steel beds occupy this space—this is the so-called dormitory, where the misses working at the hair salon sleep. Misses hang a piece of cloth on the four sides of the bed in order to have some privacy. Otherwise, customers can see the beds on the way to the "massage rooms."

The owner of that hair salon came to Shenzhen in 2003. She worked in a hair salon in the beginning, and opened her own store in 2005. Her family bought a piece of land, and built a five-story building in the center of her county. The owner is younger than 30. She told me that it was not difficult to run such a store once one knew the price and the services. The rent is 7,000-8,000 yuan per month. I asked her how much she made in a month. She said several thousand. Later, I overheard her chatting with the cashier and I learned that this store had three owners; the other two owners were her sister and another friend. She didn't become one of the owners until 2005. In 2003, there were two owners and each owner could make 5,000 yuan in a month. But now, each of them can make only two or three thousand. Misses make more money than owners. That is why some women would rather work for others than be the boss of such a business. This store is open 24 hours, seven days a week. I asked the owner if there were any customers in the morning, at around 6:00 a.m.–7:00 a.m. She told me that there were some people from Hong Kong who fooled around all night and wanted to have a nap in the morning. They would rather come to the salon and spend 50 yuan (25 yuan per hour for a massage) for a two-hour massage service than go to a hotel, which would cost them more than that sum. Obviously, they were not seeking regular massage service—based on my experience of the massage I had in that store, the misses had no training or knowledge of massage.

Owners of hair salon do not require misses to work a minimum num-ber of days each month. Misses make the decision on how many days they want to work. But when they work at the store, if they go out with a customer for more than two hours, it is assumed that they provided sex services, and they have to pay the store 100 yuan.

Nightclub/Karaoke Lounges

The size and scale of nightclubs or karaoke lounges vary significantly. Some large, high-class facilities encompass an entire two or three story building. Usually, the owner rents two or three stories of a multi-story or high-rise building, where there are also other entertainment facilities such as restaurants, hotels, or sauna parlors. Nightclubs are usually of a higher class than karaoke lounges (which are also referred to as KTV Lounges). But there is no great difference in the services provided at these two entertainment facilities. Inside, the buildings are divided into rooms installed with karaoke facilities, sofas and coffee tables. Some luxury rooms also include a restroom. Women working at nightclubs/karaoke lounges are usually not employees of that establishment. They are managed and supervised by "mammies"—who exercise the first line of supervision and management of misses at such venues. There are several mammies working at medium or large nightclub/karaoke lounges, and a mammy usually has twenty, or even forty women working for her. Some mammies work for several venues simultaneously. Managers of these venues have the mammy's phone number. When misses are needed, the owners call the mammy. The mammy and the misses divide the money earned by the latter. In addition to the managers, mammies, and misses, the people involved in this business also include security staff, waiters or waitresses, hostesses, etc. When customers arrive, the hostess at the entrance will usher them upstairs, and the manager on duty will assign them a room, based on the number of customers. There are varying sizes of rooms. People usually visit these venues in groups. After customers are seated in the room, the mammy will socialize with them and ask whether they need misses. If they do, several misses will enter the customer's room in order to be selected—the mammies usually refer misses to customers based on the customers' preferences, or recommend misses whom they like to customers.

Usually the mammy was herself a miss before she became a mammy. A mammy's responsibilities include introducing misses to customers, solving problems between misses and customers, developing and maintaining regular customers, and assuring the misses' safety if they *"chutai"* (this term denotes going out with customers and providing sex services). A responsible mammy should make sure that the misses are not at risk when they go out with customers; she must know where the misses go with their customers. Thus, the mammies are expected to protect the interests of the prostitutes. The misses don't get any payment from the establishments.

Instead, they depend on tips paid by customers. In case of tension between a customer and a miss, if the customer refuses to offer a tip, the mammies will ask the customer for a tip. Thus, to a certain extent, misses depend on mammies to do business. But a mammy does not always stand for the misses' interest. In order to maintain and develop regular customers, some mammies would like the misses to do their best to cater to all. As a matter of fact, there are some rules that apply. Lily said that she would be fined if she refused to go out with customers (e.g., if she did not want to go out with certain customers because they used drugs).

Mammies have three sources of income: the first is a management fee (it is usually 300 yuan a month) and the second is a "chutai" fee earned when the misses go out with customers (it is usually 100 yuan). The third one is deductions from customers' expenditure on beers, snacks, etc. One mammy I interviewed also said that she would get 50 yuan from the hotel upstairs if customers rented a room for sex services. She oversees more than 30 misses and more than 20 of these work everyday. Some mammies are flexible regarding the management fee, that is to say, the misses may pay their management fee based on the number of days they work. Usually it is 20 yuan each night.

The mammy is not a necessary actor in the operation of the karaoke lounge. At some small-scale karaoke lounges, there are fewer mammies and misses, and some venues even do not have a mammy. The misses are supervised by a manager of the venue. This is the case of a karaoke lounge I visited during my fieldwork:

> This KTV has a little over 40 misses. They are all from other provinces, mainly from Sichuan and Hunan. 25 of the 40 misses are married. They were introduced by their friends. There is a lot of flexibility in working here. They do not need to pay a management fee to a mammy, we do not have mammies here. The misses are managed by the corporation. They pay us 10 yuan each day they work. The misses can leave if they do not have customers. In some places, they have to wait until 1:00 or 2:00 a.m. even when they do not have customers. We do not categorize misses. Customers choose misses by themselves. Some customers are shy and so then we will refer misses to them. In such a situation, we will refer those who usually have fewer opportunities to zuotai because we must make sure everyone makes money. If customers want misses who are experienced and not dull, we will introduce them to such kind of misses (Manager of a KTV).

In addition to paying their mammy 300 yuan per month, which is referred to as a management fee, the misses need to pay 300 yuan for their work uniform when they first accept the job. Some KTV lounges will not charge a management fee if there are customers who reserve two rooms on behalf of her, which serves as an incentive for misses to develop and maintain regular customers.

Massage/Sauna Parlors

Venues falling in this category have multiple alternative names, such as "foot bath city," "entertainment center," or "leisure center," etc. Services provided at these venues are very similar, basically including baths, massage, and sex services. The size of the premises, the construction and layout of interior facilities, the complexities of operating such a business, the luxurious exterior decoration, etc. are all very similar to those of nightclubs/karaoke lounges. However, a massage/sauna parlor is more complex than other venues in terms of the services it provides. Prostitutes at this venue are euphemistically referred to as "technicians"—and the managers who supervise and oversee these technicians are called "ministers." Prostitutes at such high-class venues are classified into two categories (A and B), and the prices and services each category provides vary. The classification is based on the technician's appearance, and the services they provide. Customers can have sexual intercourse with category A technicians, and their services don't necessarily include massage. However, the sex services do not necessarily involve just straightforward sexual intercourse. A variety of terms denote different types of luxury sex services, and the technicians must be trained before they can offer these. Category B technicians usually provide massage and hand job services. There are usually two work shifts at massage/sauna parlors, a day shift usually beginning at noon and going on to 10:00 p.m., and a night shift that runs from 9:00 p.m. until 6:00 a.m. When customers arrive, a hostess at the entrance ushers them into the building, and the "ministers" socialize with them, asking what services they are interested in. The ministers then arrange for the technicians to enter the room, and the customers can select the technician of his choice.

The people involved in the daily operation of the business include hostesses, managers, ministers, technicians, waitresses, cashiers, time recorders, and so on. The ministers are employees of the venue. They are equivalent to the mammies at the nightclub/karaoke lounges. Their duties involve receiving customers from the hostesses, assigning them to a room, arranging for technicians to service them, and resolving problems between customers and technicians. High-class venues have more than forty or fifty technicians. Smaller ones may have ten technicians or more; however these are not classified into different categories.

Technicians are usually required to work a minimum number of days in a month, ranging from 24 to 27. If they do not meet this minimum, they have to pay a fine of 100 yuan for each day they do not work. Customers have to pay 200 yuan to the establishment to take technicians out. Most venues also require technicians to bring customers to the establishment, in other words, customers must make reservations for the services of a specific technician. Some venues require technicians to bring in at least one customer a week or pay a fine of 50 yuan. Some venues have even more stringent rules regarding the technicians' behavior at work, e.g., if a customer complains about them, they will be fined 100 yuan, 20 yuan if they do not smile, 20 yuan if they are not wearing their badges, 10 yuan per minute if they are late. To avoid losing money on account of customer complaints, some technicians have to tolerate violent behavior from customers.

According to a police officer, the owners of these venues are usually local people with social connections. Hoodlums or thugs dare not bother them. However, sometimes, migrants, too, operate such businesses, e.g., the owners of some entertainment centers are from Jianli county, Hubei province. Local people are involved in their business either as partners or as "dry" owners, responsible for public relations. "Dry owners are those who do not make any investment in the business, but get dividends from the owners. To operate businesses such as nightclubs, karaoke lounges, or sauna parlors, owners must have wide social connections with a variety of government agencies, such as the Industry and Commerce Bureau, the Tax Agency, the Public Security Bureau, etc. One owner of a massage/sauna parlor I interviewed had only three years of schooling. He was 33 years old, a Cantonese from the countryside not far from Shenzhen. He started to work when he was very young, helping his parents to sell vegetables. Initially, after he came to Shenzhen, he sold pork. Later on, he was a street vendor, selling CDs and VCDs. After that, he ran a restaurant, a karaoke lounge, a dancing hall, and eventually he began to operate the hotel where sauna/massage services are provided. Another boss of a karaoke lounge refused to participate in this study. He was only 26 years old. His father was the head of a village (there is a well-know red light district in this village). He had only elementary school education.

Streetwalkers

Streetwalkers participating in this study can be divided into two categories: freelance streetwalkers, who solicit customers by themselves, and streetwalkers who depend on pimps and mammies to solicit customers for them. Freelance streetwalkers who participated in this study are usually found on their home turf after it gets dark. They hang around on the sidewalk and approach the street when they see potential customers driving through. The service and price are usually decided before she gets into the car and the sex services are usually performed in the car.

As regards the other category of streetwalkers, namely, those who depend on pimps and mammies to solicit customers on their behalf, these misses usually convene in Internet bars in the evening. Their mammy is the owner of the Internet bar. They surf online, or just hang around if there are no customers. Customers may come to the bar and choose prostitutes directly. Or they may call the mammy and tell her their preferences, and the mammy will send two or three girls to his place (usually a hotel), where he will choose one of them. Other sources for customers are women in their thirties or forties who solicit customers around the better star rated hotels. These women negotiate prices with customers and deduct half of the money for themselves. They then contact mammies, who have a bunch of women, and the mammy chooses a prostitute based on the customer's preferences. The sex service is provided in a hotel or in a customer's home, but usually in hotels. Several mammies work at the same Internet bar and almost 100 misses work there every night.

According to a streetwalker, the mammy who owns the Internet bar is a Sichuanese, about 35 years old. At one time, more than sixty misses worked with her. Now she has about twenty to thirty misses. Some misses had worked with her for two years. If she liked certain misses, she would refer them to good customers. If the misses had any trouble, for example if the customers did not pay them, they would tell the mammy, and she would help them to get their money back. Streetwalkers have a great deal of flexibility. They decide how many days they work and how long they want to work.

Price and Division of Money

Hair Salon

The price for sex service at hair salons is 130 yuan, with the miss retaining 100, and the establishment keeping 30 yuan. Sometimes customers ask for a discount, and then the price is 100 yuan, of which the miss keeps 70. The price for overnight service is 300-400 yuan, of which the establishment will retain 100. The so-called "overnight" service usually involves having sexual intercourse twice. Misses do not have to remain with customers all night long. It actually takes only two or three hours. Some misses also provide oral sex. The price for oral sex is 150 yuan, of which the miss gets to keep 120. Some stores provide hand jobs only—the price for this is 80 yuan, of which the misses retain 32. The price for a regular massage is about 25-35 yuan per hour.

Most of the women did not think that the way the money was divided was unfair. Three of the women thought that the owner had spent a lot of money to set up and run the business, and therefore it was fair that they deduct some percentage from the women's earnings. Some women said that their bosses were very nice to them, for example, cooking nutritious food for them on occasion. Two women thought the division of money was unfair, especially when the owner of the establishment got to keep 100 yuan when the women provided overnight service. One woman said that they had to pay the boss 100 yuan if they went out with a customer for more than two hours, even if they only went out for a meal.

Nightclubs/Karaoke Lounges

Services at nightclubs/karaoke lounges can be classified into three categories, with the prices varying accordingly. The usual prices for companion service (zuotai), sex service and overnight service (chutai) are 200 yuan, 500 yuan, and 800 yuan respectively. The price may go up or down, depending on the class of the venues. The price for sex services may also vary with the misses—e.g., if the misses give customers a very pleasant experience, the customers may reward them with better tips. When misses go out to provide sex service, the mammy deducts 100 yuan from what the misses earn. If the misses do not work a lot, they pay the monthly pro-rated management fee. Additionally, the miss will pay 10 percent of the "zuotai" fee to her mammy. Thus, if the companion service fee is 200, she would need to pay 20 to the mammy; if it is 100, she pays her 10 yuan. Most misses say it is fair to pay the mammy some money because the women depend on the mammy for introductions to customers, and the mammy also has other duties and responsibilities.

Massage/Sauna Parlors

In these establishments, for a category A prostitute, the price of services is usually between 400-500 yuan, and the technicians get to keep about 250 yuan of that money. Customers also give tips, and as a result, technicians can make as much as 500 yuan from each customer. Sometimes customers do not give tips, according to one technician. For category B technicians offering hand jobs, the price is 200-300 yuan, of which the women get to keep between 100-200 yuan. If customers give tips, some category B technicians can make as much as 400 yuan on occasion.

But prices at different massage/sauna parlors can vary widely. At one sauna parlor, for example, the price for category A sex service is 350 yuan, of which the technicians get 300. The price for category B is 270 yuan, of which the technicians get 240. At another parlor, the Category A price is 500, and the technicians get to keep 270; the parlor gets 200 yuan, the remaining 30 yuan pays for the condom. The service time is generally the same, usually at least 100 minutes for each customer.

Technicians usually offer a massage first. Sometimes category A technicians directly provide sex service. Category B technicians usually offer a massage first, then go on to a hand job. A hand job is also referred to as "Tuiyou"—a whole-body massage with oil, which includes massage of the penis—performed with the hands or breasts, using baby oil. If the service given is a massage, customers pay the parlor what is referred to as a room fee, 190 yuan or 98 yuan (depending on the room type), and the technicians are paid a massage fee by the store.

Therefore, in addition to tips for sex services, if they provide customers with a massage, the misses may get some money from the store for that service, and this amount may range between 20 to 38 yuan. The store usually pays them every ten days or once a month. Customers give tips directly to the technicians, or write the amount of the tip on the receipt, and the technicians get paid by the store on the same day. Some technicians complained that the owners deducted too much money; others thought that it was fair, and that since the owner provided the space for them to work, they were also entitled to make money.

Streetwalkers

Streetwalkers who do not solicit customers by themselves have to divide money with their pimps and mammies. Pimps usually charge customers around 300 yuan, with a minimum of 200 yuan. The price, however, could be as high as 1,200 yuan. The prostitutes get half of the money, and the minimum they get for each customer is 120 yuan, as long as the customers pay 200 yuan. In addition, prostitutes have to pay their mammy 80 or 90 yuan for each night they work. They do not pay the mammy any money if they do not work, and they are not required to work a minimum number of days a month.

The price for freelance streetwalkers varies greatly. Police data reveals that it could be as low as 20-50 yuan. Freelance streetwalkers who participated in this study usually charged customers 150-200 yuan. However, some prostitutes will agree to a cut price of 100 yuan, because business is sometimes slow as a result of frequent police raids.

Services

Sex services provided by prostitutes generally include intercourse, oral sex, and hand jobs. But the services offered at different venues vary, and all women do not provide all three types of sex. Some women mainly offer sexual intercourse, some only provide hand jobs, while others mainly provide oral sex. No women in this study mentioned providing anal sex.

Hair Salons

The main services offered in "hair salons" are sexual intercourse, and sometimes hand jobs. The women usually do not provide oral sex, but a few of them will do so if the customers pay more money. Misses usually require customers to use condoms. One woman was ready to engage in sex service without using a condom but would charge more money for that (at least 200 yuan). Other hair salons do not provide straight sex (sexual intercourse); their services are confined to hand jobs. Two women working at a hair salon told me that their services do not involve sexual intercourse. What they do is "tui you" (a literal translation for "push oil," a euphemism for a hand job). The women use oil, and their hands or breasts to complete sex service. Straight sex takes about half an hour. Tuiyou usually takes fifty minutes, but sometimes it can take only 20 minutes.

Nightclubs/Karaoke Lounges

The basic service at nightclubs/karaoke lounges is what is referred to as "three-companion" services—talking, drinking and singing. In addition, another very popular activity involved is playing games. Misses play games with customers and the loser is required to drink beer. This is a way to make customers spend money at the venues. The longer they stay, the more they drink. The "three-companion" service is also referred to as "zuotai," literally translated as "sitting at the table." If any sex service is requested, the misses and customers will go to a hotel, or somewhere else. This is what is referred to as "chutai"—literally translated as "leaving the table." No sex occurs on the premises. But once they are drunk, the customers do not behave themselves, and many promiscuous behaviors may occur, such as fondling, embracing, etc. One woman said that on one occasion, a customer wanted to have sex with her in the booth. She did not agree, and the customer took off her brassiere and chased her around in the booth.

Companion service can take as long as two or three hours. Misses cannot leave until the customers leave, and so they sometimes can zuotai only once each night. Usually, a few misses serve a group of customers, depending on how many customers there are and how many misses they ask for. When customers ask for sex service, it is usually straight sexual intercourse. However, it may not always be limited to that. Whether misses provide oral sex, hand jobs, or even other kinky sexual acts depends on what the misses and customers negotiate. All women said that customers must use condoms during sex.

Massage/Sauna Parlors

Services at this venue usually involve both massage and sex services. Customers usually take a bath first, and then the technicians provide massage service or sex services. This service usually lasts about 100 minutes (the duration of the service is counted in "hours"—one "hour" is generally fifty minutes long, and each customer must pay for at least two "hours"). Customers have to buy more "hours" and pay more money if the service lasts longer than 100 minutes. Sex services vary, based on the category a technician belongs to. A general rule is that category A sex service involves sexual intercourse, while category B involves only hand jobs. But sometime category B workers secretly provide more services than they are permitted to, such as sexual intercourse. They get better tips, but will be fined if discovered. Category A technicians do not have to engage in sexual intercourse if the customers ask for other sex services which cost the same.

Streetwalkers

Freelancers generally provide straight sex to their customers. But more than half the customers request oral sex. One freelancer told me that most of her customers required oral sex. If she did not offer oral sex, she would have no business. This service is mainly carried out in the car; very rarely do customers take the streetwalkers to hotels or their homes. In the case of prostitutes who do not solicit customers by themselves, sex services include straight sex, hand jobs, and oral sex. Some customers do not require sex service; they just want a companion. In such a situation, the women serve more as escorts than as streetwalkers.

> One day, the CEO of a bank, and several businessmen came by, driving a BMW. They wanted several simple, plainly dressed girls and I was selected by them. They took us to have a midnight snack (Xiao Fang).

Numbers of Customers and Working Days

Hair Salons

Misses usually have three to five customers in a day. The most number of customers they can have in a day is eight or nine. Of the women in this group, six worked 20-25 days per month, two worked 15 days a month and two misses, who provided hand jobs exclusively, worked 30 days a month. Misses can decide how many customers they want to have, who they want to work for, and how many days a month they want to work. The bosses do not get involved in these matters. There is no penalty if the women choose not to work.

Nightclubs/Karaoke Lounges

Customers usually go to nightclubs or KTV lounges in groups. Misses usually serve as least one such group of customers per day. Some more qualified women (i.e., those who are better looking, or better at entertaining customers) have two or more opportunities to zuotai per night. They work at least 20 days a month. Three of the women in this group worked 20-22 days a month, four of them worked 24-25 days a month, while four said they worked 30 days a month. No minimum number of working days per month was required.

Sauna/Massage Parlors

Women working at these venues usually have two to four customers per day. Some technicians may have as many as six or seven customers

Table 6.1   Number of "Dates" with Customers per Day

Number of dates	Frequency	Percentage
1	2	5
2	14	35
3	11	27
4	8	20
5	3	7.5
Unknown	2	5
Average number of dates		
Hair salon	4.1	
Nightclub/karaoke lounge	2.2	
Massage/sauna parlors	2.4	
Street	2.7	

Table 6.2   Number of Working Days and Average Working Days per Month

Number of working days	Frequency
12	1
15	3
20	8
22	3
24	7
25	5
26	3
27	3
30	6
Unknown	1
Average working days per month	
Hair salon	23.5
Nightclub	25.4
Massage/sauna parlors	24.1
Street	20
Unknown	1

in a day. They work 20-27 days a month. Four women in this group worked 20-22 days a month, while nine worked 24-27 days.

Streetwalkers

Most streetwalkers have two to four customers each night. Four of the six streetwalkers in the study worked 24-25 days a month, while the others worked no more than 12 or 15 days because they liked to spend time playing mahjong.

Monthly Income

The monthly income of the women is calculated based on their alleged average daily number of paid dates with customers, and the number of days in a month they work. However, for two important reasons, their self-report monthly income is not cited. Firstly, it is understandable that the women are conservative when they talk about their income. They may give a lower estimate of their earnings in order to minimize their feelings of guilt, since prostitution is viewed as a stigma. Thus, the self-report monthly income may appear smaller than what they actually make. Secondly, many women just refused to tell me how much they make in a month, and hence a lot of data is missing. Table 6.4 shows that women

Table 6.3   Monthly Income (N=34)

Income (in yuan)	Frequency
<4,000	1
4,000-5,999	6
6,000-7,999	8
8,000-9,999	5
10,000-14,999	8
15,000-19,999	5
>20,000	1
Average	10,000
Range	3,843-21,112

working at massage/sauna parlors appear to make more money when compared to women at other sex venues.

It has been ascertained that the earnings of prostitutes are much higher than those of women working in legitimate sectors. This is the decisive factor that motivates them into prostitution. What do they spend their money on? Their expenditure can be generally broken down into the following categories: living expenses, savings, contributions to family, or partying. Aside from their living expenses, some misses either save money or give some to their parents. There are also some prostitutes who squander their money by going out, buying fancy clothes or gambling. None of them were willing to tell me the amount of their savings. A total of seven women neither saved money nor gave any to their parents. They spent all their earnings. Three of them liked playing mahjong, and therefore they squandered all their money on gambling. Three others just spent all the money they earned. Sometimes they would not work for a while, fooling around, or traveling. Another woman did not save any money because her boyfriend did not work, and they both used drugs.

As Table 6.5 shows, fifteen women did not give their parents any money. Eight of them were single women, and seven were either married or

Table 6.4   Average Monthly Income of Individuals per Venue

Venue	Average	Range
Hair salon	7,448 (1,064)	3,843-12,550 (549-1,750)
Nightclub	8,862 (1,266)	4,326-14,000 (618-2,000)
Massage/sauna parlor	13,034 (1862)	4,158-21,112 (594-3,016)
Street	7,784 (1,112)	4,872-16,800 (696-2400)

(Amounts are cited in yuan, with dollar equivalents in parentheses)

Table 6.5   Money Sent Monthly to Parents (N=40)

Money (in yuan)	Frequency	Percentage
0	15	37.5
500-1,000	5	12.5
1,001-2,000	9	22.5
2,001-3,000	2	5
3,001-4,000	1	2.5
4,001-5,000	2	5
Not specified	6	15

divorced. Only three women with children were among those who gave their parents money. One woman gave her parents money on a regular basis because she was the only one of five siblings who had left their hometown. She was thus economically better off than the other siblings, and her parents would have no income if she did not give them money. Two other women, either married or divorced, said they gave their parents a little bit of money when they were in need. Women with children usually saved money, or spent it on their own family needs if they were not also financially supporting their parents. Eight single women did not give their parents money because their parents did not need it; five of them saved money, while three of them just squandered it.

Six of the forty women gave money to their parents, but did not specify how much. Four of these were single women. Three of them said that they gave their parents some money, but they did not give much, in case their parents began to suspect the source of their income. Another woman said that she gave most of her salary to her family. She was very frugal and did not spend a lot of money. In two of the six cases, the parents of the women helped them with child care. The women gave their parents some money each month, but did not specify how much they gave. Thus, five out of these six women did not give their parents much of their money. Most of the other women in the study gave their parents some money, generally no more than 2,000 yuan each month.

Lifestyle

Hair Salons

Most establishments provide their workers with lodging and food, and therefore most women live on the premises. Three women had boyfriends with whom they lived when they were not working. Only two women rented rooms by themselves. Some owners rented an apartment very close to the store, so that the misses could hasten to the salon when potential customers showed up. All the women said that they were free, that nobody controlled their movements. They usually got up at about 2:00 or 3:00 p. m., began work around 4:00-5:00 p.m., and continued until 4:00-5:00 a.m. Some women worked slightly later, from 7:00 p.m. until 6:00 a.m.

Nightclub/Karaoke Lounges

In these venues, the bosses do not provide lodging and food, so the misses rented a place by themselves. Misses were usually required to show up at 7:30 p.m. and wait for customers. They did not leave until the customers had left. If there were no customers, they could leave before 12:00 a.m. at some venues. Usually, however, they worked until 1:00-2:00 a.m. After getting home from work, they sometimes watched TV or went to bed and slept until at least noon. Some misses may sleep until 2:00-3:00 p.m. After getting up, they cooked, ate, put on make-up and then went back to work. Some misses played cards or mahjong when they were not working.

Massage/Sauna Parlors

The bosses of these parlors usually provide lodging and/or food, though the misses must pay between 50-200 yuan per month if they live at the so-called corporation dormitory. Most misses, however, rented a place by themselves. Technicians may work either the day shift from noon to 10:00 p.m. or the night shift from 9:00 p.m. to 5:00 or 6:00 a.m. When they were not working, they watched TV, played cell phone games, went shopping, played cards or mahjong, went out for dinner with customers, or hung out with them. Some misses played cards at work when there were no customers.

Streetwalkers

All streetwalkers rent a place by themselves. They begin to work around 8:00-9:00 p.m. and continue until 3:00-4:00 a.m. or 6:00-7:00 a.m. Freelance streetwalkers stop work at about 1:00-2:00 a.m., then go home and sleep until the following day. They play cards or mahjong, and gamble when they do not work. Then they come out to work or they stay home, gambling all night long.

How do these women perceive their life? When they do not work, most women watch TV, go shopping, surf online, or play mahjong, or cards. It is the usual way that they entertain themselves. As Table 6.6 shows, nearly half of them smoke and play cards or mahjong, and nine of them drink after work.

Table 6.6   Hobbies

Hobbies	Frequency	Percentage
Drinking	9	22.5
Smoking	18	45
Gambling	18	45
Drugs	1	2.5

Some women seemed satisfied with their current life and did not have unsavory hobbies. They had become used to their jobs and the "work all night" lifestyle. They were not under pressure to work, and they did not have to work if they chose not to. There was no tension with co-workers or bosses. These women did not drink, smoke, or gamble. They were complacent about their current life.

> I do not have pressures. I do not have those (bad) hobbies. I watch TV, read novels or go shopping when I do not work. To be a prostitute is already to be in a state of moral deterioration. How can we have those bad habits on top of that? (Mei Fang).

Some women were satisfied with their economic achievements and the flexible work schedule. They may have bought a house in their hometowns, or have put aside some savings for themselves. Without pressure related to work and family, they were really enjoying themselves. Drinking, smoking, or gambling were their hobbies, and the principal ways in which they entertained themselves.

> I am very satisfied with my current job. I do not have work pressure. My family bought a plot of land and built a house. It cost us more than 200,000 yuan. We also spent more than 100,000 yuan to renovate it. It is a three-story building; we can do business on the first floor (Xiao Ya).

> I do not have any pressure. I frequently entertain myself and fool around. I gamble by playing cards when I do not work. My parents do not need my money, all the money I earn is squandered in gambling. I work when I want; I do not work if I do not want to. It depends on whether I am in the mood to work (Ah Lian).

> This job is not bad. If I did not take this job I would have got married and had several children. My life would have been very tough. This work changed my destiny (Lily).

> I get up at 10:00 a.m. have my meals, and surf online. Sometimes I go jogging. But most often I play mahjong. I have rarely lost money when I play mahjong. Customers are very nice to me. I have no work pressure. Many customers like me (Wang mei).

> This work is very flexible. If you work in a factory or as a cashier, you do not have as much flexibility as you do by working here. I have no work pressure. Sometimes I smoke or play mahjong when I work (Lan Lan).

But some women become so addicted to playing mahjong that they do not even want to work. Lin Yan used to work more than 20 days a month. But she now works only 15 days, sometimes playing mahjong continuously for more than 24 hours without sleeping. Furthermore, some women lose a lot of money when they play mahjong, and this eventually affects their financial condition. The women take risks and prostitute themselves with the hope of making money, but they then squander it by gambling.

> I smoke and gamble. Some customers are really disgusting. I do not have any interest in them. But I have to have sex with them for money. I have thought of giving it up for a long time. Now I want to earn some money so that I can start a business. If I had not played mahjong and lost money last month, I would have opened a business this month. But I like gambling, I cannot stop. I regret being a prostitute, but what I regret most is gambling. My life is like this because of gambling. I told you just now that I would not be a prostitute if I were to go back to six years ago (before I started gambling after my divorce) (Li Wen).

> I do not work if I want to play mahjong. I lost 700 yuan last night and won 200 yuan back this afternoon. In order to come here, I borrowed 2,000 yuan from my sister to cover my travel expenses, and I have not repaid her yet. I lost all the money I made on gambling, even though I know it is not easy to make money (Xiao Ju).

Being a prostitute earns the women a lot more money than if they worked in other legitimate sectors, and it has many other advantages, such as a flexible working schedule. They become financially better off. But being rich does not necessarily make them happy. Many women expressed their anxiety, frustration, confusion, and self-contempt because of the stigma associated with this profession, work and family pressures, and tension between co-workers. Some of them resorted to smoking, drinking or gambling to deal with these pressures.

> I am depressed. I am wondering if it is right or wrong to do this; and what my family thinks. I did not work for the first 10 days after I came here. I wondered everyday what others would think about me and this job. I was also aware that there was no way to turn around once I stepped into this line of work. I look down when I walk on the street everyday—I feel that I am inferior and I am afraid that other people know what I am doing. When people look into the store, I feel that they know I am a prostitute, and I feel very sad. I feel better when I am not in the store and when I have my period, because I feel that I am like other women (Sha Sha).

> Working here is mentally tiring. I become sad when I have bad customers, and I feel better with nice customers. It is not unusual for us misses to cry. I have cried several times (Na Na).

> I will smoke and drink when I am anxious. I attempted suicide in 2006, when I got drunk and missed my mother very much. I really wanted to die. I hate my father for not being responsible for my family. But he is my father. I have to

take care of him now. My brother just came here and is an apprentice with a hair designer. My father has a health condition. He broke his back bone and cannot do heavy work. My jailed brother has to depend on me after being released. My sister got married, but my brother-in-law looks down upon my family and won't help us (Li Xue).

I feel pressure when I deal with customers. I become worried if customers choose me, because I do not know whether they are good or bad. I also have pressure from my family, I have to lie sometimes. I feel hypocritical (Nan Nan).

I am very anxious when I work, because of the bad reputation of being a prostitute. I am not pleased when I work. Women here are different from those in factories. They all love money and compete with each other. I looked down upon prostitutes when I was in a factory, and now I look down upon myself (Xiao Ke).

I have pressure at work. Some customers are not easy to deal with, they give us a hard time. The competition between the girls is fierce. I do not want to have any connections with these girls. They are all dishonest (An Wen).

This is not a job for a human being. I do not want to do this. When I work, I tell myself that I just want to make money. I wish the customer lets me leave as soon as possible. I smile when I meet customers, but my heart is bleeding, especially when customers make us suffer. I cry by myself frequently (Ding Ding).

Concerns

All subjects were asked about their concerns regarding their work. Some of them had more than one concern (N=60). The most cited concerns include: being found out by family/friends (N=19), exposure to sexually transmitted diseases (STDs) (N=10), being arrested (N=9), and not being able to date (N=6). Some subjects reported having no concerns (N=8). Other less frequently cited concerns include: not being able to bear children (N=2), being short-tempered with customers (N=1), not being able to make money as age catches up (N=1), drinking (N=1), feeling uncomfortable (N=1), being subjected to perverted customers (N=1) and robbery (N=1).

Being found out by family and/or friends was the most cited concern. As a member the police stated, these women feel ashamed when their activity is discovered by their family or friends. Being found out by family or friends is such a big concern that some women dared not invite their friends to visit.

I am afraid of being discovered by my family and friends. I become nervous when my father calls me. I dare not let my friends come to see me (Ah Ying).

Table 6.7   Concerns (N=60)

Concerns	Frequency	Percentage (%)
Being found out by family/friends	19	32
STD	10	17
Arrests	9	15
No Concerns	8	13
Not being able to date	6	10
Others	8	13

My concern is being found out by my family and friends. I dare not ask my friends to come to see me (Na Na).

One woman worried more about being found out by her friend, rather than by her family. She also said that she felt very hypocritical.

There is no way that my family can get to know this. But I am afraid of being found out by my friends. I have to tell them that I am not working, when I am actually working at night; that I am not sleeping when I am indeed sleeping. I feel very sorry that I am a hypocrite. I have never been arrested, I have never thought about that (Ah Mei).

The chief concerns on the list point to the deterrent effects of formal and informal social control on women's involvement in prostitution. However, this does not mean that these concerns exercise an actual effect of deterrence because the women believe, at the same time, that their fears are not very likely to be realized. Some women (N=8) explicitly said that they had nothing to worry about. They believed that it was not very likely that their families or friends would find out, or that they would catch a sexually transmitted disease. Their families did not live in Shenzhen, and if any relatives lived in Shenzen, the women rarely communicated with them. In addition, the women took precautionary measures to prevent the possibility of being found out by their friends or families. For example, one woman shared an apartment with her friend. Her husband, who also works in Shenzhen, had to give her advance notice when he visited her, and she took days off when her husband came to visit. Furthermore, some women did not have any connections with the friends or fellow villagers who might disclose their activity to their family. Regarding STDs, most of them believed that they would not be infected if they used condoms. Some of them were very cautious when they work—they observed everything keenly, and would not provide sex services if they saw anything abnormal. Some of them get regular medical examinations. As far as being arrested is concerned, six of the forty women have had that experience since they began this trade. Four of the six arrestees were streetwalkers, while two were technicians at sauna parlors. A total of 31 women talked about the likelihood of being arrested. There is a variation in terms of their belief in the likelihood of arrest. Only three of them believed it was very likely they would be arrested, three believed it was likely to happen, 13 believed that it was less likely, six believed arrest was unlikely, and six had never even considered the possibility, which implies they were unconcerned, or did not think it was possible they would be arrested.

Some women thought that there was little chance they would be arrested since they were very cautious when they provided services. Moreover, they believed that since they did not work everyday, the chances of being arrested remained low.

> I have never been arrested. I've thought about it, but it is not my concern because it hasn't happened yet. I don't worry about being arrested very much. I would not do this if I thought it wasn't safe. I can have the job done in 30 minutes upstairs, so the possibility of being arrested is small (Xiao Xiu).

> I do not have any concerns. I have never been arrested. It is possible to be arrested, depending on your luck. I don't work a lot, so it is less likely that I will be arrested (Ah Lian).

> I have nothing to worry about. I was caught by the police once. I was standing on the street when I was caught. But they did not have any evidence, and released me several hours later. If they detained me more than 24 hours, I would sue them. We don't have any cause for worry. We usually ask the customer's name, age, etc. in case we are caught; we also know which hotels are dangerous. Usually the star-hotels are safe (Lin Dan).

In truth, the most important reason why being arrested was not a concern, or the possibility of arrest appeared trivial, is that many women believed that their bosses had connections with the police and that the bosses would notify them in advance about possible police raids. It was the bosses' responsibility to guarantee their safety, and the women, therefore, did not worry about police raids. Taking all this into account, some women declared that they only worked at safe venues.

> I had never been arrested. I thought of the possibility. But the owner usually has a relationship with the police if she/he wants to run such a business (Sha Sha).

> I have never been arrested. I have thought about it. But the boss has social connections, and furthermore, I am very cautious when I do this (Li Xue).

> I have never been arrested and never thought about it. The boss has connections with the police (Xiao Yu).

There is a slight possibility of being arrested. Generally, however, you won't be arrested unless there is a police campaign. The boss would notify and caution us (Liu Yan).

One woman disclosed the measures her boss had taken in order to deal with unexpected police raids:

Our boss has a "hard back stage" (i.e. he has connections with government officials). He will notify us in advance if the police are going to come. The reception desk is on the second floor, we work on third floor. The person who is responsible for keeping time has a button underneath her desk, which operates a light in our room. In case of a police raid, she steps on that button, the light in our room will flash and we will put on our pants very quickly (An An).

Another reason for the low rate of concern about being arrested was the false impressions the women had regarding the consequences of being arrested. Some women believed that they would not be jailed if they were arrested. They would be released upon paying a fine and their boss would bail them out.

My concern about being arrested is that my family will find out. I have never thought of being arrested. If it happens, you will be fined; if you cannot afford to pay the fine, you will go to jail (Ah Hong).

My biggest concern is that you will be fined if you are arrested. I just started, and don't have much money. So the fine will be a huge loss to me. Generally you won't be detained if you are arrested—police arrest you just because they want money (Cheng Hong).

If I were arrested, my boss would bail me out; it costs about 3,000-4,000 yuan. What we are most concerned about is that being arrested would make it public (Lin Lin).

However, according to Chinese prostitution laws and law enforcement practices, punishment for prostitutes and their customers is very severe. Both prostitutes and customers may be jailed for periods ranging from six months to two years. According to one police officer I interviewed, "the general punishment for prostitutes and customers is at least five days detention if they are arrested for the first time. Very few people are fined for prostitution. But most prostitutes are not aware of the severity of the punishment." Regarding whether their bosses will bail them out if they are arrested, during my field observation, I had the opportunity to talk to a prostitute who had been arrested the night before I met her at a police station. Two other technicians, three customers and their minister had also been arrested during the police raid. The woman in question was working the day shift on the day she was arrested. She had been ready to leave, when she was asked to serve one more customer. During our conversation, she kept saying that she would not have been arrested had she left—being arrested seemed to her an accident. She thought that her boss would bail them out. But her boss did not show up for almost 24 hours after the arrest, and the prostitute would be detained for ten days.

A total of eight women stated directly that they had nothing to worry about, because all the concerns described above were rarely realized. Or, the women used to worry about being discovered by their families. However, once their families knew the truth, the women were relieved and had no further concern.

> I used to be afraid of being found out by my husband. He knows now, and I have nothing to worry about. He fought with me initially. I reasoned with him, saying that I wanted to make money so that my daughters could have an education and would not have to struggle like me. I would not work here if I had an education. He worried that I would divorce him (after working here for a while). He has stopped fighting now because I go straight home after work (Li Ying).

Ke Ke told me that she had nothing to worry about. When I asked whether she was concerned about being arrested or being infected with a STD, she replied with a smile:

> My desire to make money outweighs those concerns. Regarding STDs, I am very cautious. I won't do it if I observe something wrong. Regarding arrest, the boss won't run such a store if he had no social connections. The boss will bail you out if you are arrested. The worst that can happen is being detained for half a month, and it is not a big deal. The boss has social connections and will let us know in advance if there is a police raid (Ke Ke).

Some women did not mention these three main concerns, or at least these were not their top worries. Instead, these women had other concerns, mainly the ways in which being a prostitute affected their personal life—they could not date while working in this seedy trade.

> I dare not date. I just broke up with my boyfriend because I was afraid that he knew what I was doing. My ex-boyfriend loved me very much and he wanted to see me. I don't want him to know that I am a prostitute, so I broke up with him (Ah Mei).

> It is very difficult to find a boyfriend. You will feel sorry for him because you feel guilty about what you are doing (Lan Lan).

> I often wonder how I can get married if I go home. If I get married here, what would I do if one of my customers attended my wedding? Yet, I would make only a little over 1,000 yuan a month in a factory, and I can make the same here in a day if I am lucky. So I do not want to work in a factory. Furthermore, my time is flexible, and I can do whatever I want. Sometimes I feel jealous when I see other girls date. But in this trade, I have to forget about dating. I did not work for several days last week

and I bought a lot of DVDs. I felt very lonely and wished for some one to keep me company and to talk to me. I feel very sad when I think that my future husband may have had affairs with other women (Xiao Fang).

I would be lying if I told you that I had no regrets. Sometimes I wonder why I am doing this. I met a guy who liked me very much. He had a girlfriend and broke up with her because of me. However, I felt that I was not good enough for him. I thought that I would be good enough even if I were a working-sister, because I would be "clean." Later, I went home and did not contact him. I do not know how his life turned out, and I miss him very much. I won't date when I am doing this (Mei Fang).

Because they cannot date when they work as prostitutes, some of their other concerns included not being able to get married and not being able to bear children. One woman worried that this might affect her personality.

What I am concerned about includes the thought that nobody will marry me, that I will not bear children, and that I cannot make money when I get older (Lily).

What I am concerned about is that I cannot bear children. I also worry that being a prostitute for a long time will affect my temperament. Some prostitutes become short-tempered after working for a long time (Xiao Yu).

Force and Violence at Work

In studies on human trafficking, violence against prostitutes has been well documented and exhaustively explored. Violence may be used not only during the stages of recruitment and transportation, but also in the work institution. Customers, managers and brothel keepers are the perpetrators of violence against respondents. They also exert stringent control over the lives of the trafficked women, withholding food and money, inflicting violence, punishment, isolation and threats (Raymond et al., 2002: 108).

Table 6.8 Force and Violence

Type of experience	Frequency
Force	5
Violence	17
Violence report to police	
Yes	6
No	29
Unknown	5

The present study did not find evidence of violence perpetrated against prostitutes by sex ring operators. Force and violence against women came exclusively from their customers. No woman said that she was forced by owners or operators of venues to provide sex services; nor was any violence perpetrated by owners or operators. A few women mentioned that some customers forced them to do what they did not want to do, or that they experienced violence when they provided services to customers.

A total of five women mentioned that they were forced to do certain things by the customers. Two women working at karaoke lounges said that their customers would force them to drink a lot of beer. A woman working at a sauna parlor said that customers would not force her if she reasoned with them when they tried to force her to do something she was not willing to do. One woman working at a hair salon provided overnight service for a customer. When they had finished, the customer did not let her leave. Another woman was forced to take off her clothes, and eventually her boss called the police.

Violence can be physical or verbal. Physical violence by customers was mentioned by 17 women. Physical violence can take the following forms: rape (N=1), robbery (N=2), physical assault including beating, biting or slapping (N=7), forced kiss (N=2), and verbal assault (N=5).

Ah Rong was raped when she worked at a hair salon that provides massage service and hand jobs. The customer deceived her by asking her to go to downstairs and bring him a cup of water before she started the massage. She left her own cup upstairs. After she brought up water, the customer asked her to drink water in her cup. Later, her cousin went upstairs upon realizing that Ah Rong had not come back down for a long time, and found her lying on the bed without clothes. There was blood on the sheet. The owner found the customer by reviewing the store's security video. The matter was resolved with the customer paying Ah Rong 5,000 yuan, and the owner paying her a bonus of 1,000 yuan.

Many studies on violence against prostitutes find that working the streets is much more risky than working in other venues in terms of police arrests, and incidents of violence against prostitutes (see Shaver, 2005; Benoit and Millar, 2001; Chapkis, 2000). That streetwalkers take the most risks, compared to off-street prostitutes, is confirmed by the present study. Two streetwalkers were robbed by their customers. Being aware of this danger, streetwalkers usually do not carry much money when they work.

> I was robbed by people disguised as customers. They forced me with a knife to give them money. I did not have a lot of money, only 20 or 30 yuan. The main item of value is the cell phone. It has happened two or three times.

Another streetwalker was robbed by customers in their car. She lost 500 yuan and a cell phone. However, the risk of such intense violent crime is not limited to streetwalkers alone. Women working at other venues are also vulnerable to kidnapping, rape, blackmail etc. A mammy told me about an incident that happened in 2006. Several customers went to a nightclub one day. They did not choose pretty misses to chutai—instead, they chose those having expensive cell phones and wearing expensive jewelry. Their mammy had never met these customers before, and refused to let the misses leave with them. It appears that the customers paid the mammy 1,000 yuan to let the misses go with them. After getting in the car, the misses were blindfolded with a piece of cloth, and taken to Dongguan. They were raped and beaten. Eventually, the misses' boyfriends had to pay 4,000 yuan to redeem each of them.

In addition to violence by customers, streetwalkers also experience police violence and high risk of being arrested.

One time I was arrested. I was hit by the police, so I requested to speak to their chief. I also threatened to call the media and expose this. I said: "What evidence do you have to arrest me? Do I bother you by standing there? Even if I were a prostitute, you are not allowed to hit me. I called an ambulance and pretended that they hurt my stomach because I had a stomach condition already. Later, the police had to pay my hospital costs (Li Wen).

They grabbed my hair and pulled me into their car. They also said dirty words, called me names, insulted us and did not view us as human beings (Liu Yan).

Each time I conducted observations on the street, police cars were driving through. One day, I was talking with a man who was obviously a resident on that street. He told me that there used to be over 100 women standing along this street at night, but the situation had greatly improved now (only about four or five women were standing across the street on that day). While we were talking, a police car appeared. I realized that it was a good opportunity to observe how these women respond to the situation. When I turned around, however, all the women were already out of sight. They had run away and hidden in a narrow alley.

The interview with Liu Yan was conducted in my friend's car. I was deeply grateful that my friend had generously allowed me to conduct this interview in the car. A typical evening in early June in Shenzhen, it was hot and humid and the temperature was about 90 degrees. I was sweating and had to open the door in the middle of the interview because my friend had not left the car keys with me and I could not turn on the air-conditioning. Mosquitoes started to fly into the car and bite us. Right before I wrapped up the interview, I could not endure the sweating and mosquito bites anymore and decided to get out of the car. On the street, as I was asking her to refer her friends to me for interviews, a police car came along the street toward us. She became nervous. I tried to calm her by saying: "You are talking with me, don't be scared by them." I was thinking that the police could not assume that a woman was soliciting a customer when she was talking with another woman. However, she said: "No, the police would arrest both of us."

Women from different venues in this study experience varying intensities of violence. Streetwalkers may have a higher likelihood of being robbed, or arrested by police than women at other venues. However, women at nightclubs/karaoke lounges and massage/sauna parlors experience more physical and verbal assaults than streetwalkers. Physical or verbal assaults are the most frequently cited forms of violence, especially in the case of those working at nightclub/karaoke lounges and massage/sauna parlors. Three-companion service at nightclubs/karaoke lounges may last for two or three hours and services provided at massage/sauna parlor take at least 100 minutes. The longer duration of service at these establishments increases the likelihood of physical and verbal assaults from customers. Several operators of such venues admit this, saying that some drunken customers use dirty words, smash objects, beat the misses or waitresses, and do not pay the money they owe. This is confirmed by many prostitutes. They agree that most customers are not bad, and some customers are in fact very nice to the misses. But sometimes they come across drunken customers who call them names, use dirty words and behave badly. One prostitute showed me a light scar on her arm during the interview. A few days earlier, a customer had tried to take off her clothes and scratched her arm, leaving that scar. Of course, this kind of physical assault may occur even when customers are not drunk. They may beat the misses if the misses do not allow them to touch sensitive parts of their body, or bite the misses' breasts when they have sex. On the whole, the overwhelming impression appears to be that assault, especially verbal assault by drunken customers, is an integral part of the job, and prostitutes have to tolerate and accept it. To prevent assault from occurring, some misses are very wary not to provoke customers, or else they try to compromise or negotiate with customers. As a result, these misses will not experience assault, or will experience it less than those who are not good at these skills. When these efforts fail to work, misses usually call the minister or manager.

There are all sorts of customers, nice or rude. ... The main problem is that some customers force me to drink, to say dirty words. I do not quarrel with them, I just pretend not to hear (Li Ying).

Some customers want to have sex with category B technicians, or want to have oral sex. We will tell them that it is impossible for us to do this, that we will be fined. There is no violence. Some drunken customers are very demanding. If we cannot deal with them, we will tell the minister. The main issue is that drunken customers do not pay us, and then we will call the minister (Ah Xiang).

Some technicians are wily and adept at dissuading customers. When customers insist on having sex, the technicians will call us to solve the problem (Manager of a sauna parlor).

A few bold and resolute women fought with their customers when customers physically assaulted them.

One customer was drunk, called me names and touched me. He beat me when I didn't let him touch me. I smashed his glasses and I was fined 1000 yuan by the sauna center (Xiao Xiu).

Customers dare not force me to do anything. There are so many people in our store, how dare he force me? No customer is violent. If any violence happens, I will call my boss. I dare to fight back. Some time ago, a customer slapped me once, I slapped him back twice. I was not afraid of him (Ah Mei).

There are both good and bad customers. The bad customers do not behave themselves; they disrespect us (because we are misses), verbally insult us and request us to drink a lot of beer. One time when I worked in another nightclub, a customer was drunk. He became rude and beat me. I fought back. Later he refused to give a tip. My mammy helped me to get it. I would report to the police if I was really hurt (Na Na).

In a nutshell, not all women experience violence from customers. Just as they said, most customers are good. But when some get drunk, they cannot behave themselves and both verbal and physical violence may be inflicted on the women, especially those who work at nightclubs/karaoke lounges and massage/sauna parlors. This has rarely happened to women working at hair salons, or to streetwalkers, because they provide straight sex service, and the time period during which the customers and women are together is shorter than that involving those working at the two other venues. Among the forty women, seven reported physical assault. Among these, four worked at massage/sauna parlors, one at a hair salon, and one on the street. Five women reported incidents of verbal assault. Three of them worked at nightclubs/karaoke lounges.

Some customers want to have anal sex, I will not agree. They must use condoms. No customers use violence against me. There are customers who ask me to beat them; no customers beat me (Wen Wen).

> It is very rare that women are hurt by their customers. It almost never happens at hair salons because both parties just take what they need. It may happen at clubs because some customers may beat people after becoming drunk (A member of the police).

Subjects were also asked whether they would file a report with the police if they were assaulted by customers. While six women said they would report such incidents to the police, most women said they would not, but they would tell their boss, mammy, or minister. Reasons for not reporting assault incidents include the belief that reporting incidents to police will not bring any good to the women on account of the nature of their work, the belief that they will not be taken seriously, and the fact that the women do not want to make a big scene because they do not want their family or others to find out about the nature of their profession.

The Extent of Sex Trafficking and the "Boyfriend" Issue

As stated in the preceding chapters, a significant objective of this study is to explore the extent and scope to which Chinese women in the sex industry are victims of trafficking. Due to the nature of the study and the limited number of women participating in it, the conclusions may present a biased picture of Chinese women in commercial sex. Therefore, in order to achieve a more comprehensive picture and enhance the validity of this study, the interviewer also asked participants the following two questions. 1) Have you known women who are involved in prostitution because of force, deception, or coercion? 2) Have you heard about women who are involved in prostitution because of force, deception, or coercion?

As Table 6.9 shows, almost half the prostitutes in the study indicated that they had heard about women who were forced to work as prostitutes, or who had no control over the money they earned even if they may have been willing to work as prostitutes. Eight women personally knew such women. However, we do not know the specific circumstances under which these women became trafficking victims, such as whether they were aware of the nature of job before they were trafficked, whether or not they were initially willing to work in the sex industry. However, based on interviews with prostitutes, sex ring operators and law enforcement officials, a general picture can be constructed of women who are "brought" into the world of prostitution. Certain prominent features are involved in the scenario.

First, young women from inland provinces are usually brought to Shenzhen and made to work as prostitutes by their friends or peers. It is not unusual that some people (usually men) cultivate it as a business. They

Table 6.9   Victims Known or Heard of
by Study Subjects

Victims	Frequency
Known	8
Heard of	18

live off these women and are referred to as "chicken-heads" (prostitutes are called chickens). This kind of "business" has become increasingly prominent in the sex industry over the past few years.

Second, there appears to be a pattern as regards the source areas of "chicken-heads." They hail mainly from Sichuan, Hunan, Hubei or the northeastern provinces. This pattern is similar to that of source areas for prostitutes. It is very common that chicken-heads come from the same place as the women they deceive.

Third, these women usually work initially at hair salons or as street-walkers, and will be beaten or threatened if they refuse to work. They have no control over the money they make, and have to turn it over to their chicken-head. Some chicken-heads have more than one woman making money for them.

Fourth, a very prominent feature is the personal relationship between chicken-heads and the women. Usually they are boyfriend and girlfriend. Many men initially date a woman, and then make her work as a prostitute. There may be no physical force involved in the process. But coercion, seduction, coaxing, cajoling or other invisible means of force are present. The most common tactics employed to make women work as prostitutes include: 1) Coaxing and seduction: The man asks the girlfriend not to work. He is generous to her, buys her clothes and other things, and acquaints her with girls who have been prostitutes. After a while, the woman may fall in love with him. The boyfriend then asks her to provide sex services after he becomes penniless. He may also promise to marry her if she makes a lot of money. After falling in love with a boyfriend, some young women may be willing to work or may feel obliged to work and support their boyfriends financially. 2) Coercion and snaring: Some chicken-heads intentionally bring to Shenzhen women who they think are likely to work as prostitutes. The chicken-heads are responsible for all the travel expenses. Upon arrival, the women will be told to work as prostitutes. If they refuse, they are asked to pay off the debt they have incurred. The young women usually have no money to pay off the so-called debt, and thus are forced to work, and to divide the money they make with the chicken-head. 3) Drifting into prostitution:

Some women initially begin work in legitimate sectors such as factories or restaurants. They may meet an evil character who does not have a regular job, but may know some people in the sex sector. This individual may not initially mean to let his girlfriend work as a prostitute. However, when they run out of money, or the man wants to break up with the girl, he makes use of her and asks her to work in sex venues. Girls are willing to do this when neither of them have any money. Furthermore, once they get involved in prostitution, they find it hard to quit because of the easy money they are making. They believe their boyfriends love them, and they give them most of their income. In some cases, they are compelled to give money to their boyfriends, or they will be beaten.

Love is a major medium by which pimps get women involved in prostitution, and get the women to support them (Perkins, 1991). This is a significant issue, as there is a high rate of misses who have boyfriends that are financially dependent on them.

> A lot of men I know do not work, and their women are willing to support them. Half of the misses working at this nightclub are in such a situation. They are willing to make money and support these men. The men are mainly from Hunan, Henan, Sichuan. A man who usually plays mahjong with me is supported by one of the misses in this nightclub. One time he lost 600 yuan, and called his girlfriend, saying: "Don't sleep, hurry up and send me money." Usually such couples are from the same place (Wang Mei).

> 90% of misses have a boyfriend who depends on them. Some men have several women working for them. I know that there is a man who has two misses, and he requires them to give him 300 yuan a day. The misses would borrow money from their mammy if they could not make enough for him (Lily).

> There are some women whose boyfriends bring them to work here. The men do not work. Some women are controlled by men and I know one woman who is in such a situation. The man takes away the money she makes (Ding Ding).

Both misses and sex ring operators view this as a common occurrence. They know that many misses are brought to work at sex venues by their boyfriends; they do not know whether or not they are forced or deceived. Some women love their boyfriends and are willing to work and support them. Some misses do not tell people even if they are being forced to work.

The reality is that in some cases, force, deceit and coercion come into play, and this fits the definition of human trafficking. In other cases, the aforementioned elements may not be present, and therefore the situation may not fit the definition of human trafficking. A mammy told me that 80-90 percent of these women were being used by their boyfriends to make money for them, and that more than half of these men were married. Yet, there are some prostitutes who also end up marrying their boyfriends. A prostitute told me her experience with her boyfriend:

> Regarding whether the man will marry her, it depends. Take me and my boyfriend as an example. Neither of us initially wanted to get married. He had money, I just wanted to spend his money and he just wanted to play with me. Later, we ran out of money, and I started to work. I gave him the money I made and this touched him. All his prior girlfriends just wanted to spend his money; none of them gave him money. I feel that he is a nice man. Therefore we want to get married (Lin Dan).

No matter how many prostitutes end up getting married, the perplexing question still remains: Why are these women deceived? If women are working as prostitutes in order to make money, why they are willing to support the "little white face" (a designation for a good looking man who financially depends on his wife or girlfriend). This study proposes some tentative explanations.

Some of the women are from the countryside. They have rarely ever left their hometown and lived somewhere else by themselves. They are not like sophisticated women from cities who are experienced, and have a wider vision. These girls are also naïve and simple in terms of their understanding of love. They trust their so-called boyfriends, and don't doubt the truth of their boyfriends' promises. A manager of a karaoke lounge has insightful comments about this.

> There are some immature girls who make money and support their boyfriends. They love these men and perceive it as unselfish love. They may justify (what they do for their boyfriend) by saying that you cannot resist it when you fall in love. They may think that when they are bullied by customers or somebody else, their boyfriend will stand up. Some men just make use of them, won't marry them and these women's purpose is to make money for themselves (Manager of a karaoke lounge).

Materialism is another reason that makes these women vulnerable to being deceived. "They love indolence and loathe working hard. They cannot make big money by working at legitimate jobs, but they usually like to spend a lot of money" (Lan Lan). "They are deceived because they want to make a lot of money. Work in the sex industry pays a lot of money, this is why they are deceived" (An An). This observation implies that some women are willing to work as prostitutes. However, they then have to turn over their earnings to their so-called boyfriend.

In addition to the above mentioned psychological factors making some women vulnerable to exploitation by their boyfriends, there is also a practical reason, namely, that the women need such persons to help her start the business and keep her company. According to a member of the police, some men bring their girlfriends, who are generally fellow villagers, to Shenzhen. The men are responsible for renting rooms, looking for hair salons, or asking for money when customers do not pay the girls. Some girls do not want to be bothered by these things or they do not have the necessary social connections. They want to find somebody to help them deal with these matters, and are willing to divide their money with the man. To some extent, they develop a cooperative business relationship, and both parties gain from this partnership.

As a manager said:

> I know a venue run by a man who has a group of technicians who make money for him. There are a lot of such things going on. Some girls are naïve, they do not have the social connections and therefore they need somebody to bring them into this line of work; then they get rid of the man after they become independent and work at a place where the man cannot find them. Therefore, they are willing to do this work. But they may have never left their hometown, or dared to come out by themselves. Thus they need someone to bring them out.

> Customers do not respect these technicians, regarding them as whores. Those who eat soft food (this refers to men who depend on women) treat them very well. Therefore these girls support them economically and they are emotionally compensated (Manager of a sauna parlor).

This kind of psychological dependence on a boyfriend is confirmed by Lin Dan whose boyfriend does not work and depends on her financially.

> I work here voluntarily. I work from 7:00 p.m. until 6:00 or 7:00 a.m. My boyfriend does not work. He cooks and does the laundry for me everyday. Without him, I would have to cook and do the laundry myself. Furthermore, I would feel lonely if I were home by myself. One time, we fought, and he left to work in his brother's factory. Later, I asked him to come back (Lin Dan).

It is very well known that some women work at sex venues because of their boyfriends, and that violence, coercion, or other means of force may be involved when women refuse to work or to turn over their money. Many prostitutes, all sex ring operators, and police officers participating in this study are well aware of this. In the meantime, the belief is that women who get involved in prostitution in this way account for only a small proportion of women working in the sex industry in general. It appears, as a matter of fact, that very few women work in the sex industry because of force, deception, or coercion. According to a police agent who used to work in a jurisdiction within which there is a famous red light district, there are cases where women call the police asking to be rescued. Some women may have been cajoled or deceived into prostitution in the beginning, but they accept it later. They do not report it to the police until they are beaten or until they realize they have no control of the money they earn. Some women are acquaintances of their chicken-heads, and fear of reprisal and revenge prohibits them from contacting the police. In addition, if they call the police, their peers, who are usually fellow villagers, regard their actions as a betrayal. In Shazui village, there are many women from Hunan and Hubei provinces. Back in their hometowns, some families started to build mansions two years after their daughters left to go to work. People are jealous of this prosperity, yet at the same time, they know how so much money can be made. Therefore, they come out of the villages to go work in this profession. This is why the source areas from where the women originate present a specific geographic pattern. In Shazhui village, many women come from the same town in Hubei province. The local people have accepted this profession as a means of making money.

A manager at a sauna parlor said:

> There are almost no women forced to do this now. I have known some receptionists, ministers, or cashiers who cannot resist the enticement of the high salary of technicians, and so they become technicians, too. They used to make only a little more than 1,000 yuan a month. Some technicians can make 1,000 yuan in a day. The gap is too big. Some people become technicians after straightening their thoughts.

It is not rare in the world of prostitutes for "pimps" to be the boyfriends or husbands of prostitutes, who financially depend on their girlfriends or wives (see Perkins, 1991; Raymond and Hughes, 2001; Sharpe, 1998). Some studies have found that "these men act as protector or 'sitter,' driver, or have some other task established for them by their prostitute girlfriends or wives" (Perkins, 1991: 325). The extent to which these relationships are exploitative or based on violent coercion cannot be easily established, and vary significantly. Whether what appears as a partnership in some cases constitutes a fair exchange or not is a matter of perspective. No matter how controversial this issue is, there is no disagreement about the fact that the chicken-heads are low-class hoodlums or small thugs who are not employed on a regular basis and have a limited education; or that they are "petty criminals with one foot outside the law, or men seeking petty power" (Perkins, 1991: 325).

7

Prostitution and Human Trafficking: Underlying Reasons

The preceding chapters examined the lives of women before they began to work in the sex industry, as well as after they had embarked upon this path. The women have been grouped into several categories based on the most proximal factor that influenced their initial involvement in prostitution. However, as stated in Chapter 3, these immediate factors cannot fully explain why these women work in the sex industry. According to the Rational Choice Perspective, a variety of factors, both background and situational, must be taken into account in explaining women's involvement in the sex trade. This chapter, therefore, will explore a wide range of factors, at both the aggregated and individual levels, responsible for the re-emergence of prostitution, and its rampant nature, and will also examine the related issue of sex trafficking in contemporary China.

As discussed before, most women in the sex industry hail from families with low socio-economic status, and have limited education and skills. Therefore, the legitimate jobs available to them are strenuous and low-paid. A few of the women are in dire need of money, or are in a bad financial situation right before they get involved in prostitution for the first time, or become victims of human trafficking, A number of women also adopt prostitution because they want more than what routine jobs can provide, or are overwhelmed by other physically demanding jobs, or by the poverty they have experienced in their childhood. Their incentives for wanting to make money vary, ranging from maintaining a regular life, helping their families, coping with unusual events, buying a house, paying off debt, or, generally, to improving their financial status. Overall, they migrate with the hope of solving their financial problems or improving their economic status, but end up in prostitution or fall into the hands of traffickers.

Superficially, it appears that most women enter into prostitution because they are enticed by the prospect of high incomes. However, the monetary incentive alone cannot trigger women's involvement in prostitution or render them vulnerable to human trafficking. As discussed in preceding chapters, an individual's current circumstances are affected by factors in their background, as well as the context in which they find themselves. Both distal and proximal factors, as well as factors at the aggregated and individual levels must be taken into account to fully explain women's involvement in prostitution.

Economic Reasons

Lim (1998) asserts that prostitution has a long history, and its existence in South East Asian countries has strong economic foundations, as well as social bases involving the unequal relationship between men and women. This is the case with China. Over the past 30 years, China has made huge strides in its battle against poverty, as it has transformed itself into one of the most dynamic economies in the world. A variety of economic reform strategies have stimulated rapid economic growth, and reduced poverty in China. However, the rapid growth has also resulted in inequality, materialism, and a high cost of living. As mentioned in the preceding chapter, the poverty rate in China has dropped dramatically since the initiation of economic reform. Many people are perplexed by the apparent paradox: during the pre-reform era, most people lived in poverty, but incidents of prostitution were rare, if not completely eradicated. In contrast, in the reform era, China has achieved enormous economic success, many people have been lifted out of poverty and their economic situation has improved dramatically. Why then, is prostitution so prevalent, and what is its relation to economic progress? Chinese officials describe the phenomenon as "dying embers flaring up again" as a result of "the opening up to the west" (Hershatter, 1997). Before the Communist party took power, it was assumed that women went into prostitution as a result of socioeconomic factors (Anderson and Gil, 1994). In contrast, some scholars believe that contemporary prostitutes get involved in prostitution voluntarily (Si, 1997; Xiao, 1999; Zhu, 1994). Prostitutes are described as being "addicted to hedonism, loving indolence and hating work" (Si, 1997); they are "fallen" women, they are considered "shameful' and "immoral," and are criticized for employing "improper methods of sustaining a living." It would appear, thus, that the first and foremost reason for prostitution is that the women concerned are morally degenerate, and second, that they are individualistic pleasure seekers (Kang et al., 1988: 55). In this way, the prevalence of prostitution is attributed to individual psychological reasons. To emphasize psychological factors, however, is to dismiss the role played by socio-economic factors in the proliferation of prostitution, and to ignore the existence of forced prostitution. In the context of economic growth, both relative poverty and inequality contribute to the expansion of prostitution and to sex trafficking.

Uneven Development

While economic reform has improved the general living conditions of the Chinese people, it has also broadened the gap between the rich and the poor. China's economic development is uneven. Based on survey data spanning 1980-2001, Ravallion and Chen (2004) find that, while the incidence of poverty in China has fallen dramatically, progress has been uneven. Although absolute poverty has been reduced, inequality in incomes has been rising. The average per capita income of peasant households increased from 367.7 yuan in 1985 to 657.4 yuan in 1990, to 2,129.6 yuan in 2000 and to 2,326.8 yuan in 2002 (*China Agricultural Yearbook*, 1999 and 2003). However, the income of Chinese peasants still lags behind that of their counterparts in cities. While urban workers' per capita salary averaged 12,964 yuan (1,878 dollars) in the first half of 2008, the per capita cash income of farmers stood at 2,528 yuan (369 dollars) during the same period (China Net, 2008).

The Gini index is a measure of inequality of income distribution. A low Gini coefficient indicates a more equal distribution of income. The Gini index in China increased from 28 percent in 1981 to 39 percent in 2001 (Ravallion and Chen, 2004). Rapid economic growth in China has been accompanied by rising social inequality (Fu, 2004). Another aspect of relative poverty can be demonstrated by the geographic pattern of China's economic growth. The Eastern coastal areas received greater attention from the government and/or investors, and have therefore developed much faster than remote inland provinces. Before the economic reform, a low standard of living was almost universal for all Chinese, and income inequality was not an issue (Ravallion and Chen, 2004; Wu, 2002). However, inequality among different geographical areas, and the increasing disparity of incomes have now emerged as important concerns. This pattern of development is the major factor motivating people to migrate to coastal provinces in order to explore economic opportunities.

One of the results of the disparity between rich and poor is the emergence of a new class of poor people, and the appearance and increase of relative poverty. It has become a trend to pursue pleasure and money with all possible resources and methods. On the one hand, some people believe that sex is one of the available resources to be taken advantage of, and they pursue it relentlessly, notwithstanding that it is frowned upon by the mainstream culture. On the other hand, people have become richer and this has resulted in consumerism and a change in lifestyles. The diversity and luxury of products available make people materialistic. The role played by the growing pursuit of materialism, which has permeated even into rural villages, cannot be overestimated in the involvement of migrant women in prostitution. Some of them build beautiful houses in their hometowns, or at least send remittances to their parents, or dress nicely and spend money extravagantly when they go back to their hometowns. This arouses the envy of neighbors and inspires them to follow the same path (Hershatter, 1997). This phenomenon is confirmed by conversations with several police officers. As a result, some families, dazzled by the wealth and the new houses of their neighbors, turn a blind eye to their daughters' involvement in prostitution, even if they do not actively encourage it. Lily bought a house for her family in the center of her home county, and her father asked her to put his name on the house. Did her family know how she earned the money? According to Lily, "my family must know, because how else can a girl with no education and skills make so much money?" In addition to buying a house for her family, she also sends them several thousand a month. "My family is depending on me," she said.

Imbalances in Development Policy and Lack of Social Welfare Programs for the Working Class

As a measure to reduce the numbers of people living in poverty, Chinese economic development strategies have prioritized urbanization and industrialization. Since 1978, the number of cities in China has more than tripled, rising from 191 to 661. The urban population has more than doubled, increasing from 18 percent in 1978 to 43 percent in 2005 (China Labor Bulletin, 2007). China is being transformed from a traditional agricultural nation to a modern industrial one. Priority in economic development has been accorded to the development of secondary and tertiary industries (the service and industry sectors) thus encouraging rapid urban development. This has contributed, either directly or indirectly, to the relative neglect of the primary industry, namely, the agricultural sector, and consequently disfavored the rural areas. A variety of taxes and fees imposed on farmers, combined with the widening disparity in rural and urban income, natural disasters and limited arable land, have reduced farmers' incentives to continue working on farms, resulting in the creation of a huge rural migrant population. As stated in Chapter 1, in some rural villages, no people between the ages of 20 and 40 can be found. The pattern of development and the macroeconomic policies adopted have much to do with the continued expansion of the sex sector.

For rural migrants, employment opportunities in cities are limited to the construction industry and the service sector. Male rural migrants naturally have advantages over female migrants in the former. Female migrants, therefore, flood the service industry (Li, 2004). 90 percent of female rural migrants work in the service industry (Deng, 1998). The relationship of the sex industry to the service industry is obvious. The possibility of women who work in the service industry getting involved in the sex industry is much higher than in the case of women working in other industries. Service sector women become a potential source group for the sex industry.

In the past, the Chinese government used to provide comprehensive welfare benefits for urban residents. A full employment policy meant that the majority of urban residents were covered under this welfare system. When this system was dismantled in the reform era, a new urban welfare system—the socialized welfare system—was created for the urban employed. However, during the period of transition between the old and the new systems, some urban workers (such as those who had been laid-off) were excluded from the system. Rural people, on the other hand, have never been covered by welfare systems, unlike their urban counterparts. The continuing dichotomy between rural and urban areas excludes millions of rural migrants from the welfare system (Fu, 2004). No universal welfare system benefiting the whole society has been established. Farmers migrating to urban areas do not get a change of status in the welfare system. They do not get included in the social welfare system. Social welfare programs are inaccessible to rural families. When a family member falls sick, especially if the illness is severe, the entire family will be dramatically affected. Among the forty women in this study, some got involved in the sex industry as a direct result of illness, either their own, or that of a family member. Some women did not continue going to school for the same reason. Without a system of health benefits, it is very expensive to see a doctor. In serious cases, medical expenses can wipe out years of saving.

Lack of Legal Protections

Part of the reason why a large supply of women is available for the sex sector is that the legitimate sectors of the economy do not pay wages adequate enough to allow them to remit funds to their families. The Chinese Labor Law (1995) prescribes the minimum wage and the maximum permissible working hours per week. According to labor laws, employees shall work for no more than eight hours a day and no more than 44 hours a week on the average (article 36); the employer shall guarantee that workers have at least one day off a week (article 38); if work hours are to be prolonged, in general, it shall be for no longer than one hour a day, or no more than three hours a day, if such a prolongation is called for due to special reasons, and providing that the physical health of workers is guaranteed. The excess working hours, however, shall not exceed 36 hours a month (article 41). The state is required to implement a system of guaranteed minimum wages; the employer shall pay laborers wages no lower than the local standard on minimum wages (article 48).

However, in the case of migrant workers, inspections are rare, and these provisions are seldom enforced. Many enterprises violate regulations, and their employees have to work overtime. Ah Lian worked overtime until midnight, and she made only 17 yuan per day when she worked in a factory. An An worked ten hours everyday in a hotel. Beginning in the latter half of the year 2006, the China Labor Watch has conducted research on several factories in the Pearl River Delta of Guangdong Province. This investigation (China Labor Watch, 2007) found violations of Chinese and international labor laws on a number of levels, for example, employees working without a contract, low wages, nonexistent benefits, unsafe workplaces and compulsory overtime work without adequate compensation. At some of these factories, workers put in 10 to 14 hours daily during the peak season and were not allowed even one day off per week. Factories illegally impose fines and fees. Many factories do not provide medical or work injury insurance, or even the most basic pensions to workers. Workers are not offered insurance as mandated by law. When workers are hospitalized, they sometimes do not receive any salary, and might be fired if injured (see also China Labor Bulletin, 2008).

Economic growth brings dramatic increases in the cost of living. However, according to the China Labor Watch (2004), in Guangdong, workers' wages in general, and migrant workers' wages in particular, have not witnessed any significant increase since the 1980s. The Guangdong provincial government announced its decision to raise the minimum wage level of all workers within the province, and the new minimum wage standard was implemented beginning on December 1, 2004. Under the new standard, Guangzhou's minimum wage level was raised from 510 yuan per month to 684 yuan—an increase rate of 34 percent. However, after deducting 155 yuan as the minimum social security fee, the actual wage increase was only 19 yuan—an increase rate of only 3.73 percent (China Labor Watch, 2004). According to the China Labor Watch, the minimum monthly wage in Shenzhen is 810 yuan, the highest minimum wage in China as of June, 2006 (China Labor Watch, 2006). Many private employers do not even implement the minimum wage standard at all, and never pay for their employees' medical insurance and social security. The low wages workers receive are not enough for them to eke out a normal living, and their situation is made even worse due to continually rising prices.

Low wages and the strenuous nature of work in formal sectors serve as forces that push migrant workers into prostitution when the opportunity presents itself. As Lan Lan put it: "So many women are getting involved in this trade now. There is a street in Nanshan District which is full of prostitutes. Many girls initially work in factories and later transfer to this trade." The women cannot tolerate the slavery-like work environment in the factories, and this, in combination with persuasion by fellow villagers or friends who have been working in the sex sector, makes them drift into prostitution.

Effects of Economic Development on Individuals

Economic reform has produced uneven development and relative poverty, which motivate people to migrate in search of better opportunities. On the supply side, growing income differentials and increasing materialism, coupled with the increasing cost of living an urban lifestyle, appear to provide the motivation for young women to seek higher incomes through prostitution, despite strong social norms that frown upon the profession. The women uproot themselves in the hope of earning high salaries, and being able to send money to their parents. Once they begin living in cities, the urban lifestyle and luxury products intrigue them, and stimulate an even higher degree of materialism. At the same time, their limited educational qualifications restrict them to low-status, low-income occupations—such as jobs in factories, restaurants and hotels. The possibility of earning at least several times as much money in entertainment enterprises is very tempting. When combined with other factors, prostitution becomes an acceptable and attractive alternative for migrant women who constitute the most vulnerable group for prostitution and human trafficking.

On the demand side, economic development provides men with the opportunity to travel, and their increased income makes it possible for a larger number of men to seek sex services as part of the recreation associated with the modern lifestyles. The fact that a large number of male migrants live apart from their spouses, facilitates the demand for sex services. China's transient population has reached 140 million, with the age of the migrant population falling between 16 and 40 (Legal Daily, 2007). Most of the men do not migrate with their spouses. They have money, and will look for entertainment and sexual companionship. It is this need that has, in part, fueled the rapidly growing sex industry. Buying sex has become a popular, acceptable and integral part of the lifestyle of Chinese men, and includes individuals from all walks of life. Prostitution clients may be owners of private enterprises, migrant workers, staff members of various enterprises, government officials, etc. However, the source of customers is not limited to a domestic clientele. Many foreigners, as well as men from Taiwan and Hong Kong seek services in mainland China. Due to proximity to the mainland, men from Hong Kong are an integral part of the customer population in Shenzhen. According to a government official, on an average 50,000 residents of Hong Kong come to Shenzhen per day (mainly on weekends) for sex services. This government official also told me:

> There are a lot of villages for "second-wives" in Luohu district, such as Huangbeiling, Xiangxicun villages. 80% of the apartments in this high-rise tower behind my office were bought by Hong Kong men for their second wives. One-bedroom apartments are in high demand because it is the perfect size for one woman. Why are there so many second wife villages in Luohu district? Because, firstly it is the oldest district, a symbol of Shenzhen; secondly, it is very close to the Luohu Customs facility, it does not cost more than the initial fare if you take a taxi to come here from the Customs building.

Social Factors

In addition to its economic basis, prostitution also has a strong social basis, which has remained largely unchanged over time. These socio-cultural factors are important in explaining the development of prostitution in China. As one of the countries with a history of several thousand years, China has developed its own value systems regarding the relations between men and women, sex, money, etc. In the context of China's transition, and with the influence of foreign culture as a result of the country's recent open-door policy, some of the values have undergone profound changes. Traditional attitudes or norms favoring extra-marital sex have reemerged, causing prostitution and extra-marital sex to be increasingly tolerated, accepted, or even encouraged.

Traditional Views of Woman's Body

The prevalence of prostitution is related to traditional attitudes to women's bodies. The notion that a woman's greatest asset is her body is one of the factors explaining why some women prostitute themselves (Hoigard and Finstad, 1992). In a society where women are valued based on sexuality, women may see prostitution as a viable alternative. The degree to which women regard their body as their greatest asset is crucial in their decision to adopt prostitution (James and Meryerding, 1977). The resurgence of prostitution cannot be fully explained without taking into account the resurgence of old values regarding the status of women, i.e., viewing women as commodities, thus enabling men to buy sexual services from them (Gil et al., 1994). Traditional Chinese culture created an ideology in which women's bodies and their beauty are considered their major assets. Men are valued, and women despised. Women are degraded to the status of objects, rather than being considered as human beings. Historically, men could legally have multiple wives and concubines. This practice was outlawed when the Communist Party took power, and remains illegal today. However, having a "second wife" has once again become a male status symbol. The cultural values that favor a woman's beauty, expertise in sex, ability to charm, host, and serve men for a fee, reflect ancient themes (Gil et al., 1994). This ideology is deeply entrenched in contemporary China and can be evidenced by what some women said during the interview.

> We women all think about one thing everyday: we hope to meet a man and become his mistress so that we do not have to wait for customers everyday (Xiao Fang).

> If I had the chance to start over, I won't do this. I will find a boyfriend to help solve my financial problems. I am good looking and should not have a problem dating a rich man. If we cannot get along, we can divorce (Ah Wen).

> I want to meet a man who can give me several thousands each month and I would like to be his mistress (Wang Mei).

According to Chinese sayings, ignorance is the virtue of women; the best match between a husband and wife is the man's intelligence and the woman's beauty. A more recent adage, one that has become popular over the last two decades, expresses the idea that marrying a good man spares a woman twenty years of struggle. These so-called "good" men are those who are either rich or who wield power. Such observations imply that attitudes toward women have not fundamentally changed in contemporary China. Some women believe that sex is an available resource, or that it is the only one they have; their capital is their youth and beauty, and since these are perishable assets, the women intend to use them while they last to accumulate more durable capital (Hershatter, 1997; Zhu Xudong, 2001). A survey on prostitution in three cities of northeastern China found that 46.88 percent believed that prostitution is a fair trade between customers and prostitutes and 50 percent believed that, compared to the crimes of embezzlement and theft, it is moral to trade the body for money. Of those surveyed, 51.52 percent believed that no one can resist the enticement of money; 25.81 percent believed that where women are concerned, prostitution is the easiest, shortest way to make money; and 56.25 percent thought that a woman's value lies in her attractiveness to men. These are the values, notions, and attitudes that underpin the development of the sex industry, and render it inde-structible (Zhang, 1997).

These re-emerging age-old attitudes to women's bodies have resulted in changes in attitudes towards virginity. During the pre-economic reform era, premarital virginity was promoted, encouraged and cherished. This value was considered so important in Chinese culture, that women who protected their virginity before marriage were honored. With economic development and the increasing acceptance of western sexual norms, virginity and chastity are not treated with the same respect and esteem as before. The consequences of this change are two-fold, affecting women's attitudes to sex in opposing ways but giving rise to the same results. On the one hand, the traditional importance accorded to premarital virgin-ity is gradually breaking down. Being a virgin is out of date, resulting in female adolescents engaging in premarital sex and diminishing the negative effects associated with prostitution. On the other hand, para-doxically, traditional values regarding virginity do not diminish, and may never diminish. This is illustrated by Sha Sha, who deliberately made sure just before she took the path into prostitution, that her first sexual encounter was with a man she liked. She said that she would otherwise have always regretted that her first sexual experience was with a customer. For those who have lost their virginity, the threshold of entering prostitution is lowered. Women don't worry about losing their virginity if they are not virgins when they begin prostitution. Some, in fact, may exploit their virginity by selling it off for a high price. The effects of attitudes towards virginity and chastity on the involvement of women in prostitution can be demonstrated by the following excerpts from interviews with subjects in the study:

> I used to regret what I did, but now I have changed my thinking. There is no difference in sleeping with one man or with several men. I just want to make money for my parents and get married later. Girls have a limited number of years during which to make a lot of money (Xiao Xiu).

> I agreed to work in a hair salon because my boyfriend consented, and I was not a virgin any more (Ah Hong).

Attitudes to Sex

Western sexual conceptions may have contributed to booming prostitution in the reform era in China. Elaine Jeffreys points out that the revival of prostitution during the early 1980s was initially concentrated in China's eastern coastal cities and thus "somewhat tenuously linked to the influx of foreign investment and the 'Western ideas'" (Jeffreys, 2004a: 97). Some Western scholars also acknowledge that Western culture plays a role in contributing to the revival of Chinese prostitution. David J. Lynch notes that Western culture is "transforming attitudes toward sex." Influenced by Western culture, Chinese people are experiencing their own sexual revolution (Lynch, 2003).

Prostitution had almost disappeared during the specific historical period from 1949 to 1978. Furthermore, public discussion of sex was rare—everyone was supposed to engage in "socialist construction" and political movements (especially during the Cultural Revolution). The current reform era in China is witnessing an abrupt sexual revolution, rather than a gradual evolution of sexual behaviors and relationships (Pan, 2006). Sexual promiscuity has become an accepted life-style among younger people. Rapidly changing attitudes towards sex and marriage among young people and greater political and economic freedom have contributed to the proliferation of commercial sex in China (Ren, 1993 and 1999).

As a result of the significant changes in attitudes to sex since the 1980s, the traditional ethic that "lewdness is the worst of all vices" has been replaced by "laughing at poverty, not at prostitutes" in the contemporary commercialized society. In the past, prostitutes dared not display their riches when they came back to visit their parents. Now, they wear gold and silver and there is no effort to disguise any signs that might reveal their involvement in prostitution. Meanwhile, it arouses the admiration of fellow female villagers, and instills in them the desire to follow the same path.

A survey conducted in several big cities in China found that the public does not reject the sex industry totally, but that they tolerate it to some extent (Li Wei, 2006). A study (Hong et al., 2006) on sexual attitudes among migrants showed that their perspectives about sex, and their experiences of sexual norms and values represent a wide spectrum of views and behaviors that exist in China today. While some people continue to be attached to traditional values, including concern for women's virginity, others view living with a girlfriend or boyfriend as a common practice, quite prevalent among their peers. Another study of 989 migrant women working at sauna parlors and nightclubs in Guangzhou showed that these women's sexual norms are open, and that sexual morality has limited restraining power on their sexual behavior. 61 percent have an indifferent attitude to premarital sex, and almost 20 percent did not find it objectionable to have multiple sex partners and to practice prostitution (Yang et al., 2005). Many men in China believe the purchase of sex services to be acceptable behavior. Men from very different social and age groups make use of prostitutes' services for different reasons. What is more, they even consider the purchase of sex services to be a form of charity, since they are providing prostitutes with a chance to earn a living (Pochagina, 2005).

The sexual revolution has affected both women and men, and contributed to the growth of the commercial sex industry (Ren, 1999). On one hand, the more liberal attitude toward sex has diminished the traditional stigma against prostitution, and premarital and extramarital sex, lowering the threshold for women to enter into prostitution. On the other hand, the liberal attitude toward sex and prevalent pornographic products entice men to patronize prostitutes. The traditional sense of shame relating to extra-marital sex is not strong enough to deter people from the commercial sexual trade.

Inequality in Education: Boys vs. Girls

Women in prostitution usually have limited education and skills. This fact is confirmed by the present study. The low level of education of Chinese women can be attributed to two factors: the general limited educational resources available to rural populations and fewer educational opportunities available to women when compared to those available to men. In 1986, China promulgated the law on compulsory education, which stipulates that the state should provide a nine-year compulsory education "free of tuition fees" for all primary and middle school students. However, the law has failed to guarantee funding for compulsory education, thus forcing many schools, particularly those in impoverished rural regions, to either continue to collect tuition fees or to charge various "miscellaneous fees" to their students in the name of "voluntary donations," "fund-raising for school construction" or "after-school tutoring fees." Recent surveys conducted by sociologists in several rural areas show that currently, Chinese farmers, whose annual per capita net income stood at a mere 3,200 yuan in 2005, have to pay about 800 yuan a year for a child's education at the elementary or secondary stage. Excessive charges by schools have become a major reason behind the increasing dropout rate of rural school age children who constitute nearly 80 percent of China's primary and middle school students (*China Daily*, 2006). As a result, rural people—especially women in indigent areas—have the lowest rates of education and literacy. An investigation shows that 87.9 percent of rural women have no education beyond the middle school level (Zhu Guanglei, 2001).

Another factor contributing to the low level of women's education can be traced to China's traditional culture in which boys are valued more than girls. In traditional Chinese culture, daughters are not very important; it is the son that matters. A daughter getting married means the loss of labor. Therefore, daughters are regarded as temporary family members. When a family cannot afford to send all children to school, it is usually the daughters who quit studies and support their brothers who continue studying. It is reported that some women gave up hopes of a university education and worked as prostitutes so that their brothers could continue to attend school (Goodman, 2003). As the present study demonstrates, girls start to do chores and work in the fields when they are very young. After marriage, they are regarded as instruments to give birth and do chores, and it is even more impossible for them to get an education. What makes things worse in the case of migrant women is that their limited education makes them naïve, and they have a low capacity to make informed decisions about vital aspects of their lives.

Due to limited opportunities for higher education in China, only a restricted number of people can go to college, and there is no incentive for parents to encourage their children to continue their education after graduating from middle school. While the huge cost of higher education is certainly an impediment, on the other side of the coin, children may not want to pursue education if their parents do not encourage them. Without parents' discipline and encouragement, they may not do well in school. Further, in addition to the economic impediments, there are also other physical obstacles that discourage children from going to school. This is especially true in remote indigent areas where walking to school may take as long as two hours or more. An anecdote on a website tells of a remote mountain village in China which is divided by a river. Children living on one side of the river have to cross to the other side to go to school. There is no bridge in that village, so the children have to use a steel rope to slide over the river. This may be an extreme example, but it serves to illustrate why some women in rural areas have only a few years of schooling.

Changes in Attitudes to Money

Over the past three decades, dramatic economic changes have had profound effects on values, and on attitudes to money. When everybody was poor before the reform era, people were complacent and there was no incentive to change their status. The architect of the economic reform, Deng Xiaoping, designed a path to common wealth: "let a few get rich first, then all the rest will get rich." This ideology greatly motivated people to pursue economic success as much as they could, and the government formulated a series of policies to urge people to follow an individualistic path to wealth. To advance economic development and reduce poverty, the government promoted the slogan: "Getting rich is glorious." Since then, the Chinese people feel they are permitted to aspire to wealth and the pursuit of individual wants and needs; they are no longer required to completely subordinate personal aspirations for the good of their social unit (Anderson and Gil, 1994).

The slogan "let a few get rich first" while appearing to be a clever formula, does not, however, specify how this objective is to be achieved. The emphasis on individual economic advancement stipulates economic development and serves as an incentive for individuals to get rid of poverty. However, it also has negative effects. To some people, pursuing economic success becomes the ultimate end, and they are unconcerned about the nature of means employed to reach that end. As a result, this economic development strategy is a two-edged sword. While it stipulates rapid economic development, and allows individuals to pursue their objectives, it also results in "a society characterized by a resurgence of self-centered behaviors" (Gil et al., 1994: 319); "outright, a frank celebration of material pleasures" (Hershatter, 1997: 352). Getting rich has emerged as a dominant ethos of the reform era (Deng and Cordilia, 1999). The traditional attitude "People laugh at poor people but don't laugh at prostitutes" has re-emerged. Educational achievement is not admired; instead, it is regarded as a waste of money and time when it cannot bring direct economic benefits. The words "looking forward" are transformed as "looking toward money" (in Chinese, the terms "forward" and "money" have the same sound). Many traditional Chinese virtues and values were renounced during the rapid development of the economy. Materialism is a prominent characteristic of the women in the sex industry, and this is echoed by two operators of sex venues:

> Misses are all practical and materialistic. They love money too much. I have been working here for a long time and known a lot of misses. Some misses like indolent, extravagant lifestyles. Some of them get involved in this line of work because they got hurt emotionally. Some of them are lured by the high salary, but they have limited education and no social connections and thus get involved in this line of work. There are also some misses who have had higher education. They all want to have money (Manager of a sauna parlor).

> They are materialistic, love money, and they do this just because they can make a lot of money. Sometimes they compete for good customers. Some customers give more tips than others, the miss who serves them does not want other misses getting in touch with them (Manager of a KTV lounge).

The change in values and morality in the current market economy has given rise to changes in behavior. Some people are desperate to become rich with any available means, and with no regard for morality (Xiao, 1999). Many people have become economically ambitious, and their desire for wealth knows no boundaries. People may be motivated to achieve their economic objectives in any available way, normative or not, when undue stress is placed on the importance of the ends (Deng and Cordilia, 1999). Some people don't hesitate to sacrifice the interests of others in order to make money. "People laugh at poverty rather than at prostitutes" is an adage that prostitutes believe in deeply, and this expression is also used by those who introduce and persuade other women into prostitution.

Materialism has a significant impact on people who migrate from closed rural areas to open and prosperous cities (Li, 2004). On the one hand, they used to live in poor backward areas, and thus have a strong desire to make money and change their fate. Yet, at the same time, they do not have the capacity to make the money they desire, and they cannot realize their dreams with a menial income. They cannot even make enough money to support a normal life. This relative deprivation motivates them to take a shortcut to making money. According to Deng Xiaoping, a cat is good as long as it catches mice—it does not matter whether the cat is black or white. He used this metaphor to illuminate the debate about which system was better, socialism or capitalism. However, the population applies this metaphor to justify the means used to make money—even if these means are deviant. The emphasis on getting rich, the obsession with material achievement, combined with the uneven distribution of opportunities for work in legitimate sectors motivate those with few social connections, limited education and market skills to use whatever means are available to them, including crooked ones. Several prostitutes interviewed expressed the same reasoning as Le Le:

> I just want to make a lot of money and then start a private business. People like me, with no education or money, can only work for others all their lives. If you want to change your fate, you cannot steal or rob. You have to take a crooked course.

Situational Factors

Two prominent situational factors in each of these women's lives were significantly related to their involvement in prostitution, firstly, the influence of friends, relatives or peers, and secondly, the omnipresence of advertising and entertainment establishments. Other factors acting as either inducements or impediments include formal and informal social controls, as well as a cost-and-benefit analysis of prostitution. People around these women exert significant and varying effects on their involvement in prostitution. The prevalence of advertising and entertainment establishments provides convenience for the women to start the trade. Diminished formal and informal social controls, as well as the benefits of sex work, act as pull forces in women's involvement in prostitution.

Effects of Friends/Coworkers

People do not live in a vacuum, and those involved in prostitution are no exception. The influence of people around them cannot be overemphasized. Most of the women have friends, relatives or coworkers working as prostitutes, and this serves to lower the threshold of their own entry into prostitution. Thirty-three women in the study had either friends or coworkers involved in prostitution before them. The effects of friends or coworkers on subjects' participation in prostitution vary. In some cases, friends actively talk them into this line of work, while in other cases, friends provide encouragement when the potential candidates express concerns or lack of confidence. They propose the idea, provide positive information about the job, act as role models demonstrating the attractiveness of luxurious lifestyles. The varying influence of their friends, relatives or coworkers on the women's decision to enter prostitution can be classified into the following categories: persuasion, encouragement, advice, exposure, or company.

Persuasion: As stated in Chapter 5, the influence of friends, relatives or coworkers on women's involvement in prostitution can be either direct or indirect. Direct influence refers to a situation in which a third party proposes the idea, and talks the subjects into it when they are reluctant to work as prostitutes. For example, Ah Rong was persuaded by her aunt to provide hand jobs, and Lily was introduced to this trade by her aunt when she was 15 years old. Some time later, another aunt who was a hostess brought Lily to the center of the county, where the young girl began to work as a hostess. These two subjects' aunts exerted a greater influence on their involvement with prostitution than did other friends or relatives.

Encouragement: Some people encourage their friends or coworkers to join this profession by alleviating any concerns they may have, or by providing information about the advantages of this job. Wang Hong became acquainted with another young woman when she worked in a factory. They became good friends. Wang Hong told me that she may not have got involved in prostitution had she not got to know this friend. She did not know about prostitution establishments when she worked in the factory. Her friend encouraged her by relieving her of concerns, as did the manager when she was under training.

> I worried whether or not I could do it because I am slender. My friend said that I could—many people like me do this job. It was easy to make over 2,000 yuan a month… I intended to be a formal masseuse, but the manager assigned me to category B (including sex service). I said that I was skinny, not sexy. She said that customers would touch me even if I were giving regular massage. She told me it was better to earn a lot of money while I was young, and that I could switch back to formal massage if I could not get used to it (Wang Hong).

Some friends tried to encourage subjects to start the trade by pointing out the advantages of this job. Na Na was told by her friends that prostitutes had a lot of freedom and nobody would discipline you. So she took the job. Li Ying's fellow villager who was working at a KTV lounge said that it was always better to work there than in a factory, because you were able to save some money every month. You could not save money if you worked somewhere else. Wang Xia's friend introduced her to work at a dancing hall and told her that she could make several thousand by accompanying customers, and that it was also possible to become someone's mistress. Tempted by this, Wang Xia started to work at a dancing hall. Most women are lured by the irresistible monetary benefits of working as a prostitute. No encouragement could be more efficient or effective than that provided by a trainer to some misses:

> The trainer persuaded us. She said that some people bought a BMW or Mercedes-Benz after merely working for a few years. And if you worked hard for two or three years, you would make more than some people made in their lifetime. Then you could go home and run a business, and nobody knew what you were doing if you did not tell them (An An).

Advice: Sometimes, it is friends or relatives who suggest to the women that they work as prostitutes. Xiao Ya had been in Guangdong since she was 15, working in a factory. Her friend introduced her to work at a foot massage parlor. Le Le had a friend who was a prostitute. Her friend initiated the idea of prostitution: "you are so desperate for money, why don't you make a lot of money while you are young?" Subsequently, she looked for an establishment by herself. Ding Ding took the job after being enlightened by her friend:

> I was really out of money. One of my friends who had been in Guangdong told me that you could make more money in Guangdong than in other places no matter what you did. People would laugh at you if you were poor. If you came out and made a lot of money, nobody knew you were prostitute (Ding Ding).

If the subject worked at an entertainment establishment before getting involved in prostitution, the influence of their co-worker(s) cannot be overestimated. Ah Lian washed hair at a hair salon. She started to provide sex service one week later because her colleagues did so, and her boss persuaded her to do the same. Wang Mei started to work at an entertainment facility after breaking up with her boyfriend. Following that, she was brainwashed by her coworkers.

> I got to know many women who zuotai. They told me that I was good looking and had a good temperament, and that I should have a lot of customers if I zuotai. They also said that customers would touch me even though I was just a waitress, so why didn't I zuotai? I started to zuotai three months later (Wang Mei).

Exposure: Some women get the idea of working as a prostitute on their own because they have friends who have worked in this trade. They have obtained information about this line of work from their friends. Under certain circumstances, prostitution could appear as an option to them, although, generally speaking, it would seem to be a job that they would never consider at any time. In other words, working as a prostitute is not a first option. But it presents itself as an option when the timing is appropriate. The women come up with the idea themselves. However, they may not perhaps have thought of this option had they not had friends working in the sex industry.

Sha Sha knew a fellow villager who worked at a hair salon. She approached this acquaintance when she decided to work in a hair salon. Her village friend asked whether she had made up her mind about it. Nan Nan had a girlfriend working at a nightclub. When she decided to change her factory job, she went to the nightclub for an interview. She reiterated that it was her own decision and that her friend did not influence her decision in any way. Having a friend working in these venues reduces perceived risks and lowers the threshold for women entering into sex work. In the case of some women, their friends act as role models on account of the wealth they demonstrate. Chen Hong was really jealous of her middle school friends because they were so obviously wealthy. She told a friend that salaries were very low in her hometown. Her friend told her that she could make a lot of money in Shenzhen. She knew what her friend was doing, but she did not think that it was a disgrace. Furthermore, she wanted to migrate. She did not want to get married and settle down in her hometown. Girlfriends of Lin Dan's boyfriend were all prostitutes. They all made 700 or 800 yuan each night. After finding this out, she wanted to work as a prostitute, too, because she wanted to have a lot of money. Because she had known some women who were prostitutes, she did not feel scared when she began. These were not the only women tempted by their friends' wealth. A number of women in this study were lured by the high incomes of prostitutes.

My friends who do hand jobs talk about their income very frequently. They make several thousand a month. I know they do hand jobs—no sexual intercourse. I did not feel scared when I initially did this job because many of my friends and classmates were doing this (Ah Xiang).

Some girls who worked in an entertainment center lived in a factory dorm. When they hung out together, they said that they made over 3,000 yuan a month and the work was easy. I wrote down their phone number. I quit working in the factory in the beginning of 2008, and went home for the Chinese New Year. I called them after I got back (Xiu Xiu).

I was a waitress in a sauna parlor for several months. I wanted to be a technician (prostitute) when I saw other technicians making over 10,000 yuan a month, eating well and dressing well. Gradually I accepted it. At the end of 2007, I ran out of money again and started to look for a job at a sauna parlor. There are so many women who do this job now. Many women work in factories and then transfer to this line of work (Lan Lan).

Company: Sha Sha worked at the same hair salon as her friend when she started the trade for the first time. Later, her friend left that hair salon, and Sha Sha left, too, and found another hair salon to work in because she was a little scared after her friend left. Lan Lan said that she would not be in this line of work if a prior coworker had not joined the trade together with her; she became bolder with a companion. She and her coworker used to work at the same hotel. They started to work at a massage parlor together, and both of them felt they had each other for company. Wang Hong worked at the same massage parlor as her previous coworker, too. She did not start sex service jobs until her friend began, too, half a year later. The company of their friends made them feel safer, and their choice seemed less risky.

Conclusion: The influence of friends or co-workers on women's decision to enter prostitution varies in terms of its nature and extent, suggesting the importance of specific social networks in their entry into the profession. It is not totally clear whether involvement in prostitution is a result of influence by others or not. The process of involvement is a continuum, and the third party's role is so nuanced that it is not easy to make a judgment as to whether these women got involved in prostitution on their own initiative, or whether they were introduced to it by others. At one end are women who are forced, deceived, or coerced by their peers, friends, relatives or boyfriends. At the other end are women who do not indicate having known anyone working in the sex industry. Most women fall between these two ends. They have known people who have worked in the sex industry, or they themselves have worked at entertainment establishments before beginning to provide sex services, and/or they have had co-workers who were prostitutes. As discussed above, these friends or co-workers may act as persuaders, encouragers, advisors, role models, or companions; their impact on women's involvement in commercial sex decreases along the continuum. The specific role played by boyfriends or particular events in the process are not as prominent as the role of friends, relatives, or co-workers. Those who initially get involved in prostitution because of their boyfriends or due to specific events are also, at the same time, influenced by their friends. The friends either initiate the idea, or help them to straighten out their thoughts regarding this line of work. This third party influence was prominent in the case of most women in this study.

Omnipresence of Advertising and Entertainment Establishments

Sex establishments are prevalent everywhere around Shenzhen. A general idea of the high concentration of entertainment establishments in some neighborhoods in Shenzhen may be obtained by looking at the number of entertainment establishments at a certain intersection and its immediate surroundings. For example, along a certain stretch less than 500 meters long on a main road, there are nine entertainment establishments: one night club, two sauna parlors, two foot massage parlors, and four leisure centers, which basically provide massage services. Five of them are situated in four buildings at each corner of the intersection. The proliferation of entertainment establishments creates a huge demand for female workers, and results in the large number of women providing sex services. As a mammy said: "There are a lot of entertainment venues in Shenzhen; we need more girls to work. The situation is different from the past when there were several hundred girls working in a single venue."

Advertisements are omnipresent at bus stations, on buildings housing entertainment establishments, and other public places. There are two major, impressive types of advertising –in the first, advertisements are posted at bus stations or on electrical poles; in the second, large banners are displayed on the entertainment buildings, or there are advertisements on boards at the entrance to these venues. As one waits for public transport, one cannot fail to notice the papers posted on the bulletin boards. In addition, some establishments (such as sauna/massage parlors) hang huge banners outside their premises. Some nightclubs set up a recruitment desk right at the entrance, displaying a small board detailing requirements for the types of employees desired. There are employees on the spot, ready to register new recruits. The content of all advertising is almost the same. Usually they seek to recruit male/female public relations officers (a euphemistic term for prostitutes), escorts, drivers, and waiters/waitresses. The advertisements also indicate a monthly salary for each of these jobs, ranging from 30,000 yuan for public relations officers to 1,500 yuan for waiters/waitresses. During my fieldwork in Shenzhen, I also noticed many restaurants with advertisements placed in front of their premises. The salary for various positions varied, ranging from no more than 1,500 yuan to as low as 800 yuan. The hyperbolic salary offered to public relations officers lures many women who want to make more money. The nature of the jobs is obvious.

Both Xiao Xiu and Xiao Fang found their first sex job by looking at advertisements at the bus station. Another woman was hired by a nightclub via an advertisement at the entrance. Obviously, the women cannot fail to notice all the advertising before they decide to start the trade, and they can deduce the nature of the job based on the huge salary gap between these jobs and other legitimate ones.

Diminished Formal and Informal Social Controls

Weak social control is another reason why prostitution has become prevalent in China. The market economy provides more opportunities for prostitutes and their customers (Xiao, 1999). In urban areas, during the pre-reform era, the workplace and the neighborhood used to be key areas exercising informal social control. Security departments at workplaces were closely connected to local law enforcement agencies and courts. Whenever a crime occurred at a workplace, the security department would contact local law enforcement authorities, who would get involved in the investigation. Whenever an employee displayed deviant behavior outside of the workplace, and it was brought to the attention of law enforcement agencies, the workplace would be notified. Consequently, employees were under intense supervision. Due to the fact that employees were assigned housing by their employers who usually built multiple houses constituting a neighborhood, people from the same workplace were usually neighbors. The fact of being colleagues at work, and neighbors after work, further reduced employees' privacy. Much of their life was visible, and individuals tended to be sensitive to the consequences of their behavior, whether it was normative or deviant.

In the era of economic reform, however, the role played by the workplace and the neighborhood in exercising functions of informal control has declined dramatically, if it exists at all. The practice of providing free housing is history. State-owned enterprises were replaced by private or joint-venture enterprises recruiting employees from all over the country, not just from local areas. People living side by side in the same commercial private apartment compound for many years may not know each other. People change jobs more frequently, in contrast to the pre-reform era when they worked at the same establishment until they retired. The changes in the social structure have reduced formal and informal social controls that had served as significant deterrent forces in the past.

Formal and informal social controls constitute major deterrence against deviance and crime. The stigma associated with prostitution and arrests is the main deterrent force preventing women from entering into prostitution. However it acts as an impediment only when being found out is perceived as a potential probability. As discussed in the preceding chapter, the women interviewed in this study do not perceive that their involvement in prostitution will be discovered by their family and friends, and there is little likelihood of being arrested. The low probability of these concerns materializing is a factor that minimizes perceived risks associated with prostitution and pushes the women into the profession.

Comparing Prostitution and Legitimate Jobs:
Is This an Informed Choice?

Participants in this study had worked in legitimate sectors for varying periods of time. Due to their limited education, the jobs available to them were restricted to low-paying and low status ones. Salaries from legitimate jobs can only cover their costs of living in Shenzhen. They are not able to remit money to their families, put aside some savings, or afford a luxurious lifestyle. Getting involved in prostitution does not expose them to highly risky situations. Being found out by family and friends, acquiring STDs and being arrested are their primary concerns. The possibility of these occurring, however, is very low. Living far from their hometown makes it almost impossible to be found out by family or neighbors; regular medical examinations and precautionary measures protect against STDs; corruption and authorities who turn a blind eye to prostitution lead the women to believe that arrest is next to impossible. As a result, the stigma and risks attached to prostitution fail to function as deterrents to prevent the women from embarking into prostitution. As long as the rewards of prostitution outweigh its risks, it is unavoidable that people will follow the prostitution pathway.

As stated previously, money is the incentive for every woman who gets involved in prostitution, although it may not be the only incentive. Some women are direct about the fact that they prostitute themselves just for money. The low salary and strenuousness of work in legitimate sectors serve as push factors in women's decisions to work as prostitutes. The advantages associated with prostitution, such as high incomes, flexible working schedule, easy money, and no investment or training requirements motivate women with limited education to get involved in this unsavory trade. One woman also mentioned that it would be hard to meet a rich man if you worked in a factory.

In the context of the general risks and rewards associated with prostitution as well as with legitimate work, some women also make a detailed and nuanced comparison between prostitution and other jobs they have held. This helps convince them that working in legitimate sectors is not an attractive option.

I did not take into account other alternatives. I do this because my parents need money. I could work as a secretary. But if the boss is not nice, you would get blamed, and feel upset about your work. Furthermore, you cannot work overtime and get extra money as a secretary (Sha Sha).

When I was a sales clerk at a shoe store, the customer's feet smelled bad. When I was a waitress, customers gave me a hard time. I intended to work in a factory, but you cannot even go to the restroom for a long time, and you feel dizzy every day after work. It makes you exhausted to work in factories. You will have pressure whatever you do for a living. I just want to make a lot of money and then start a private business (Le Le).

Prostitution is definitely not their first choice. Although it is lucrative, there are risks and stigma attached to this trade. Therefore, they must make sure that the risks are worthwhile. This unarticulated psychic process is illustrated by the fact that some women still go to the factories for interviews even though they have already decided to work in the sex industry before coming to Shenzhen.

I also looked for other work right after I arrived in Shenzhen. I have no degree. I had several interviews in factories, but I cannot make a lot of money this way—only 1,000 yuan a month. I cannot save money after paying my living expenses. Finally, I decided to work at a hair salon. Working here is tiring, but I feel better psychologically because I can give my family money when they are in need (Chen Hong).

I had thought of working at entertainment venues before I came here, because my family condition was not good, and I also wanted to make more money. I went to the factory and knew that you have to work eight hours a day, and four more hours overtime. I did not want to work in a factory (Yan Yan).

Some women talk about their ideal occupations. Two of them told me that their preferred occupation would be to work as a teacher at a day care center. When Sha Sha told me that her dream job was to be a teacher at a day care place, her expression revealed pleasure, and her face broke into a smile. I was moved by this smile, reminded of the tears she shed when she told me how her parents borrowed money to support her through high school. Then her father broke a bone. She wanted to repay her parents by resorting to prostitution. Another young girl, Nan Nan, has the same dream as Sha Sha. She had just come back from visiting a friend who was a daycare teacher before I interviewed her. Her friends advised her to work at the day care center, but she refused even though she was not happy with her current job.

I have considered alternatives. Sometimes I want to return to the factory where I used to work. Although I make more money now, I squander it. I feel stressed when I am with my family. I have to lie, and feel like a hypocrite. I just got back from Huizhou. I have a classmate who teaches at a daycare center. She wants me to work there. I like children very much and played with them for a long time today. But the salary is too low (Nan Nan).

When thinking about the risks and benefits of prostitution, some young subjects also appear naïve and innocent. Xiao Fang is one of them.

I often wonder how I can get married if I go home. If I get married here, what would I do if one of my customers attended my wedding? But I would make only a little over 1,000 yuan a month in a factory, and I can make the same here in a day if I am lucky. So I do not want to work in a factory. Furthermore, my time is flexible, and I can do whatever I want. I was not used to it in the beginning and wanted to quit the job several times. If I work in a factory, I can date. But when I thought about the money I would make in a factory, it is better to make more money (Xiao Fang).

Although it is obvious that these women are enticed, tempted by the lucrative nature of prostitution, the process of embarking on this profession does not appear simple. It takes the women a long time to take the last step to quit their legitimate jobs or move to Shenzhen to start the trade, and some of them want to quit after starting. Some women stated that they did not begin working in the sex industry until they lost their legitimate jobs-which serves as justification for their choice. During the process, they demonstrated caution, vacillation, concerns; after taking the job, they became anxious, frustrated or even felt contempt of themselves. They struggled with their decisions, and thought things through quite thoroughly. One subject cried and didn't start to meet customers until four days after being recruited; she quit the job and returned to her hometown after working only about two weeks. However, when she thought of the hardship of factory work, she called the owner and promised to return to work very soon. Some subjects demonstrated tremendous caution and hesitation by seeking "buffer zones"—quitting their jobs in factories and working as waitresses at entertainment establishments first, from where they could either go forward or step back, depending on further observation and the information they could gather while working at these establishments. This was evidenced by one subject who applied for an advertised position at an entertainment center. She didn't take the offer because she was afraid of being duped. Shortly after that, being dumped by her boyfriend made her determined to work as a waitress at an entertainment center and a few months later, she started to zuotai and provide sex services. Embarking on prostitution is a long, winding process. It was not a spontaneous response to a dire economic condition. Some women had accepted the idea of prostitution before they actually began the trade; they were not ready to take the last step due to concerns causing vacillation. Other women, however, may not accept the idea until they determine to take this job. One subject did not start the trade until six months after her girlfriend had worked as a prostitute, although she had determined to work at a massage parlor before she left her hometown for Shenzhen. Another subject refused to take the job even when she was nagged by her girlfriends and the owner of a sauna parlor. However, after falling into debt due to her daughter's illness, she started to have second thoughts about the work in the sauna parlor. After hesitating for over a year, she decided to take the job. Thus, prostitution appears to be an option that women can always turn back to when the timing is right for them.

In conclusion, adopting prostitution is anything but a first choice. Participants have worked in legitimate sectors and have also acquired plenty of information about working as a prostitute. They contemplate the matter, think it through, and reach their final decisions. After adopting prostitution, they still hesitate, or even want to go back to working in a factory. But they do not go back because they had been well aware of the risks and rewards associated with prostitution. The following two subjects present a good summary of what is involved in being a prostitute.

> The advantages of this job include eating well, dressing well, and playing well. I like fashionable clothes and I spent several thousand to buy clothes one month when I was in my hometown. The advantages also include freedom and an easy job. I am very practical; I won't go out with customers if they do not pay me. My concerns include not being able to bear children and not being able to make money when I get older (Lily).

> The benefits of this job include a high salary and freedom. The bad things are: it is very hard to quit once you do it; you have to figure out how to conceal your history from your boyfriend (Yan Yan).

The resurgence and prevalence of prostitution in contemporary China cannot be explained "unidimensionally" (Gil et al., 1994). Guided by the Rational Choice Perspective, this chapter explored factors associated with Chinese women's involvement in the sex industry, in the context of a society in transition. A wide range of factors have been found to be related to women's opting to engage in prostitution, and these fall into two categories: distal and proximal. The proximal factors include the women's current economic circumstances, certain situational factors, and the available opportunities for working in the sex industry. The distal factors consist of the broader socio-economic environment that has significantly affected the women's current economic circumstances, as well as certain socio-cultural factors that shape or determine the women's values, attitudes, and personality traits. In the RCP context, these distal factors predispose women to become prostitutes.

Findings of this study generally are predicted by the RCP. The RCP contends that the background and situational factors have varying effects on the occurrence of crime. Background factors affect the occurrence of crime in such a way that they shape or determine the values, attitudes and personality traits that predispose the individual to criminal involvement (Clarke and Cornish, 1985; Cornish and Clarke, 1986); they are "less directly criminogenic" (Clarke and Cornish, 1985: 167); they predispose potential offenders to crime. Or, simply put, background factors have indirect effects on the occurrence of crime, while situational factors, or foreground factors, have a direct effect on the occurrence of crime. This is confirmed by the findings of the current study.

The mechanism of how background and foreground factors intertwine, and result in women's involvement in prostitution is shown in Figure 7.1. Proximal factors are greatly affected by socio-economic and cultural backgrounds that create opportunities and situations making prostitution accessible and even desirable, when combined with dire economic circumstances. Specifically, it is both socio-economic and cultural factors that result in people either living in poverty or becoming economically ambitious; and in the latter case, prompting women in disadvantaged positions to become prostitutes. In contemporary China, opportunities to work as prostitutes are numerous, as a result of omnipresent entertainment venues and endless customers. The role of relatives, friends and/or co-workers on a woman's becoming a prostitute also cannot be overemphasized. Both formal and informal social controls are undermined; an assessment of the rewards and risks motivates women in dire need of money, or those who are economically ambitious, to embark on this profession.

The diagram also shows that socio-economic factors do not directly motivate women to enter prostitution, although they have an effect on all the other factors that do directly contribute to the women's decision. On the one hand, economic reform has lifted millions of people out of poverty; on the other hand, unintended consequences have resulted from economic reform, e.g., uneven development across the country, growing inequality, an imbalance in economic policies, and lack of labor law protections, which have also given rise to poverty, in either absolute or relative terms. The most negatively affected are the people at the bottom of the social hierarchy, specifically, farmers and those uprooting themselves in search of better lives. The economic context also creates convenient opportunities for entering prostitution, and situations that lower the threshold and reduce the risks associated with prostitution. Therefore, in the long run, to contain the development of commercial sex in China, it appears that efforts must be focused on adjusting the policy

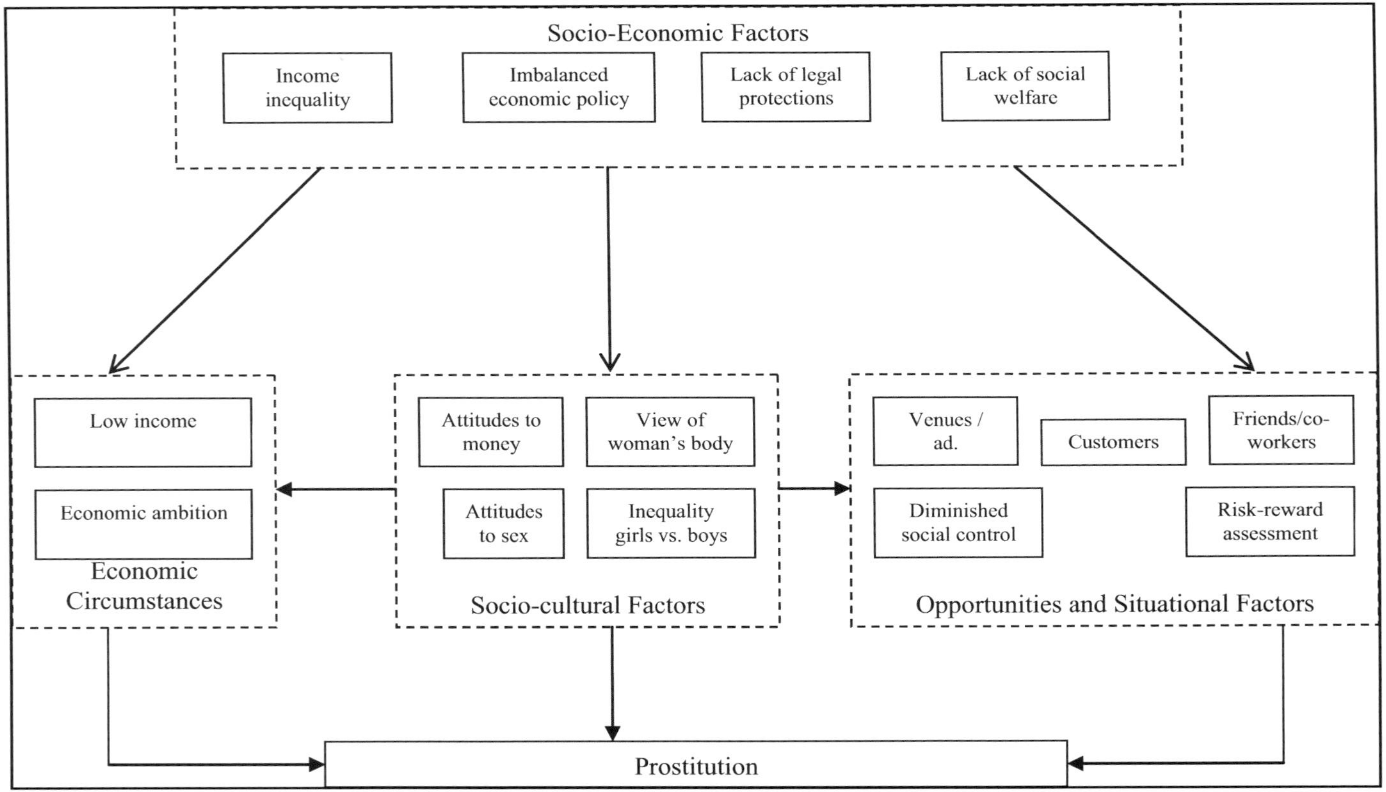

Figure 7.1 Factors Associated with Women's Entering Prostitution

of economic reform from one that principally emphasizes industrialization and urbanization, to one that prioritizes the welfare and interests of people at the lower end of the social hierarchy.

The second aspect by which this study is consistent with the RCP lies in the fact that these women do make decisions, and in doing so, they select the optimum choice available to them. The RCP implies "soft" determinism (Clarke and Cornish, 1985), which means that while offenders do indeed make choices, they are not free to choose what choices are available to them. The choices available to them are heavily constrained, not only by the women's current life circumstances and opportunities, but also by their backgrounds and social context. Thus, a combination of these factors affects the nature of choices available to them.

As demonstrated in the preceding part of this chapter, most, if not all, of the women interviewed had worked in legitimate sectors before becoming involved in prostitution. They are well aware of the risks and benefits associated with prostitution, as well as those associated with legitimate jobs. When women uproot themselves from indigent isolated villages to move to growing cities, such as Shenzhen, prostitution appears to be lucrative. Many, if not all of them, have alternatives. However, while these alternatives are not starvation, they are usually grueling, menial, and low-paid jobs. The choices are constrained by the characteristics of China's economic reforms, as well as by both the entrenched and the newly emerging cultural attributes of the Chinese nation, which include, but not limited to, poor economic resources in rural areas when compared to urban areas, limited rights for migrant workers as opposed to those for urban workers, the inferior status of women when compared to that of men, and more liberal attitudes toward sex. These background factors restrict and shape the choices of Chinese migrant women in particular, and thus their choices are "bounded," in rational choice perspective terms.

Among the findings of this study not predicted by the RCP, is the fact that socio-cultural factors, as background factors, have both direct and indirect influence on women's embarking on the sex trade. Attitudes toward sex and money have been fundamentally changed as a result of China's economic reforms and open door policy. Traditional views of women's status as being subordinate to that of men have reemerged. More liberal attitudes toward premarital and extramarital sex are being increasingly accepted. One consequence has been the fueling of an expansion of the commercial sex business, impacting both the demand and supply sides. When these cultural factors dominate some women's ideologies, especially those in dire need of money, and those who are materialistic and desire luxurious lifestyles, prostitution becomes acceptable, viable, and even desirable, making women psychologically ready to embark on this trade. This demonstrates the indirect influence of background factors on women's involvement in prostitution, which is consistent with the RCP.

The diagram also shows that socio-cultural factors have a direct effect on women's decision to enter prostitution. In the context of a society in transition, social norms, values, and attitudes toward wealth and sex are experiencing an unprecedented shift—from traditional and conservative to more diverse and liberal. The extent to which a woman accepts these liberalized attitudes toward sex, how she views her body, and her attitudes about money are the decisive forces determining whether she will embark on prostitution, given certain financial circumstances. Individual attitudes and acceptance help explain why all women do not choose prostitution, despite living under similarly negative economic circumstances.

In conclusion, these women's experiences reveal that their involvement in prostitution is a result of the interaction of a variety of factors. Some of factors have direct effects on women's involvement in the sex trade; while others exert indirect influences. Prostitution is certainly not the only option open to them. However, while other options available to them are not necessarily starvation, they are often grueling or low-paid jobs that cannot provide them a flexible, secure or luxurious lifestyle. Embarking on the sex trade is regarded by them as the optimal choice which can help fulfill their aspirations and life objectives, and their perceptions of this option is bounded by their background, attitudes, and values. In the prostitution and human trafficking discourse, nothing is more controversial than the debate of force vs. choice. Abolitionists emphasize the influence of backgrounds factors, i.e., structural factors, in women's involvement in prostitution; while regulationists highlight free choices made by these women. A proper analogy to these opposing perspectives is the proverbial cup of water. Whether it is half empty or half full depends on one's perspective. Unfortunately, people form the wrong impression that it is either empty or full, and this consequently misinforms what in fact really occurs.

8

Legal Responses and Conclusions

Laws, Regulations, and Policy Implications

Prostitution laws vary significantly from one country to another but generally fall into three categories: prohibition, regulation and abolition (Barry, 1995). These three perspectives differ in the way they define the legal status of prostitutes and their clients. Under prohibition all prostitution is illegal, and both prostitutes and their customers are in violation of the law. Under regulation, the prostitution industry is legalized and regulated, and working as a prostitute is viewed as a woman's right. This approach makes a distinction between voluntary and forced prostitution by decriminalizing consensual sexual practices and placing the sex sector under the jurisdiction of commercial and labor laws, as opposed to criminal laws. Abolition refers to the abolition of laws and regulations that legalize or criminalize prostitution. It contends that prostitution constitutes a form of violence against women and is hence a violation of human rights. Prostitutes are therefore victims, and prostitution should be prohibited. The abolition perspective works towards the eradication of prostitution by decriminalizing prostitution and providing support and protection for women in prostitution, whilst simultaneously criminalizing those who live off prostitution. Laws prohibiting or regulating prostitution should be abolished while laws against pimping and procuring should be strengthened. In all three systems and their variations, pimping—living off the earnings of a prostitute—is illegal (see Barry, 1995 for details). What is the nature of Chinese prostitution laws? Before we come to any conclusion, it is necessary to examine the evolution of prostitution laws in China.

It was widely accepted after the Chinese Communist Party's (CCP) accession to power that prostitution was a product of the capitalist system of exploitation and it denigrated the position of women under capitalism and under patriarchal systems (Barry, 1995; Jeffreys, 2006; Zhang, 2006). Prostitution was viewed as social disease that would affect the stability and health of society as a whole, were it not dealt with in a timely and drastic fashion. This understanding produced an attitude of intolerance toward the existence of prostitution, and the CCP therefore announced that it would resolutely eliminate the system of prostitution in China (Barry, 1995; Jeffreys, 2004a; Ren, 1993; Ruan, 1991; Zhang, 2006). The government proudly claimed several years later that China was a country free of prostitution. Thus, prostitution was not a subject of concern for the government for almost 30 years. However, since the 1980s, with the resurgence and proliferation of prostitution in mainland China, governmental authorities have realized that it constitutes a widespread and growing problem (Jeffreys, 2006). The Chinese government reiterated its previous prohibitionist stance: the selling and buying of sex is not to be tolerated in China. The desired goal of eradicating prostitution led to the promulgation of various laws and regulations, and periodic police campaigns against prostitution and human trafficking.

Generally speaking, prostitution laws in China fall into one of two groups. In the first are administrative laws that prohibit prostitution, and subject prostitutes and customers to administrative penalties. In the other are the criminal laws and their amendments by which pimping, procuring, organizing and/or forcing prostitution is considered criminal, and is subject to severe criminal penalties. Accordingly, offenses related to prostitution fall into one of two categories under Chinese legal systems. Those involving the first party (prostitutes and their clients) are generally viewed as administrative offenses and fall under the purview of administrative law. In contrast to administrative offenses, criminal offenses involving third parties fall under the purview of the Criminal Code and its amendments.

Administrative Laws

According to the 1957 Regulations of the People's Republic of China for Security Administration, a female who sells sex could be placed in detention for a maximum of 10 days and fined up to 20 yuan, or she could simply be given a warning (Anderson and Gil, 1994). In 1987, in response to the increasing presence of prostitution activities, a new administrative penalty law, namely, the Regulations on Administrative Penalties for Public Order (hereafter referred to as Administrative Regulations) was enacted, and further amended by the Chinese People's Congress (CPC) Standing Committee, in May 1994. Article 30, in Chapter 3 of the Regulations, states that (a) it is forbidden to sell sex and have illicit relations with a prostitute, to introduce others into prostitution and to provide accommodation for the purposes of prostitution. (b) Offenders shall be detained for a maximum of 15 days, given a warning, made to sign a statement of repentance, or subjected to reform through education and labor, and may be concurrently fined a maximum of 5,000 Yuan. (c) Those whose behavior constitutes criminal offenses are subject to criminal punishment. (d) Buying sex service from girls who are younger than 14 shall be considered as rape and offenders will be punished. (Administrative Regulations, 1987).

The Administrative Regulations were replaced by the current Law on Administrative Penalty for Public Order (hereafter referred to as Administrative Penalty Law) which came into effect on March 1, 2006. Generally speaking, the Administrative Penalty Law explicitly subjects three categories of people to administrative penalties, including fines and administrative detention: firstly, the sellers and buyers of sex services, secondly, the third parties who induce, accommodate or introduce others to sell sex in cases where the offenses are not severe enough to be punished under the Criminal Code, and thirdly, personnel working at restaurant, hotels, entertainment enterprises or taxi companies who tip off offenders when police investigate prostitution (Administrative Penalty Law, 2005). Furthermore, the Administrative Penalty Law prohibits soliciting or seeking sex services in public places. It holds owners, operators or other employees of the entertainment or service industries accountable for the prevention of prostitution on their premises and for cooperation with law enforcement investigations.

Criminal Law

The first Criminal Code since the Chinese Communist Party took power was promulgated in 1979, and came into force on January 1, 1980. Only two articles of the Criminal Code dealt directly with the subject of prostitution (Jeffreys, 2006). Articles 140 and 169 of that Code banned all third-party attempts to profit from the prostitution of others, but made no explicit reference to the activities of first party participants in the prostitution transaction, or those who buy and sell sex.

In 1991, the CPC Standing Committee enacted and promulgated the Decision Strictly Forbidding the Selling and Buying of Sex (hereafter referred to as the 1991 Decision), a legal response to the proliferation of prostitution in China. Its objectives are to amend and supplement the prostitution provisions in the 1979 Criminal Law. It aims to educate and redeem prostitution offenders and also to prevent the spread of sexually transmitted diseases (Zhang, 2006). With the aim of severely punishing third parties, this law criminalizes those who organize, force, induce, accommodate, or introduce others to prostitution, and subjects them to severe criminal punishment for these behaviors. In the presence of aggravated circumstances, provided for in this Decision, offenders may be subject to life in prison or the death penalty.

The 1991 Decision introduces a system of sanctions against any person who takes advantage of their business in the entertainment and service industry to organize, force, facilitate, or introduce other persons to participate in prostitution. (1) Personnel of hotels, restaurants, entertainment venues or car rental companies who take advantage of their business locations to force, organize, lure, accommodate or introduce others to prostitution will be subject to criminal penalty. (2) Managers in the entertainment industry and hotel business are held responsible for prohibiting the occurrence of prostitution in their establishments. Those who adopt an attitude of ignorance shall be punished with fines. (3) Personnel working at restaurant, hotels, entertainment enterprises or taxi companies who conceal information or tip off offenders when police investigate occurrences of prostitution shall be subject to criminal punishments.

While stipulating that those who sell or buy sex shall be punished according to the Administrative Penalty Regulation, the Decision specifies that those who sell or buy sex may be subject to mandatory educational detention with a period of six months to two years. This is an innovative administrative measure incorporated in the 1991 Decision. Another significant innovation included in the Decision is that, for the first time, the first parties involved in prostitution may be subjected to criminal penalty under certain circumstances—i.e., prostitutes or their clients who buy or sell sex with knowing that they have syphilis, the clap, or severe venereal diseases, or customers having sex with people younger than 14.

The 1991 Decision criminalizes those who organize the sex business, or get others involved in prostitution. But it keeps sellers and buyers under the purview of administrative law and regulations. The 1979 Criminal Code was revised in 1997, retaining the relevant criminal items of the Decision. The Chinese have been fairly consistent in their response to third parties who organize, force, induce, accommodate, or introduce women into prostitution (Anderson and Gil, 1994).

Regulations on Entertainment Facilities

The operations of places of leisure and entertainment are also subject to governmental intervention. The PRC State Council promulgated Regulations Concerning the Management of Entertainment Places (hereafter referred to as Management Regulations) in January 2006, and these became effective in March 2006. These Regulations provide that cubicle rooms or compartments in entertainment facilities must install clear windows and doors, and they should not be lockable from the inside (Management Regulation, 2006). The Ministry of Commerce has ordered all public bath houses to make their premises more accessible to public inspections. If bath houses have massage rooms, it must be possible to view these openly from the outside. Foot-massage parlors must have unlocked cubicle doors (*China Daily*, 2007). Some cities have already taken the lead in cracking down on the sex trade. For example, the administration of Guangzhou issued a regulation as early as 2004, forbidding masseuses in beauty salons from massaging customers below the shoulder, in an effort to curb possible prostitution (*China Daily*, 2004).

The numerous legislation activities represent the Chinese government's perspective, and its response to prostitution and human trafficking. Although prostitution itself, by and large, remains a problem that is handled administratively under the complex systems of law and regulations in China, the degree of state intervention has escalated to a level more in line with criminal conduct (Anderson and Gil, 1994). Based on the 1991 Decision, both prostitutes and their customers are subject to penalties that could be educational detention or reform through labor. These are currently two most controversial punishments in China.

What is the nature of educational detention? Chinese legal scholars construe it as an administrative measure, rather than an administrative punishment (Li Kejie, 2006). However, it is more akin to a criminal penalty because its prominent feature is the deprivation of freedom for a period ranging from six months to two years. Furthermore, the decision is made by the police without the involvement of judges or prosecutors. It is one of the two systems (the other one is Reform through Labor) that deprive people of their freedom without due process.

Thus, the punishment of prostitution is very severe. This can be evidenced by police data, according to which 41 of 43 arrested women were punished with six months of educational detention, while the other two women were administratively detained for five and two days respectively for attempting trade in sex. In addition, police data demonstrates that customers were also punished with six months of educational detention, except in the case of three offenders who were detained for 14 days and one who was detained for 10 days. However, according to interviews with a police officer, the imposition of educational detention is very rare now because the educational facilities do not have enough space to detain more defendants. The police officer further told me what penalties may be imposed upon prostitutes and their customers.

> If it is proved that they have committed prostitution, they are usually subjected to detention of at least ten days; if it is proved that they attempted prostitution, the punishment is detention lasting no more than five days or the payment of a fine. But fines are rarely imposed now because the police cannot keep the fine and have to submit it to the treasury department; they have no incentive to impose the fine penalty (Interview with a police officer).

Ineffectiveness of Police Campaigns

In addition to the adoption of laws and regulations containing and preventing prostitution and human trafficking, the authorities have launched periodic intensified campaigns against prostitution and human trafficking. The actions taken in China have been enormous in both scale and scope. During a particularly harsh crackdown on prostitution in the late 1980s and early 1990s, death sentences were awarded to a number of pimps and brothel owners (Davidson, 2001).

Shenzhen is not an exception. The resurgence of the sexual trade has become increasingly visible in Shenzhen since the 1980s. There are streets full of pink-lit karaoke lounges and massage parlors. Due to its proximity to Hong Kong, the commercial sex trade is rampant, and Shenzhen has to take significant measures to contain it. An initiative referred to as "Strike Hard" culminated in a parade of 100 or so prostitutes and clients in front of a jeering crowd on November 29, 2006. This was intended as the first step in a two-month campaign by the Public Security Bureau of Futian district, Shenzhen, to crack down on prostitution. The prostitutes and their clients were all detained for 15 days after the parade (*Washington Post*, 2006).

The ban on prostitution, the measures carried out by law enforcement entities, and the severe punishments for forcing, coercing, or introducing people into prostitution are not restraining the growth of the sex industry. In spite of these efforts, prostitution activities keep rising. Prostitutes ply their business openly in many areas with little or

no official intervention and prostitution businesses continue to prolifer-
ate throughout China (Anderson and Gil, 1994; Jeffreys, 2006; Zhang,
2006). Some liberal scholars have begun to critique the effectiveness of
the campaign style response and the prohibitive policy (Jeffreys, 2006;
Li, 2000; Zhang, 2006).

A range of factors may be identified as contributing to the failure to
contain and control rampant prostitution. The most cited reason is corruption (Jeffreys, 2006; Liu, 2007; Ren, 1999). Widespread corruption
among law enforcement and government officials is a serious obstacle
to eliminating prostitution in China. Some of these officials not only
ignore the existence of prostitution in certain business premises, but
may also tip off suspects so they can escape when an investigation is
launched (Ren, 1999). As shown in the preceding chapters, owners of sex
venues must have social connections to open and run such businesses. It
is next to impossible for prostitutes to be arrested. Anecdotes frequently
disclose that police officers or government officials are involved, and
make a profit from the operation of entertainment establishments. Consequently, police officers have no incentive to investigate prostitution
cases. Suspects, i.e., prostitutes and customers, once arrested, have to
be released because their owners have connections with government
officials (Interview with police).

The practice of fining minor prostitution offenders, rather than de-
taining them for re-education, has become a way in which the Chinese
police can generate much-needed finances. Thus, they contribute to
the prevalence of the commercial sex trade (Jeffreys 2006; Zhu, 1994).
Furthermore, anti-prostitution campaigns target the most vulnerable
and marginalized population within the sex industry, i.e., the prostitutes
and customers. Those with social connections, that is to say, the owners and operators of entertainment establishments are left untouched.
The 1991 Decision stipulated stiff punishment for hotels, restaurants
and entertainment facilities permitting the occurrence of prostitution.
In practice, however, there are very few convictions, because the local
government worries that this may have negative effects on the economy
(Si, 1997). Campaigns against prostitution in China do not appear to aim
at the organizers and facilitators of the prostitution industry; instead,
they tend to further disadvantage the already marginalized and exploited
prostitutes, making them scapegoats, while those who are exploiting
them evade punishment (Zhang, 2006).

The ineffectiveness of the anti-prostitution campaign is also related to false
perceptions of prostitution, which are partly responsible for the increasing

acceptance of prostitution. A review of Chinese literature on prostitution led to a recognition of the following false concepts of prostitution (e.g., Li, 2000; Liu, 2007; Zhu, 1994): (1) Prostitution has a positive function: commercial sex services can improve the investment environment and stimulate the development of the service industry. Containing prostitution may discourage foreign investment and negatively affect economic development. (2) Prostitution is not a big deal: the prevalence of sex services will not affect social stability. (3) Prostitution is unavoidable: it has existed historically and internationally, and it is normal to expect that it will become prevalent in the era of economic reform. (4) Prostitution is hard to eradicate. It is almost impossible to eradicate prostitution, and therefore it is not worth expending a lot of effort in dealing with it. Due to these false perceptions, some local authorities approach prostitution with "one eye open, one eye shut," mindful of the need to protect and develop the local economy (Zhang, 2006). The discrepancy between policy goals and the effectiveness of their implementation can thus be attributed to both ideological and practical reasons.

With the rapid growth of entertainment establishments, commercial sex services are increasingly accepted, and are gradually becoming a popular means of entertainment, entrenching themselves in the social life of the Chinese people. Prostitution became rampant around the country after 1998 and it has long passed its growing stage in Shenzhen, according to the interview with a police officer. The paradox is that, on the one hand, local governments allow these establishments—the frontline of sex services disguised as legitimate businesses—to be opened in order to improve the investment environment, attract foreign investment and stimulate the economy. On the other hand, to keep in line with the central government's anti-prostitution policy, they have to convey the message that prostitution is a social evil, that local governments are serious about tackling it, and that it should be eradicated. This dilemma is also articulated by a massage parlor manager who was arrested during a police raid.

> This kind of establishment is prevalent; several hundred new establishments are opened every year. Everyone knows the services provided are illegal and misses provide sex services secretly like thieves. You should let these establishments to exist once you allow them to open (Interviewing with an operator).

Identifying Victims of Human Trafficking: A Perpetual Dilemma

To assess the extent and magnitude of human trafficking, a consistent unambiguous definition at both conceptual and operational levels must be obtained. Despite the passage of the UN Protocols to Prevent, Suppress, and Punish Trafficking in Persons (United Nations, 2000), many fundamental questions remain unanswered at both the theoretical and practical levels. Lack of a precise, consistent, and unambiguous definition of the phenomenon is one of the two reasons identified by Wijers and Lap-Chew (1997) to achieve reliable statistics on the extent of trafficking (the other reason is lack of systematic research).

A comprehensive interpretation of the 2000 UN Protocol definition of human trafficking must take into account three significant elements: a number of diverse means of trafficking, the exploitation purpose, and the various stages of trafficking, which include not only the recruitment and transportation of victims, but also the context in which they work. As previously stated, however, the debate on what constitutes human trafficking has never ended since the promulgation of the Protocol. Ambiguities are still inherent in this definition, and in the way it is actualized. There has never been consensus on the meaning of the term "coercion," on what represents a position of vulnerability, and on what constitutes exploitation. This complicates the task of identifying victims of trafficking.

The present study has found that the supply of labor for the sex industry does not rest entirely upon force, deceit or coercion, for it is possible to openly recruit women and girls into prostitution. As a police officer pointed out, Shenzhen is a highly developed city, where salaries are much higher compared to most of the rest of China. In some undeveloped areas where the women's hometowns are located, the construction of infrastructure lags far behind. There is not even running water, nor electricity and no good roads. Rural women and girls, therefore, do not want to go back home after arriving in cities, no matter how hard their lives are in cities. They are generally eager to migrate, not simply because they need employment or higher paying jobs, but also because the idea of uprooting themselves to look for fortune and luck in developed cities holds a good deal of charm for them.

Therefore, force, deceit and coercion were rarely the means of recruiting women into the sex trade or for retaining them in this line of work. Only a few of the women in this study were locked up, raped and abused until they agreed to prostitute themselves. Similarly, only a few found themselves in situations where, depending on a third party for information and financial help, they were subsequently exploited by the third party. The present study found that, at the recruitment stage, most women chose to work in the sex industry without the involvement of a third party. Once the women began to work in the sex industry, however, they had to depend on the owners of the hair salons, the mammies at nightclubs/karaoke lounges, the operators of massage/sauna parlors, or the pimps to enable them to make money. Therefore they had to divide the money they made with those third parties. The third party deducts money based on a percentage of what they make from each customer. In addition, some third parties also make money from women in the name of what they call a management fee, i.e., women pay a fixed amount of money per day or per month when they work, no matter whether or how many customers they have. This arrangement is commonly found at off-street venues and among streetwalkers who depend on third parties to send them customers. Some women do not feel it's a burden, or that it is unfair to divide money with the third party; others may feel that it is unfair that they have to divide money with their bosses. Also, there are a number of rules regarding the operation of venues, such as minimum work days in a month, or other rules specified by the establishments. The women have to comply with these operating rules and may not be able to control where, when, how, and for whom they work. How should these practices be interpreted? Should they be considered regular business operating rules or should they be viewed as forced work? Is the relationship between the women and the third parties a business partnership, or is it a relationship based on exploitation? Brunovski and Tyldum (2004) view this as a less obvious type of exploitation because, "if the fixed price is high, or demand is low, such an arrangement may limit a woman's room for action, and make it difficult to take one day off, or to decide not to take a particular client" (2004: 86). However, what is the threshold at which women feel forced to work, and what constitutes exploitation? If the practice is viewed as exploitation, no matter how much they are paid, can it be considered exploitation if freelance prostitutes pay for their own sex service advertising? If there are elements of forced work or exploitation involved, there is no doubt that these women should be regarded as victims of human trafficking, according to the UN Protocol. However, it is still open to debate whether working under such circumstances constitutes forced work or exploitation, and therefore the women should be viewed as victims.

Another question that emanated from this study is: Is exploitation the only motive or purpose behind human trafficking? The present study finds that some recruiters do not make money from forcing others to work in sex industry. Meifang's friend dragged her into the sex trade for the purpose of having a companion. Liu Yan's cousin forced her to work at a hair salon to improve her family's financial condition. Xiao Yu's boyfriend brought her to Shenzhen and introduced her to work at a hair salon without making money. Therefore, the motive of trafficking is not limited to monetary purposes. However, the means used by the friend or cousin in the abovementioned examples included withholding money, debt bonding, brainwashing and taking advantage of the subject's position of vulnerability. Thus, women can be trafficking victims without necessarily being exploited by recruiters. Or, in other words, the incentives for trafficking include not only exploitation, but also a variety of other motives, such as wanting company.

Violence, insults and other dangers are intrinsic to commercial sex, and also a prelude to human trafficking. Women may fall in the hands of unscrupulous traffickers although they might have voluntarily begun to work as prostitutes. The possibility of being trafficked is inherent in this choice, rendering the women vulnerable to human trafficking. The identification of trafficking victims requires clarification of the key concepts contained in the UN Protocol definition, in particular on aspects such as what constitutes exploitation, what constitutes forced work when a woman has willingly chosen to work in the sex industry. The answers to all these questions depend on one's perspective, and therefore, there are still a lot of inconsistent and controversial debates regarding these issues.

The 2000 UN Protocol provides a comprehensive list of criminal means by which trafficking takes place, including not only palpable means, but also less explicit ones, such as coercion and abuse of a victim's position of vulnerability. As far as the stages during which trafficking may occur, what gets easily ignored in the human trafficking discourse is that even if women consent to work as prostitutes, they can be victims of trafficking if at their work place elements of criminal means are present or if they work under situations of exploitation. Thus, women working voluntarily the sex industry can be victims if exploitation or forced work is involved (Kelly, 2002; Vocks and Nijboer, 2000). However, this expanded interpretation of the UN Protocol definition does not seem adequate at answering questions emanating from this study. We still have a long way to travel in order to come up with a definition, at both the conceptual and operational levels, that would make it easy to determine whether or not a woman in the sex industry is a victim of trafficking.

Discussion: Driven by Poverty or Motivated by Money?

Prostitution in China has attracted enormous interest and academic attention since its re-emergence in the 1980s, and many academic outlets have been devoted to discussions of the reasons for its resurgence and prevalence. People generally agree that a wide range of factors have given rise to this phenomenon which was purportedly eradicated (see Liu, 2007; Pi and Ma, 2001; Ren, 1999; Si, 1997; Xiao, 1999; Zhao, 2001; Zhou, 2006; Zhu, 1994; Zhu Xudong, 2001). These factors can be classified as psychological, socio-sexual, or economic (Hershatter, 1997). However, two distinct perspectives have emerged in this discourse. Some researchers regard prostitution mainly as a moral issue, while others emphasize the effects of structural factors, such as relative poverty, unemployment and gender inequality, on women's involvement in prostitution.

One perspective highlights psychological reasons, citing materialism, deterioration of morality, lack of aspirations, desire for luxurious lifestyles, etc. As a result, some Chinese scholars attribute the proliferation of prostitution to the women themselves. It has been variously asserted that most prostitutes voluntarily prostitute themselves in order to pursue money and materialism (Xiao, 1999); that working as a prostitute becomes a short cut to wealth for young women with little education (Zhu, 1994); and that prostitution is used as a means to become rich (Zhang, 2000). Prostitutes are seen as one group of people who loose the "natural" psychological equilibrium (Hershatter, 1997). They are "shameful," "immoral," and "greedy for material luxuries" (Evans, 1997: 176); they are "morally degenerated," and "individualistic pleasure seekers" (Kang et al., 1988: 55). While acknowledging the effects of structural factors in women's involvement in the commercial sex trade, this perspective emphasizes women's willingness to enter into prostitution as a result of the attractive and lucrative nature of this profession (Si, 1997; Zhang, 2000; Zhu, 1994).

Some Chinese scholars move beyond applying standards of morality and argue that prostitution is related to a number of social problems. The main causal factor is economic, rather than moral: to some extent, women become prostitutes on account of the forces of poverty (Zhao, 2001; Pi and Ma, 2001). The re-emergence and proliferation of prostitution is regarded mainly as a result of poverty, unemployment, inequality, and so on. Women are "forced" into prostitution because of these invisible forces. Therefore, they are victims of systems of inequality and patriarchy, and should be protected instead of punished (Zhang, 2006; Zhao, 2001; Zhu Xudong, 2001).

There is no doubt that most women in prostitution are individuals who come from marginalized and disadvantaged backgrounds. They work as prostitutes, voluntarily or by force, as a result of numerous factors. Some of these factors, namely, the social, cultural, or political ones, are out of their control. At the same time, however, not all women take the same life paths under similar circumstances. This implies that there is some leeway for people to control their own lives. Prostitution appears as a reasonable option to some women at a certain point in their lives. Even though it is undesirable, it appears attractive and acceptable.

Poverty is the factor most often cited as contributing to women's involvement in prostitution or in their becoming trafficking victims. However, the extent to which they get involved in prostitution because of poverty, or the relevance of poverty to their involvement in the commercial sex trade has never been the object of research on prostitution and within the human trafficking discourse. Through the analyses of prison records and interviews of 2,057 prostitutes arrested in Sichuan province, Gil et al. (1994) found that a primary motivator is money, but most of these prostitutes did not come from a poor or unstable home life, nor were they emotionally unstable themselves. In the present study, many women characterized their childhood life as poverty ridden. However, all women did not come from poor families. Furthermore, given the fact that some women's parents constituted the first generation of migrants, their family's economic circumstances had been improving gradually. At the time when they started to work as prostitutes, they were not as poor as they had been when they were children. Some of them helped their family with the money they made and in a few cases, their families were financially dependent on them. It is not clear to what extent they prostituted themselves because of their family's financial need. One subject told me that no parents ask their children for money. Only about half of the women in this study sent money to their parents. Some women even told me that their parents did not or would not allow them to return home after finding out what they were doing. Yet, it is also true, as a police officer pointed out, that even if parents do not ostensibly encourage their daughters to embark upon prostitution, they nevertheless at least tolerate or accept the fact, because of the remittances their children can send them.

Money was a powerful motivation. Indeed, most of the prostitutes rationalized and justified their decision to work as prostitutes because of a "sister's tuition," "family debt," "buying a house," "low salary from menial jobs," "dire need of money," or even "earning money for dowry." In many of these cases, poverty is relative. None of the women had to make a choice between selling sex and starvation. Instead, the choices were between making more money and less money; between flexible, easy jobs and rigid, strenuous, routine work. Prostitution emerged as a premium alternative among limited choices. This is the only job in which people with limited resources can make maximum money with minimum effort.

As to why these women get involved in the sex trade, law enforcement officials provide insightful comments:

> Easy money, no sense of shame, indolence, lavish lifestyles… these are the factors motivating women to work as prostitutes. Once they start, they won't stop. They are not necessarily forced by poverty. Some women are initially forced by poverty, but it is very rare. Some women are young, naïve and they have no people to depend on when they initially come here. They come out, and see people around them all making money in this way. Therefore, they accept these values and norms gradually. Plus, they are far away from their hometown, nobody knows what they are doing; they have no skills and factory work is hard. Gradually they drift into prostitution. Just as ambitious people won't become panhandlers, women who have aspirations won't become prostitutes (Interview with a police officer).

> If they tell you that they are doing this to help their parents build a house, help their siblings go to school or make money for their brother's wedding, they are making excuses. These are their justifications (Interview with a police officer).

These police officers' views about women's incentives may over-emphasize economic motivations and the rational choices made by individual migrant women in the sex industry; they fail to take into account the macro socio-economic and cultural constraints that shape women's decision-making. However, it is a reflection of the views held by the public at large regarding the involvement of Chinese women in prostitution. Even some of the women involved hold a similar view about themselves.

> Only those who are unmarried with little education, incapable and afraid of strenuous jobs work as prostitutes. Some married women do this secretly if their husbands are not capable of making big money. I regret it, and feel morally degenerate. Those with aspirations won't degrade themselves to become prostitutes (Lan Lan).

Some women in this study entered into prostitution because of a dire need of money for various reasons. Some women did not like routine, physically demanding jobs, and prostitution was the only way to make easy money. However, it is erroneous to believe that none of them have higher aspirations. They are a group of people who want to change their destinies. Their family background, lower socio-economic status, limited education and the resultant narrow horizon restricted their capability and the possibility of moving upward in a society full of inequities. Furthermore, in a period of great social change, social reform and development strategies and policies rarely worked in their favor. Instead, they belong among those most negatively affected and the most harmed. Without social resources to depend on, they struggle to change their destiny and in the process they may display "remarkable initiatives, resilience and tenacity" (Zhang, 2006). In this sense, they are not a group of people distinct from the rest of the population. But they may be more adventurous, more determined than the general populace. They share the same aspirations as those of most people in general.

What Wang Anyi, a female Chinese fiction writer, said in an interview may best describe the character of women who sell sex for a better life.

> Don't feel contempt for them. Most have ideals in life and dream of something higher than the sky.... Lots of them did it to secure a happy life. Money was one element. Without money, you cannot live that kind of life.... They simply do not want to fall into the fate of common female factory workers, crushed each day on the bus, with a tiny little pay packet every month and then to make everything worse, getting saddled with a baby. They don't want their lives to fall that low and that I think is very normal. Many of them are the most ambitious among us (Hershatter, 1997: 356).

References

Administrative Penalty Law. Law of the People's Republic of China on Administrative Penalty. 2005. Retrieved on November 25, 2008 from http://www.cecc.gov/pages/newLaws/adminPunishmentENG.php.)

Agence France Presse. 2000. China's Prostitution Capital Stirred, not Shaken by Vice Crackdown. 18 December 2000. Retrieved on January 23, 2008 from http://www.hartford-hwp.com/archives/55/319.html.

AMC (Asian Migrant Center). 2000. *Asian Migrant Yearbook 2000: Migration Facts, Analysis and Issues in 1999.* Hong Kong: Asian Migrant Center.

Agustin, Laura. 2000. Working in the European Sex Industry: Migrant Possibilities. Retrieved on September 6, 2007 from http://www.swimw.org/engver.html.

Agustin, Laura. 2003. Sex, Gender and Migrations: Facing up to Ambiguous Realities. *Soundings* 23: 84-98.

Agustin, Laura. 2005. Migrants in the Mistress's House: Other Voices in the 'Trafficking' Debate. *Social Politics* 12: 96-117.

Agustin, Laura. 2006. The Disappearing of a Migration Category: Migrants Who Sell Sex. *Journal of Ethnic and Migration Studies* 32: 29-47.

Alexander, Priscilla. 1996. Trafficking v. Sex Migration. New York: North American Task Force on Prostitution.

Anderson, Allen F. and Vincent E. Gil. 1994. Prostitution and Public Policy in the People's Republic of China: An Analysis of the Rehabilitative ideal. *International Criminal Justice Review* 4: 23-36.

Barry, Kathleen. 1995. *The Prostitution of Sexuality.* New York: New York University Press.

Bamgbose, Oluyemisi. 2002. Teenage Prostitution and the Future of the Female Adolescent in Nigeria. *International Journal of Offender Therapy and Comparative Criminology* 46: 569-585.

Bell, Shannon. 1994. *Reading, Writing and Rewriting the Prostitute Body.* Bloomington: Indiana University Press.

Bennett, Trevor and Richard Wright. 1984. *Burglars on Burglary.* Aldershot, Hants, England: Gower.

Bindman, Jo and Jo Doezema. 1997. Redefining Prostitution as Sex Work on the International Agenda. Retrieved on May 20, 2007 from www.walnet.org/csis/papers/redefining.html.

Boonchalaksi, Wathinee and Philip Guest. 1998. Prostitution in Thailand, in Lin Lean Lim (ed.), *The Sex Sector: The Economic and Social Bases of Prostitution in South-East Asia.* Geneva: International Labor Organization (ILO).

Brunovskis, Anette and Guri Tyldum. 2004. Crossing Borders: An Empirical Study of Transnational Prostitution and Trafficking in Human Beings. Retrieved on September 17, 2007 from www.eldis.org/static/DOC18956.htm.

Brunschot, Erin Gibbs Van and Augustine Brannigan. 2002. Childhood Maltreatment and Subsequent Conduct Disorders: The Case of Female Street Prostitution. *International Journal of Law and Psychiatry* 25: 219-234.

Bullough, Bonnie &Vern Bullough, 1996. Female Prostitution: Current Research and Changing Interpretations. *Annual Review of Sex Research* 7: 158-80.

CATW. 1999. Prostitutes Work, But Do They Consent? Coalition against Trafficking in Women (CATW). www.uri.edu/artsci/wms/hughes/catw.

Caouette, Therese M. and Yuriko Saito. 1999. *To Japan and Back: Thai Women Recount Their Experiences.* International Organization for Migration (IOM), Geneva.

Caldwell, Gillian, Steven Galster and Nadia Steinzor. 1997. *Crime and Servitude: An Expose of the Traffic in Women for Prostitution from the Newly Independent States.* Washington: Global Survival Network.

China's Agricultural Yearbook. 1999. Beijing: China Agricultural Press.

_____. 2003. Beijing: China Agricultural Press.

China Daily. 2004. Below-shoulder Massage Banned to Curb Prostitution. *China Daily.* December 5, 2004. Retrieved on June 6, 2007 from http://www.chinadaily.com. cn/english/doc/2004-12/05/content_397447.htm.

China Daily. 2006. China Pledges Elimination of Rural Compulsory Education Charges in Two Years. *China Daily*, March 5, 2006. Retrieved on December 1, 2008 from http://english.peopledaily.com.cn/200603/05/print20060305_248042.html.

China Daily. 2007. Tighter Rules on Bath Houses, Massage Parlors. *China Daily.* September 1, 2007. Retrieved on October 23, 2007 from http://www.chinadaily.com. cn/china/2007-09/01/content_6073061.htm.

China Industry. 2008. Economy of China. Retrieved on March 10, 1008 from www. chinaindustryhub.com.

China Labor Watch. 2004. Guangdong Province Raises Minimum Wage Level. China Labor Watch. December 4, 2004. Retrieve on December 1, 2008 from http://www. chinalaborwatch.org/en/web/article/php?article_id=50226.

China Labor Watch. 2006. Minimum Monthly Wage Standards in Selected provinces/Municipalities/Cities in China. China Labor Watch. July 24, 2006. Retrieve on December 1, 2008 from http://www.chinalaborwatch. org/2006%20Editorials/07-24-2006%20Minimum%20Wage.

China Labor Watch. 2007. Investigations on Toy Suppliers in China: Workers are still Suffering. *China Labor Watch*, August 2007.

China Labor Bulletin. 2007. Unemployment in China. http://www.china-labour.org. hk.en.node/100060, retrieved on December 15, 2008.

China Labor Bulletin. 2008. "Dagongmei"-Female Migrant Labourers. Retrieved on December 18, 2008 from http://www.china-labour.org.hk/en.

China Net. 2008. Urban Workers' Per Capita Salary up 18% in the First Half. Retrieved on December 1, 2008 from http://www.china.org.cn/business/news/2008-07/28/content_16083817.htm.

Chinese Labor Law. 1995. Labour Law of the People's Republic of China. Retrieved on November 26, 2008 from http://www.usmra.com/china/Labour%20Law.htm.

Chapkis, Wendy. 1997. *Performing Erotic Labor.* New York: Routledge.

Chapkis, Wendy. 2000. Power and Control in the Commercial Sex Trade. In R. Weitzer (ed.) *Sex for Sale: Prostitution, Pornography and the Sex Industry.* PP. 181-201. New York: Routledge.

Chapkis, Wendy. 2003. Trafficking, Migration and the Law: Protection Innocents, Punishing Immigrants. *Gender and Society* 17: 923-937.

Clarke, Ronald V. 1995. Situational Crime Prevention, in M. Tonry and D. Farrington (eds), *Building a Safer Society. Strategic Approaches to Crime Prevention: Crime and Justice: A Review of Research* Vol. 19. Chicago: University of Chicago Press.

Clarke, Ronald V. and Derik B. Cornish. 1985. Modeling Offenders' Decisions, A Framework for Policy and Research. In M. Tonry and N. Morris (eds), *Crime and Justice: An Annual Review of Research* Vol. 6. Chicago: University of Chicago Press.

Clarke Ronald V. and Marcus Felson. 1993. Introduction: Criminology, Routine Activity, and Rational Choice. In Clarke and Felson (eds) *Routine Activity and Rational choice, Advances in Criminological Theory* Vol. 5. New Brunswick, NJ: Transaction Publishers.

Cody, Edward. 2006. Public Shaming of Prostitutes Misfires in China: Traditional Discipline Draws Angry Outcry. Retrieved on August 31, 2009 from http://www.washingtonpost.com/wp-dyn/content/article/2006/12/08/AR2006120801480_p...

Cook, Philip J. 1980. Research in Criminal Deterrence: Laying the Groundwork for the Second Decade. In Tonry, M. and Morris, N. (Eds.) *Crime and Justice: An Annual Review of Research.* 2. Chicago: University of Chicago Press.

Coontz, Phyllis and Catherine Griebel 2004. 2004. International Approaches to Human Trafficking: the Call for a Gender-Sensitive Perspective in International Law. *Women's Health Journal* 4: 47-58.

Copes, Heith. 2003 Streetlife and the Rewards of Auto Theft. *Deviant Behavior: An Interdisciplinary Journal* 24: 309-332.

Copes, Heith and Andy Hochstetler. 2006. Why I'll Talk. In Paul Cromwell (ed.) *In Their Own Words: Criminals on Crime* (4th ed). Los Angeles, CA: Roxbury Publishing Company.

Cornish, Derik B. and Ronald V. Clarke (eds). 1986. *The Reasoning Criminal*, New York: Springer-Verlag.

Cromwell, Paul, James Olson, and D'Aunn Avary. 1991. *Breaking and Entering: An Ethnographic Analysis of Burglary*. Newbury Park, CA: Sage.

Cusick, Linda. 2002. Youth Prostitution: A Literature Review. *Child Abuse Review* 11: 230-251.

Dalla, Rochelle L. 2001. Et Tu Brute? A Qualitative Analysis of Streetwalking: Prostitutes' Interpersonal Support Networks. *Journal of Family Issues* 22: 1066-1085.

Dalla, Rochelle L. 2006. *Exposing the "Pretty Women" Myth: A Qualitative Investigation of Street-Level Prostituted Women*. Maryland: Lexington Books.

Davidson, Julia. 2001. Children in the Sex Trade in China. Published by Save the Children Sweden online http://www.no-trafficking.org/content/web/05reading_rooms/China/children_in_the_sex_trade_in_china.pdf.

Davis, Kathleen. 2006. Human Trafficking and Modern Day Slavery in Ohio. Retrieved on September 6, 2007, from http://216.128.14.181/polarisproject/programs_p3/Ohio_Report_Trafficking.pdf.

Davis, Nanette J. 1993. *Prostitution: An International Handbook on Trend, Problems, and Policies*, edited by Nanette J. Davis. Westport, CT: Greenwood Press.

Delacoste, Frederique and Priscilla Alexander. 1998. *Sex Wok: Writings by Women in the Sex Industry*. San Francisco: Cleis Press.

Deng, Meifang. 1998. Report on the Investigation of AIDS and Prostitutes. *Yangcheng Evening Paper*, October 22, 1998.

Deng, Xiaogang and Ann Cordilia. 1999. To Get Rich is Glorious: Rising Expectations, Declining Control, and Escalating Crime in Contemporary China. *International Journal of Offender Therapy and Comparative Criminology* 43: 211-229.

Department of Census &Statistics. 2001. Hong Kong resident departures by destination, Hong Kong in figures (online) retrieved April 27, 2001.

Doezema, Jo. 2000. Loose Women or Lost Women? The Re-emergence of the Myth of 'White Slavery' in Contemporary Discourses of 'Trafficking in Women'. *Gender Issues* 18: 23-50.

Doezema, Jo. 2002. Who Gets to Choose? Coercion, Consent and the UN Trafficking Protocol. *Gender and Development* 10: 20-27.

Earls, Christopher M. and Helene David. 1989. Male and Female Prostitution: A Review. *Annals of Sex Research* 2: 5-28.

Evans, Harriet. 1997. *Women and Sexuality in China: Female Sexuality and Gender since 1949*. New York: Continuum.

Felson, Marcus. 1994. *Crime and Everyday Life*. Thousand Oaks, CA: Pine Forge Press.

Findlay, Christopher and Chunlai, Chen. 2001. A Review of China's Grain Marketing System Reform. ACIAR China grain market policy project paper No. 6, retrieved on March 31, 2006 from http://apseg.anu.edu.au/research/9721_papers.php.

Flowers, R. Barri. 2001. *Runaway Kids and Teenage Prostitution: America's Lost, Abandoned, and Sexually Exploited Children*. CT, Westport: Greenwood Press.

French, Howard W. 2006a. Letter from China: The Sex Industry Is Everywhere but Nowhere-Asia-Pacific-International Tribune. December 14, 2006. Retrieved on January 23, 2008 from http://www.iht.com/articles/2006/12/14/news/letter.php.

French, Howard W. 2006b. Chinese Success Story Chokes on its Own Growth. The New York Times. December 19, 2006. Retrieved on March 19, 2008 from http://www.nytimes.com/2006/12/19/world/asia/19shenzhen.html?_r=1&oref=slogin&pag...

Fu, Wulong. 2004. Urban Poverty and Marginalization under Market Transition: The Case of Chinese Cities. *International Journal of Urban and Regional Research* 28: 2 (401-23).

Gil, Vincent E. and Allen F. Anderson. 1998. State-Sanctioned Aggression and the Control of Prostitution in the People's Republic of China: A Review. *Aggression and Violent Behavior* 3: 129-42.

Gil, Vincent E.; Marco Wang, Allen F. Anderson, and Guao Matthew Lin. 1994. Plum Blossoms and Pheasants: Prostitutes, Prostitution, and Social Control Measures in Contemporary China. *International Journal of Offender Therapy and Comparative Criminology* 38: 319-337.

Glassner, B. and Carpenter, C. 1985. *The Feasibility of an Ethnographic Study of Property Offenders: A Report Prepared for the National Institute of Justice*. Mimeo., Washington, D.C.: National Institute of Justice.

Goodman, Peter S. 2003. Sex Trade Thrives in China: Localities Exploiting a Growing Business. *Washington Post*, January 4, 2003, p. A01.

Gordy, Molly. 2000. A Call to Fight Forced Labour. *Parade Magazine*. February 20, 2000.

Gozdziak, Elzbieta. M. and Elizabeth A. Collett. 2005. Research on Human Trafficking in North America: A Review of Literature. *International Migration* 43: 99-128.

Graham, John and Benjamin Bowling. 1995. *Young people and crime*. Home Office Research Study 145. London: Home Office: A Research and Planning Unit.

Graham, Nanette and Eric D. Wish. 1994. Drug Use among Female Arrestees: Onset, Patterns, and Relationships to Prostitution. *Journal of Drug Issues* 24: 315-29.

Hammersley, Marty and Paul Atkinson. 1995. *Ethnography: Principles in Practice* (2nd ed.). New York: Routledge.

Hardman, Karen. 1997. A Social Work Group for Prostituted Women with Children. *Social Work with Groups* 20: 19-31.

Heckathorn, Douglas D. 1997. Respondent-driven Sampling: A New Approach to the Study of Hidden Populations. *Social Problems* 44: 174-198.

Henriot, Christian. 1996. From a Throne of Glory to a Seat of Ignominy: Shanghai Prostitution Revisited (1984-1949). *Modern China* 22: 155.

Hershatter, Gail. 1997. *Dangerous Pleasures: Prostitution and Modernity in Twentieth-Century Shanghai.* California: University of California Press.

Hoigard, Cecilie and Liv Finstad. 1992. *Backstreets: Prostitution, Money and Love.* Pennsylvania: Pennsylvania State University Press.

Hobson, Perry and Vincent Heung. 1998. The Modern Chinese Concubine. In Oppermann M. (ed.), *Sex Tourism and Prostitution: Aspects of Leisure, Recreation, and Work.* New York: Cognizant Communication Corporation.

Hong, Yan, Boita Stanton, Xiaoming Li, Hongmei Yang, Danhua Lin, Xiaoyi Fang, Jing Wang, and Rong Mao. 2006. Rural-to-Urban Migrants and the HIV Epidemic in China. *AIDS and Behavior* 10: 421-430.

Huang, Yingying and Pan Suiming. 2003. Female Sex Workers in Northeastern China Labor Market. *Sociological Research.* 2003 Issue 3.

Hughes, Donna M. 2002. Trafficking for Sexual Exploitation: The Case of the Russian Federation. Retrieved on September 7, 2007 from http://www.uri.edu/artsci/wms/hughes/russia.pdf.

Huizinga, David and Delbert S. Elliott. 1986. Reassessing the Reliability and Validity of Self-report Delinquency Measures. *Journal of Quantitative Criminology* 2: 293-327.

Human Trafficking. 2007. Human trafficking highlighted in China. Retrieved on October 23, 2007 from http://www.humantrafficking.org/updates/407.

Human Trafficking. 2008. China. Retrieved on January 24, 2008 from http://www.humantrafficking.org/countries/china.

IOM (International Organization for Migration). 1995. *Trafficking and Prostitution: the Growing Exploitation of Migrant Women from Central and Eastern Europe.* Geneva, IOM.

_____. 2001. *Victims of Trafficking in the Balkans: A Study of Trafficking in Women and Children for Sexual Exploitation to, through and from the Balkan Region.* Geneva, IOM.

John Irwin. 1972. Participant Observation of Criminals. In *Research on Deviance.* ed. Jack K. Douglas. New York: Random House.

Jacobs, Bruce A. 1996. Crack Dealers and Restrictive Deterrence: Identifying Narcs. *Criminology* 34: 409-431.

_____. 2000. *Robbing Drug Dealers: Violence Beyond the Law.* New York: Aldine De Gruyter.

_____. 2006. Researching Crack Dealers: Dilemmas and Contradictions. In Paul Cromwell (ed.) *In Their Own Words: Criminals on Crime* (4th ed). Los Angeles, CA: Roxbury Publishing Company.

Jacobs Bruce A., Volkan Topalli and Richard Wright. 2003. Carjacking, Streetlife and Offender Motivation. *British Journal of Criminology* 2003: 673-688.

Jacobs, Bruce A. and Richard Wright. 1999. Stick-up, Street Culture, and Offender Motivation. *Criminology* 39: 149-173.

James, Jennifer and Jane Meyerding. 1977. Early Sexual Experience and Prostitution. *American Journal of Psychiatry* 134: 1381-85.

Jeffery, C. Ray and Diane L. Zahm. 1993. Crime Prevention through Environmental Design, Opportunity Theory, and Rational Choice Models. In Clarke and Felson (eds) *Routine Activity and Rational choice, Advances in Criminological Theory*, Vol. 5. New Brunswick, NJ: Transaction Publishers.

Jeffreys, Elaine. 2004a. *China, Sex and Prostitution*. London and New York: RoutledgeCurzon.

2004b. Feminist Prostitution Debates: Are There Any Sex Workers in China? In Anne E. Mclaren (ed), *Chinese Women—Living and Working*. New York: Routledge Curzon.

2006. Governing Buyers of Sex in the People's Republic of China. *Economy and Society* 35: 571-593.

Jesson, Jill. 1993. Understanding Adolescent Female Prostitution: A Literature Review. *British Journal of Social Work* 23: 517-530.

Jupp, Victor 1989. *Methods of Criminological Research*. London: Routledge.

Kang, Shuhua, Liu Canpu and Zhao Ke. 1988. *On Female Offenders*. Lanzhou: Lanzhou University Press.

Kelly, Liz. 2002. Journeys of Jeopardy: A Commentary on Current Research on Trafficking of Women and Children for Sexual Exploitation within Europe. Retrieved on October 20, 2007 from childtrafficking.org/pdf/user/journeys_of_jeopardy.pdf.

Labor Law. 1995. Labor Law of the People's Republic of China. Retrieved on November 26, 2008 from http://www.usmra.com/china/Labour%20Law.htm.

Laczko, Frank. 2002. Human Trafficking: The Need for Better Data. *Migration Information Source*. Migration Policy Institute, Washington, DC.

Lau, Joseph T.F. and Thomas, J. 2001. Risk Behaviors of Hong Kong Male Residents Traveling to Mainland China: a potential bridge population for HIV Infection. *AIDS Care* 13: 71-81.

Lau, Joseph T.F., Hi Yi Tsui, P.C. Siah, and K.L. Zhang. 2002. A Study on Female Sex Workers in Southern China (Shenzhen): HIV-related Knowledge, Condom Use and STD History. *Aids Care* 14: 219-233.

Lazaridis, Gabriella. 2001. Trafficking and Prostitution: The Growing Exploitation of Migrant Women in Greece. *The European Journal of Women's Studies* 8: 67-102.

Lee, June JH. 2005. Human Trafficking in East Asia: Current Trends, Data Collection, and Knowledge Gaps. *International Migration* 43: 166-201.

Legal Daily. 2007. The Number of Migrant People Has Reached 140 Million. *Legal Daily*. December 13, 2007.

Li, Kejie. 2006. Educational Detention: Is There any Legitimacy and Rationality? *Procuration Daily* November 29, 2006. A6.

Li, Wei. 2006. Research on Public Opinion on Eroticism. *Journal of Jiangxi Public Security College* 2006 Issue 1: 25-30.

Li, Yinhe. 2000. Reasons for Uneradicability of Prostitution. *People's Police*. 2000 Issue 18.

Li, Zhengdong. 2004. An Investigation of Prostitutes Migrating from Rural to Urban. *Society* 2004 Issue 5: 60-63.

Liang, Zai and Zhongdong Ma. 2004. China's Floating Population: New Evidence from the 2000 Census. *Population and Development Review* 30: 467-488.

Lim, Lin Lean. 1998. The Economic and Social Bases of Prostitution in Southeast Asia. In Lin Lean Lim (ed.) *The Sex Sector: The Economic and Social Bases of Prostitution in Southeast Asia*. International Labor Office: Geneva.

Liu, Jintao. 2007. An Analysis of Forbidding Prostitution and the Function of Police. *Journal of Shanghai Police College* 17: 44-46.

Lu, Hong, Juanhong Liu and Alicia Crowther. 2006. Female Criminal Victimization and Criminal Justice Response in China. *British Journal of Criminology* 46: 859-874.

Lynch, David J. 2003. Today's Chinese Revolution is Sexual. *USA Today*, 16 Sept. 2003, A15.

Maher, Lisa. 1997. *Sexed Work*. Oxford: Clarendon Press.

Management Regulations. 2006. Regulations on Management of Entertainment Places. Retrieved on November 25, 2008 from http://202.123.110.5/zwgk/2006-02/13/content_187029.htm.

Maxfield, Michael G. and Earl Babble. 2001. *Research Methods for Criminal Justice and Criminology*. 3rd ed. CA, Belmont: Wadsworth.

Maxwell, Joseph A. 1996. *Qualitative Research Design: An Interactive Approach*. CA: Sage Publications.

McCall, George. 1978. *Observing the law*. New York: Free Press.

McDonald, Lynn, Brooke Moore, and Natalya Timoshkina. 2000. Migrant Sex Workers from Eastern Europe and the Former Soviet Union: The Canadian Case. Retrieved on September 6, 2007 from http://www.swc-cfc.gc.ca/pubs/pubspr/0662653351/200011_0662653351_e.pdf.

Meaker, Linda. 2002. A Social Response to Transnational Prostitution in Queensland, Australia. In Susanne Thorbet and Bandana Pattanaik (ed.): *Transnational Prostitution*. Zed Books: New York.

Miethe, Terance D. and Richard C. McCorkle. 2001. *Crime Profiles: The Anatomy of Dangerous Persons, Places, and Situations*. Los Angles: Roxbury.

Nandon, Susan M., Catherine Koverola & Eduard H. Schludermann. 1998. Antecedents to Prostitution: Childhood Victimization. *Journal of Interpersonal Violence* 13: 206-221.

Outshoorn, Joyce. 2005. The Political Debates on Prostitution and Trafficking of Women. *Social Politics* 12: 141-155.

Pan, Suiming. 2000. Study on Underground Red Light District in Mainland China. *Research Report on Mainland Chinese Sex Workers*. Hong Kong: Zi Teng.
2006. Transformations in the Primary Life Cycle: The Origins and Nature of China's Sexual Revolution. In Elaine Jeffreys (ed.) *Sex and Sexuality in China*. New York: Routledge.

Perkins, Roberta. 1991. *Working Girls: Prostitutes, their Life and Social Control*. Australia Institute of Criminology.

Pi, Yijun and Kai Ma. 2001. The Symbiosis Pattern in Prostitution. *Research on Crime*, 2001 Issue 1: 30-32.

Pickup, Francine. 1998. Deconstructing Trafficking in Women: The Example of Russia. *Journal of International Studies* 27: 995-1021.

Pochagina, Olga. 2005. The Sex Business as a Social Phenomenon in Contemporary China. *Far Eastern Affairs*. 2005 4: 118-134.

Potterate, John, J., Richard B. Rothernberg, Stephen Q. Muth, William W. Darrow, and Lynanne Phillips-Plummer. 1998. Pathways to Prostitution: The Chronology of Sexual and Drug Abuse Milestones. *The Journal of Sex Research* 35: 333-40.

Quangquo Renda, 1991. Quanguo renda changweihui fazhi gongzuo weiyuanhui xing-fashi. Beijing.

Raymond, Janice G. 2001. Guide to the New UN Trafficking Protocol to Prevent, Suppress and Punish Trafficking in Persons, Especially Women and Children. Retrieved on September 20, 2007 from http://www.catwinternational.org.
2002. The new UN Trafficking Protocol. *Women's Studies International Forum* 25: 491-502.

Raymond, Janice G. and Dona M. Hughes. 2001. Sex Trafficking of Women in the United States: International and domestic Trends. Retrieved on April 17, 2007 from www.uri.edu/artsci/wms/hughes/sex_traff_us.pdf.

Raymond, Janice G., J. D'Cunha, S.R. Dzuhayatin, H. P. Hynes, Z. R. Rodriguez, A. Santos. 2002. A Comparative Study of Women Trafficked in the Migration Process." Retrieved on September 6, 2007 from http://action.web.ca/home/catw/attach/CAT W%20Comparative%20Study%202002.pdf.

Ravallion, Martin and Shaohua Chen. 2004. Learning from Success: Understanding China's (Uneven) Progress Against Poverty. *Finance & Development*. December 2004: 16-19.

Ren, Xin. 1993. China. In Nanette J. Davis (ed.), *Prostitution: An International Handbook on Trend, Problems, and Policies*. Westport, CT: Greenwood Press.

1999, Prostitution and Economic Modernization in China. *Violence against Women* 5: 1411-1436.

2000. Prostitution and Employment Opportunities for Women under China's Economic Reform. Lola Press. Retrieved on May 25, 2007 from http://www.lolapress.org/artenglish/xinre13.htm.

Reuters, 1998a. China Petrol Stations Offer Fill up with Flair. September 21, 1998.

1998b. Condom Vending Machines a Hit in China. Reuters, September 21, 1998.

Rosenthal, Elisabeth. 2002. Migrants to Chinese Boom Town Find Hard Lives. *The New York Times*. July 2, 2002. Retrieved on March 19, 2008 from http://query.nytimes.com/gst/fullpage.html?res=9506EEDA1631F931A35754C0A9649C8.

Ruan, Fang Fu. 1991. *Sex in China: Studies in Sexology in Chinese Culture*. New York: Plenum.

Salt, John and Hogarth, Jennifer. 2000. Migrant Trafficking and Human Smuggling in Europe: A Review of the Evidence. In F. Lazko and D. Thompson (ed.), *Migrant Trafficking and Human Smuggling in Europe: A Review of the Evidence with Case Studies from Hungary, Poland and Ukraine*. Geneva, IOM.

Sanders, Teela. 2004. The Risk of Street Prostitution: Punters, Police and Protesters. *Urban Studies* 41: 1703-1717.

Selfe, David and Vincent Burke. 2001. *Perspectives on Sex, Crime, and Society* (2nd ed.) London: Cavendish Publishing Limited.

Seng, Magnus J. 1989. Child Sexual Abuse and Adolescent Prostitution: A Comparative Analysis'. *Adolescence* 24: 665-75.

Sharpe, Karen. 1998. *Red Light, Blue Light: Prostitutes, Punters and the Police*. Aldershot, UK: Ashgate Publishing Ltd.

Shaver, Frances M. 2005. Sex Work Research: Methodological and Ethical Challenges. *Journal of Interpersonal Violence* 20: 296-319.

Shaw, Victor N. 2006. China under Reform: Social Problems in Rural Areas. *China Report* 42: 341-368.

Shover, Neal. 1985. *Aging Criminals*. Beverly Hills, CA: Sage.

_____. 1996. *Great Pretenders: Pursuits and Careers of Persistent Thieves*. Boulder, CO: Westview.

Shover, Neal and David. Honaker (1992), "The Socially Bounded Decision Making of Persistent Property Offenders." *The Howard Journal* 31: 276-293.

Si, Qinshan. 1997. Macro-Strategy on Preventing Prostitution. *Journal of Police Academy of Jiangxu*. 1997 Issue 1: 33-37.

Simons, Geoffrey L. 1987. *The Illustrated Book of Sexual Records*. Maryland: Ransom House Value Publishing.

Simons, Ronald L. and Les B. Whitbeck. 1991. Sexual Abuse as a Precursor to Prostitution and Victimization. *Journal of Family Issues* 12: 361-79.

Skeldon, Ronald. 2000. Trafficking: A Perspective from Asia. *International Migration* Special Issue, pp. 7-30.

Skrobanek, Siriporn, Nataya Boonpakdee and Chutima Jantateero. 1997. *The Traffic in Women: Human Realities of the International Sex Trade.* London: Zed Books.

Sunday, Maureen Fan. 2007. Oldest Profession Flourishes in China. *Washington Post.* August 5, 2007; A16 http://www.washingtonpost.com/wp-dyn/content/article/2007/08/04/AR2007080401309_pf.html. Retrieved on January 23, 2008.

The 1991 Decision. 1991. The Decision on Strictly Forbidding the Selling and Buying of Sex. Retrieved on November 25, 2008 from http://news.xinhuanet.com/ziliao/2003-09/08/content_1068870.htm.

The Economist. 2000. Shenzhen's Sex Industry-New China, Old Vice. August 11, 2000.

The Administrative Regulations. 1987. Regulations on Administrative Penalties for Public Order. Retrieved on November 25, 2008 from http://law.chinslawinfo.com/newlaw2002/SLC/slc.asp?db=chl&gid=2959.

The U.S. Department of State. 2005. Distinctions between Human Smuggling and Human Trafficking. *Fact Sheet.* The Human Smuggling and Trafficking Center at the U.S. Department of State. Washington, DC. January 1, 2005.

The U.S. Department of State. 2006. The United States Department of State Human Rights Report 2006. Retrieved on September 17, 2007 from www.state.gov/g/drl/rls/hrrpt/2006/78771.htm.

Tyldum, Guri and Anette Brunovskis. 2005. Describing the Unobserved: Methodological Challenges in Empirical Studies on Human Trafficking. *International Migration* 43: 17-34.

United Nations. 2000. Protocol to Prevent, Suppress and Punish Trafficking in Persons, Especially Women and Children, supplementing the United Nations Convention on Transnational Organized Crime. www.uncjin.org.

Vocks, Judith and Jan Nijboer. 2000. The Promised Land: A Study of Trafficking in Women from Central and Eastern Europe to the Netherlands. *European Journal on Criminal Policy and Research* 8: 379-388.

Wang, Zhuoqiong. 2007. More Forced into Labor, Prostitution. Retrieved on July 13, 2009 from www.chinadaily.com.cn/cndy/2007-07/27.content_544326.htm.

Washington Post. 2006. Public Shaming of Prostitutes Misfires in China: Traditional Discipline Draws Angry Outcry. Saturday, December 9, 2006; A10.

Weitzer, Ronald (2005a). Flawed Theory and Method in Studies of Prostitution. Violence Against Women 11: 934-49.

2005b. New Directions in Research on Prostitution. *Crime, Law and Social Change* 43: 211-235.

Wijers, Marian, and Lin. Lap-Chew. 1997. *Trafficking in Women: Forced Labour and Slavery-Like Practices in Marriage, Domestic Labour and Prostitution.* Utrecht, the Netherlands: STV.

Wijers, Marian. 2001. European Union Policies on Trafficking in Women. In Mariagrazia Rossilli (ed.) *Gender Policies in the European Union.* New York: Peter Lang.

Wright, Richard T., Scott H. Decker, Allison K. Redfern, and Dietrich L. Smith. 2006. A Snowball's Chance in Hell: Doing Fieldwork with Active Residential Burglars. In Paul Cromwell (ed.) *In Their Own Words: Criminals on Crime* (4th ed). Los Angeles, CA: Roxbury Publishing Company.

Wright, Richard, Fiona Brookman, and Trevor Bennett (2005), "The Foreground Dynamics of Street Robbery in Britain." *British Journal of Criminology* 46: 1-15.

Wright, Richard T. and Decker, Scott H. 1994. *Burglars on the Job: Streetlife and Residential Break-Ins*. Boston, MA: Northeastern University Press.

Wright, Richard T. and Trevor Bennett. 1990. Exploring the Offender's Perspective: Observing and Interviewing Criminals. In Kimberly L. Kempt (ed.) Measurement Issues in Criminology. New York: Springer-Verlag.

Wong, J. 1992. Prostitution Flourishing in China's Capitalist Enclave. San Francisco Chronicle, March 22, 1992.

World Bank. 2005. Fighting Poverty: Findings and Lessons from China's Success. Retrieved on March 10, 2008 from http://econ.worldbank.org/WBSITE/EXTERNAL/EXTDEC/EXTRESEARCH/0,, contentMDK:20634060~pagePK:64165401~piPK:64165026~the SitePK:469382,00.html.

The World Factbook: China. 2008. https://www.cia.go/library/publications/the-world-factbook/print/ch.html. Retrieved on December, 18, 2008.

WHO (World Health Organization). 2001. Sex Work in Asia. July 2001. Retrieved on July 20, 2007 from http://www.wpro.who.int/NR/rdonlyres/D01A4265-A142-4E19-99AE-6CC7E44F995C/0/Sex_Work_in_Asia_July2001.pdf.

Wu, Xiangang. 2002. Work Units and Income Inequality: The Effect of Market Transition in Urban China. *Social Forces*, 80: 1069-1099.

WuDunn, Sheryl. 1991. Economic Progress in China has a Seedy Side. *New York Times*. April 21, 1991, retrieved on March 19, 2008 from http://query.nytimes.com/gst/fullpage.html?res=9D0CE7D61F3DF932A15757C0A967958260&sec=&spon=&pagewanted=print.

Xiao, Yi. 1999. The Social Causes and Countermeasures of Prostitution. *Contemporary Jurisprudence*. 1999, Issue 5: 70-71.

Xinhuanet. 2005 Yunnan Public Security Agencies (China) Rescued over 2,000 Trafficking Women and Children over Last Five Years. Retrieved on January 24, 2008 from http://www.xinhuanet.com/chinanews/2005-11/22/content_5646288.htm.

Xinhua News Agency. 2005. www.china.org.cn/english/life/139288.htm. Retrieved on December 15, 2008.

Xu, Jingyong. 1999. Rural Economic Structure Evolution and the Movement of Rural Surplus Labor. *Zhejiang Social Science*. 1999 Issue 3.

Yang, Yi, Sidong; Cheng, Ya Xu; Jiaming Lu; Boning Yao and Zhijian Yan. 2005. Analysis of Sexual Norms and Values of Migrant Women in Entertainment Industry. *Journal of Guangdong College of Pharmacy*. 2005 Issue 2: 187-189.

Zhang, Chunli. 2000. A Report on Research of Prostitution. *Law and Life*. 2000 Issue 11: 20-21.

Zhang, Heqing. 2006. Female Sex Sellers and Public Policy in the People's Republic of China. In Elaine Jeffrays (ed.) *Sex and Sexuality in China*. New York: Routledge.

Zhang, Yibin. 1997. Investigation and Analysis of Public Opinion on Pornographic/Erotic Services. *Zhejiang Academic Journal*. 1997 Issue 3: 119-124.

Zhao, Jun. 2001. Report on Investigation of Prostitution in China. *Chinese Youth Research*. 2001. Issue 1: 13-20.

Zhou, Jinghao. 2006. Chinese Prostitution: Consequences and Solutions in the Post-Mao Era. *China: An International Journal* 4: 238-262.

Zhu, Guanglei. 2001. Preliminary Exploration of Factors of Inequality. *Opening Times* 2001 Issue 8.

Zhu, Xudong. 2001. A Review of Research on Prostitution after the Economic Reform. *Research on Police*. 2001 Issue 4: 92-96.

Zhu, Yong. 1994. The Characteristics and Causal Analysis of "Hostesses" at Entertainment Establishments. *The Journal of Public Security University* 1994 Issue 4: 99-11.

Index

Abolitionism, 37-38
Administrative
  Penalty Law, 176-177
  detention, 177
Attitudes
  toward money, 158, 172
  toward sex, 154-155, 172

Brothels, 9, 14-15, 27, 37, 42
  government-owned, 8
  state-owned, 9
Beauty salons, 14, 179

Chicken
  store, 110
  head, 100, 139, 143
Childhood experience, 25, 49-52, 59, 71
Chutai, 112-113, 117, 119
Circumstances
  personal, 53
  individual, 25
Coalition against Trafficking in Women
  (CATW), 37-39
Communist
  party, 9, 146, 153, 175, 177
  government, 4, 9, 14
Companion service, 117, 119, 136
Concern, 9, 29, 33,44, 86, 96-97, 109,
  128-133, 147, 156, 160-161,
  166-167, 169-170, 179
Criminal Code, 176-178

Decision (1991), 177-179, 181
Developmental factors, 71

Economic reform, 1-7, 9-11, 62, 107,
  146-147, 151, 158, 166, 171,
  173, 182
Educational detention, 178-180
Employment history, 59

Entertainment establishment, 72, 89-90,
  92-93, 96, 110, 160, 162, 164-165,
  169, 181-182
Exploitation, 12-13, 33-37, 42, 44, 47,
  58, 109, 141, 175, 183-185
Extra-marital sex, 152-153, 156

Family production responsibility system
  (FPRS), 3
Family condition, 62-67, 71-73, 93, 97,
  101, 168
Feminist
  radical, 36-37, 54, 58
  liberal, 54
Field observation, 15, 22, 24, 29, 31,
  110, 131
Floating population, 3-4, 6-7, 62, 72
Forced labor, 12-13, 34
Forced work, 109, 184-185
Free will, 38, 56-57

Gatekeepers, 18
Global Alliance against Trafficking in
  Women (GAATW), 38
Grain rationing system, 3
Guanxi, 18

Hair salon, 11, 17-18, 20, 22, 24, 62,-63,
  65, 67, 72, 77-79, 81-84, 90, 95,
  98-101, 103-106, 110-111, 116,
  119, 134, 137-139, 142, 155,
  162-164, 168, 183-184
Hand job, 77, 83-88, 95, 98, 100,
  102, 114, 116-121, 134, 161,
  163
Hidden population, 17
Human trafficking, 12-13, 33-42, 44-49,
  53-54, 58-59, 72, 96, 105-106,
  109, 133, 140, 145-146, 151, 174,
  176, 179-180, 182-187

For Product Safety Concerns and Information please contact our EU
representative GPSR@taylorandfrancis.com Taylor & Francis Verlag GmbH,
Kaufingerstraße 24, 80331 München, Germany

Printed and bound by CPI Group (UK) Ltd, Croydon, CR0 4YY

11/04/2025

01844008-0010